500
U

C.2

U-X-L science fact
finder.

34880030013176

$135

Science
fact
finder

DATE DUE	BORROWER'S NAME	ROOM NUMBER
10/12/07	Diego Damian	305
1/29/08	Zayuri Martinez	207
4/7/08	Bryant Angel	207

BAKER & TAYLOR

W9-ATF-122

U·X·L
SCIENCE
FACT
FINDER

U·X·L
SCIENCE
FACT
FINDER

VOLUME 2: THE PHYSICAL WORLD

Phillis Engelbert, Editor

AN IMPRINT OF GALE

DETROIT • NEW YORK • TORONTO • LONDON

U•X•L *Science Fact Finder*

Edited by Phillis Engelbert

Staff

Julie L. Carnagie, *U•X•L Associate Developmental Editor*
Carol DeKane Nagel, *U•X•L Managing Editor*
Thomas L. Romig, *U•X•L Publisher*

Shanna P. Heilveil, *Production Assistant*
Evi Seoud, *Assistant Production Manager*
Mary Beth Trimper, *Production Director*

Margaret A. Chamberlain, *Permissions Specialist*

Michelle DiMercurio, *Art Director*
Cynthia Baldwin, *Product Design Manager*
The Graphix Group, *Typesetting*

Engelbert, Phillis.
    U•X•L science fact finder / Phillis Engelbert.
        p.   cm.
    Includes bibliographical references and index.
    Contents: v. 1. The natural world. v. 2. The physical world. v. 3. the technological world.
    Summary: Presents information on a variety of scientific subjects
as answers to frequently asked questions.
    ISBN 0-7876-1727-X (set)
        1. Science—Miscellanea—Juvenile literature.   [1. Science-
-Miscellanea.   2. Questions and answers.] I. Title.
    Q173.E537 1997
    500—dc21   97-24046
                                                                CIP
                                                                AC

ISBN 0-7876-1728-8 (vol. 1); 0-7876-1729-6 (vol. 2); 0-7876-1730-X (vol. 3)

☺™ This book is printed on acid-free paper that meets the minimum requirements of American National Standard for Information Sciences—Permanence Paper for Printed Library Materials, ANSI Z39.48-1984.

Printed in the United States of America

The editor dedicates this work to her life-long friend and fellow science enthusiast, Diane Surati.

CONTENTS

VOLUME 3: THE TECHNOLOGICAL WORLD

READER'S GUIDE

"What are the parts of a flower?" "How hot is lightning?" "How did the quark gets its name?" The answers to these — and 750 more — science-related questions can be found in this intriguing reference from U•X•L.

Written in nontechnical language, *U•X•L Science Fact Finder* answers the most commonly asked sci-tech questions, from the inner workings of the human body to outer space and from math and computers to planes, trains, and automobiles. A cornucopia of science facts, this three-volume set presents clear, concise questions and answers. Volume 1, The Natural World, covers biology, animals, plants, the human body, health and medicine, and food and nutrition. Volume 2, The Physical World, provides answers to questions related to Earth, energy, the environment, metals and other materials, weather and climate, and space. The Technological World, Volume 3, features general science and technology, chemistry, physics, communication, modes of transportation, buildings and bridges, mathematics, computers, and systems of measurement.

ADDITIONAL FEATURES

U•X•L Science Fact Finder contains 19 subject-arranged chapters that make it easy to locate particular topics. Sidebar boxes call out fun and interesting facts and approximately 200 photos, diagrams, and charts keep the volumes lively and entertaining. Each of the three volumes ends with a cumulative index, making it simple to find terms, topics, and people discussed throughout the text.

ACKNOWLEDGEMENTS

Special thanks are due for the invaluable comments and suggestions provided by the *U•X•L Science Fact Finder* advisors:

Valerie Doud, Science Teacher at Peru Junior High School in Peru, Indiana; Jon Engelbert, President of Beige Bag Software in Ann Arbor, Michigan; Bonnie Raasch, Media Specialist at Vernon Middle School in Marion, Iowa; Frances Smith, Mathematics Faculty at Oakland Community College, Orchard Ridge Campus in Farmington Hills, Michigan; and Frank Zuerner, Science Department Head at James Madison Memorial High School in Madison, Wisconsin.

Special thanks goes to Julie Carnagie, Associate Developmental Editor at U•X•L, for her careful attention to detail; copyeditor Paulette Petrimoulx for verifying the accuracy of this writing; and Julian N. Smith for answering questions about computers and electric cars.

COMMENTS AND SUGGESTIONS

We welcome your comments on this work as well as your suggestions for topics to be featured in future editions of *U•X•L Science Fact Finder*. Please write: Editors, *U•X•L Science Fact Finder*, U•X•L, 835 Penobscot Bldg., Detroit, Michigan 48226-4094; call toll-free: 800-877-4253; or fax: 313-961-6347.

PICTURE CREDITS

FURTHER READING

BOOKS

AAMA *Motor Vehicle Facts and Figures '95*. Washington, D.C.: American Automobile Association, 1995.

Abel, Bob. *The Book of Beer*. Chicago, IL: Regnery, 1976.

Abell, George O. *Realm of the Universe*. 3rd ed., Philadelphia, PA: Saunders College Publishing, 1984.

Academic American Encyclopedia. vol. 3. Danbury, CT: Grolier, 1992.

Adler, Bill. *The Whole Earth Quiz Book: How Well Do You Know the Planet*. New York: Quill, 1991.

Agent Orange and Its Associated Dioxin: Assessment of a Controversy. New York: Elsevier, 1988.

Agress, Clarence M. *Energetics*. New York: Grosset & Dunlap, 1978.

Ahrens, C. Donald. *Meteorology Today: An Introduction to Weather, Climate, and the Environment*. 5th ed. St. Paul, MN: West Publishing Company, 1994.

Aldridge, Susan. *The Thread of Life: The Story of Genes and Genetic Engineering*. New York: Cambridge University Press, 1996.

Ali, Sheikh R. *The Peace and Nuclear War Dictionary*. Santa Barbara, CA: ABC-CLIO, 1989.

Allaby, Michael, ed. *Illustrated Dictionary of Science*, Rev. ed. New York: Basic Books, Inc., 1984.

Amazing Animals. Alexandria, VA: Time-Life Books, 1990.

American Academy of Dermatology. *Poison Ivy* (pamphlet). Washington, D.C.: American Academy of Dermatology, 1990.

The American Geological Institute. *Dictionary of Geological Terms*, Rev. ed. Garden City, NY: Anchor Press, 1976.

The American Heritage Dictionary of Science and Technology. Houghton Mifflin.

American Kennel Club. *The Complete Dog Book*. New York: Howell Book House, Inc., 1985.

American Medical Association Encyclopedia of Medicine. New York: Random House, 1989.

The American Medical Association Family Medical Guide, Rev. ed. New York: Random House, 1987.

American Nuclear Society. *Personal Radiation Dose Chart* (leaflet).

Anderson, Kenneth. *Orphan Drugs*. Los Angeles, CA: The Body Press, 1987.

Anderson, Norman D., and Walter R. Brown. *Ferris Wheels*. New York: Pantheon Books, 1983.

Angelo, Joseph A. *The Extraterrestrial Encyclopedia*, Rev. and updated ed. New York: Facts on File, 1991.

Arem, Joel E. *Color Encyclopedia of Gemstones,* 2nd ed. New York: Van Nostrand Reinhold, 1987.

Argenzio, Victor. *Diamonds Eternal.* New York: David McKay, 1974.

Armstrong, Joseph E. *Science in Biology.* Prospect Heights, IL: Waveland Press, 1980.

Ashworth, William. *The Encyclopedia of Environmental Studies.* New York: Facts on File, 1991.

Asimov, Isaac. *Asimov on Numbers.* New York: Doubleday, 1977.

Asimov, Isaac. *Asimov's Biographical Encyclopedia of Science and Technology,* 2nd Rev. ed. Garden City, NY: Doubleday & Company, Inc., 1982.

Asimov, Isaac. *Asimov's Chronology of Science and Discovery.* New York: Harper and Row, 1989.

Asimov, Isaac. *Asimov's New Guide to Science,* Rev. ed. New York: Basic Book, Inc., 1984.

Asimov, Isaac. *The Human Body,* New rev. ed. New York: A Mentor Book, 1992.

Asimov, Isaac. *Isaac Asimov's Guide to Earth and Space.* New York: Random House, 1991.

Asimov, Isaac. *Understanding Physics.* 3 vols. New York: Dorset Press, 1988.

Astronauts and Cosmonauts Biographical and Statistical Data: Report to the Committee on Science, Space, and Technology U.S. House of Representatives 1989. Washington, D.C.: Committe on Science, Space, and Technology, 1989.

Automotive Encyclopedia, Rev. ed. South Holland, IL: Goodheart-Willcox Company, 1989.

Bagel, Marilyn, and Tom Bagel. *The Bagels' Bagel Book.* Herndon, VA: Acropolis Books, 1985.

Bagenal, Philip, and Jonathan Meades. *The Illustrated Atlas of the World's Great Buildings.* London: Salamander Books, Ltd., 1980.

Bailey, Janet. *Keeping Food Fresh,* Rev. ed. New York: Harper & Row Publishers, 1989.

Bair, Frank E. *The Weather Almanac,* 6th ed. Detroit, MI: Gale Research, Inc., 1992.

Balfour, Henry H. *Herpes Diseases and Your Health.* Minneapolis, MN: University of Minnesota Press, 1984.

Bali, Mrinal. *Space Exploration: A Reference Handbook.* Santa Barbara, CA: ABC-CLIO, 1990.

Barnard, Christiaan. *The Body Machine.* New York: Crown, 1981.

Barnes-Svarney, Patricia. *The New York Public Library Science Desk Reference.* New York: Macmillan, 1995.

Barnhart, Robert K. *The American Heritage Dictionary of Science.* Boston, MA: Houghton Mifflin, 1986.

Barrett, James A. *Biology.* Englewood Cliffs, NJ: Prentice-Hall, 1986.

Barr, Roger. *Radios: Wireless Sound.* San Diego, CA: Lucent Books, 1994.

Bates, Robert, and Julia A. Jackson. *Glossary of Geology,* 3rd ed. Alexandria VA: American Geological Institute, 1987.

Battan, Louis J. *Weather in Your Life.* New York: W. H. Freeman, 1983.

Baylin, Frank, and Brent Gale. *Home Satellite TV Installation and Troubleshooting Manual,* 1986 ed. Boulder, CO: Baylin/Gale Productions, 1985.

Beatty, J. Kelly, Brian O'Leary, and Andrew Chaikin. *The New Solar System,* Cambridge, MA: Sky Publishing Corp., 1981.

Beeching, W. A. *Century of the Typewriter.* New York: St. Martins's Press, 1974.

Bennett, Albert B. Jr. and L. Ted Nelson. *Mathematics for Elementary Teachers: A Conceptual Approach,* 3rd ed. Dubuque, IA: Wm. C. Brown Publishers, 1992.

Bergamini, David. *Life Science Library: Mathematics.* New York: Time Incorporated, 1963.

Berliner, Barbara. *The Book of Answers.* Englewood Cliffs, NJ: Prentice-Hall, 1982.

Bernard, Josef. *The Cellular Connection.* Mendocino, CA: Quantam Publishing, 1987.

Berry, James. *Exploring Crystals.* New York: Crowell-Collier Press, 1969.

Beyer, Don E. *The Manhattan Project.* New York: Watts, 1991.

Beyer, William H. *CRC Standard Mathematical Tables,* 25th ed. Boca Raton, FL: CRC Press, 1987.

The Biocycle Guide to Maximum Recycling. Emmaus, PA: JG Press, 1993.

The Biographical Dictionary of Scientists: Chemists. New York: Oxford University Press, 1994.

The Biographical Dictionary of Scientists: Physicists. New York: Oxford University Press, 1994.

Bishop, Peter. *Fifth Generation Computers.* Hempstead, Eng.: Ellis horwood, Ltd., 1986.

Blair, Ian. *Taming the Atom*. Bristol, Eng.: Adam Hilger, 1983.

Block, E. B. *Fingerprinting: Magic Weapon Against Crime*. New York: McKay, 1969.

Blocksma, Mary. *Reading the Numbers*. New York: Penguin, 1989.

Bogner, Bruce F. *Vehicular Traffic Radar: Handbook for Attorneys*. Mount Holly, NJ: The Brehn Corporation, 1979.

Bohren, Craig F. *Clouds in a Glass of Beer*. New York: Wiley, 1987.

Bonnet, Robert L. *Botany: 49 Science Fair Projects*. Blue Ridge Summit, PA: Tab Books, 1989.

Booth, Nicholas. *The Concise Illustrated Book of Planets and Stars*. New York: Gallery Books, 1990.

Bothamley, Jennifer. *Dictionary of Theories*. London: Gale Research International, 1993.

Brady, George S. *Materials Handbook*, 13th ed. New York: McGraw-Hill, 1991.

Brandreth, Gyles. *Your Vital Statistics*. New York: Citadel, 1986.

Branson, Gary D. *The Complete Guide to Recycling at Home*. Whitehall, VA: Betterway Publications, 1991.

Braun, Wernher von, and Frederick I. Ordway III. *Space Travel: A History*. New York: Harper & Row, 1985.

Brennan, Richard P. *Dictionary of Scientific Literacy*. New York: John Wiley & Sons, Inc., 1992.

Brennan, Richard P. *Levitating Trains and Kamikaze Genes*. New York: Harper Perennial, 1990.

Broadcasting and Cable Yearbook 1995, vol. 1. New Providence, NJ: Bowker, 1995.

Brody, Jane E. *Jane Brody's Good Food Book*. New York: W. W. Norton, 1985.

Burnam, Tom. *The Dictionary of Misinformation*. New York: Perennial Library, 1986.

Burroughs, William J., Bob Crowder, et. al. *The Nature Company Guides Weather*. New York: Time-Life Books, 1996.

Burton, Benjamin T., and Willis R. Foster. *Human Nutrition*, 4th ed. New York: McGraw-Hill, 1988.

Burton, Maurice, and Robert Burton. *Encyclopedia of Insects and Arachnids*. New York: Crescent Books, 1975.

Burt, William Henry. *A Field Guide to the Mammals*, 3rd ed. Boston, MA: Houghton Mifflin, 1976.

Bush, Grace A. *Foundations of Mathematics*. New York: McGraw-Hill, 1968.

Bynum, W.F., et al. *Dictionary of the History of Science*. Princeton, NJ: Princeton University Press, 1985.

Cairis, Nicholas. *Cruise Ships of the World*. Boston, MA: Pegasus, 1988.

Calder, Nigel. *The Comet Is Coming*. New York: Penguin Books, 1982.

Callahan, Philip S. *Bird Behavior*. New York: Four Winds Press, 1975.

The Cambridge Dictionary of Science and Technology. New York: Cambridge University Press, 1988.

The Cambridge Encyclopedia of Space. New York: Cambridge University Press, 1991.

Cancer Free: The Comprehensive Cancer Prevention Program. New York: Simon & Schuster, 1995.

Can Elephants Swim? New York: Time-Life Books, 1969.

Carlson, Neil R. *Foundations of Physiological Psychology*. Needham Heights, MA: Allyn Bacon, Inc., 1988.

Carnegie Library of Pittsburgh, Science and Technology Department. *Handy Science Answer Book*. Detroit, MI: Visible Ink Press, 1994.

Cartnell, Robert. *The Incredible Scream Machine: A History of the Roller Coaster*. Fairview Park, OH: Amusement Park Books, 1987.

Carwell, Hattie. *Blacks in Science: Astrophysicist to Zoologist*. Oakland, CA: Exposition Press, 1977.

Cassel, Don. *Understanding Computers*. Englewood Cliffs, NJ: Prentice-Hall, 1990.

Cassens, B. *Preventive Medicine and Public Health*. New York: Harwal Publishing Co., 1987.

Cazeau, Charles J. *Science Trivia*. New York: Berkley Books, 1986.

Cecil Textbook of Medicine, 18th ed. Philadelphia, PA: Saunders, 1988. 2 vols.

Chalmers, Irena. *The Great Food Almanac*. San Francisco, CA: Collins, 1994.

Chambers Science and Technology Dictionary. Cambridge, Eng. & Edinburgh, Scotland: W&R Chambers, Ltd., and Cambridge University Press, 1988.

Christian, Spencer, and Tom Biracree. *Spencer Christian's Weather Book*. New York: Prentice-Hall, 1993.

Churchman, Lee W. *Survey of Electronics*. San Francisco, CA: Rinehart Press, 1971.

Cipolla, Carlo M., and Derek Birdsall. *The Technology of Man*. New York: Holt, Rinehart, and Winston, 1980.

Coated Abrasives: Modern Tool of Industry. New York: McGraw-Hill, 1958.

Cody, John. *Visualizing Muscles*. Lawrence, KS: University Press of Kansas, 1990.

Columbia University College of Physicians and Surgeons. *Complete Home Medical Guide*. New York: Crown, 1985.

The Complete Encyclopedia of the Animal World. London: Octopus Books, 1980.

Conant, Roger. *A Field Guide to Reptiles and Amphibians: Eastern and Central North America*, 3rd updated ed. Boston, MA: Houghton Mifflin Company, 1991.

Concise Encyclopedia of Chemistry. Berlin: de-Gruyter, 1994.

Cone, Robert J. *How the New Technology Works*. Phoenix, AZ: Oryx Press, 1991.

Congressional Institute for the Future. "Emerging Issues" (pamphlet).

Considine, Glenn D. *Van Nostrand's Scientific Encyclopedia*, 8th ed. vols. 1 and 2. New York: Van Nostrand Reinhold, 1995.

Conway, W. Fred. *Discovering America's Fire Museums*. New Albany, IN: FBH Publishers, 1993.

Coombes, Allen J. *Trees*. New York: Dorling Kindersley Publishing, Inc. 1992.

Corbeil, Jean-Claude. *The Facts on File Visual Dictionary*. New York: Facts on File, 1986.

Cornell, James. *The Great International Disaster Book*, 3rd ed. New York: Charles Scribner's, 1982.

Cortada, James W. *Historical Dictionary of Data Processing: Technology*. Westport, CT: Greenwood Press, 1987.

Costello, David F. *The World of the Porcupine*. Philadelphia, PA: Lippincott, 1966.

Council on Environmental Quality. *Environmental Quality*. Washington, D.C.: Council on Environmental Quality, 1992.

Couvering, John Van. *Encyclopedia of Human Evolution and Prehistory*. New York: Garland Publishing, 1988.

Cruickshank, Allan D. *1001 Questions Answered About Birds*. New York: Dodd, Mead, 1958.

Cuff, David J. *The United States Energy Atlas*, 2nd ed., New York: Macmillan, 1986.

Cunningham, William P., and Barbara Woodhouse Saigo. *Environmental Science: A Global Concern*. Dubuque, IA: Wm. C. Brown Publishers, 1990.

Cunningham, William P., et al. *Environmental Encyclopedia*. Detroit, MI: Gale Research, Inc., 1994.

Curtis, Anthony R. *Space Almanac*. Woodsboro, MD: ARCsoft, 1990.

Curtis, Helena, and N. Sue Barnes. *Invitation to Biology*, 4th ed. New York: Worth Publishing, Inc., 1985.

D'Adamo, James. *One Man's Food—Is Someone Else's Poison*. New York: R. Marek, 1980.

Daintith, John. *The Facts On File Dictionary of Physics*. New York: Facts On File, 1988.

Darwin, Charles. *On the Origin of Species*. Cambridge, MA: Harvard University Press, 1964.

Davie, Michael. *Titanic: The Death and Life of a Legend*. New York: Alfred Knopf, 1987.

Davis, G. J. *Automotive Reference*. Boise, ID: Whitehorse, 1987.

Day, John, and C. Eng. *The Bosch Book of the Motor Car*. New York: St. Martin's Press, 1976.

De Blij, Harm J. *Nature on the Rampage*. Washington, DC: National Geographic Society, 1986.

De Bono, Edward. *Eureka!* New York: Holt, Rinehart, and Winston, 1974.

Deming, Richard. *Metric Power*. Nashville, TN: Nelson, 1974.

DeVoney, Chris. *MS-DOS User's Guide*, 2nd ed. Indianapolis, IN: Que Corporation, 1987.

Diagram Group Staff. *Comparisons*. New York: St. Martin's Press, 1980.

Diamond, Freda. *The Story of Glass*. San Diego, CA: Harcourt, Brace, and Co., 1953.

Dictionary of Scientific Biography. vol. 8. New York: Charles Scribner's Sons, 1989.

Dictionary of Scientific Biography. vol. 14. New York: Charles Scribner's Sons, 1989.

Dictionary of Scientific Biography. vol. 16, suppl. 1. New York: Charles Scribner's Sons, 1989.

Diseases and Disorders Handbook. Springhouse, PA: Springhouse Corporation, 1990.

Ditzel, Paul C. *Fire Engines, Firefighters*. New York: Crown, 1976.

Doctor, Ronald M. *The Encyclopedia of Phobias, Fears, and Anxieties*. New York: Facts On File, 1989.

The Doctors' Book of Home Remedies II. Emmaus, PA: Rodale, 1993.

Dowling, Harry F. *Fighting Infection*. Cambridge, MA: Harvard University Press, 1977.

Downing, Douglas, and Michael Covington. *Dictionary of Computer Terms*, 2nd ed. Hauppauge, NY: Barron, 1989.

Downs, Robert B. *Landmarks in Science: Hippocrates to Carson*. Littleton, CO: Libraries Unlimited, Inc., 1982.

Downs, Robert B. *Scientific Enigmas*. Littleton, CO: Libraries Unlimited, Inc., 1987.

Drake, George R. *Weatherizing Your Home*. New York: Reston Publishing Co., 1978.

Drug Testing in the Workplace. Chicago, IL: ASCP Press, 1989.

Duensing, Edward. *Talking to Fireflies, Shrinking the Moon*. New York: Penguin, 1990.

Dunbar, Ian. *Dog Behavior: Why Dogs Do What They Do*. Neptune, NJ: T.F.H. Publications, 1979.

Dunne, Levon J. *Nutrition Almanac*, 3rd ed. New York: McGraw-Hill, 1990.

DuVall, Nell. *Domestic Technology*. Boston, MA: G. K. Hall, 1988.

Duxbury, Alyn C., and Alison Duxbury. *An Introduction to the World's Oceans*. Reading, MA: Addison-Wesley Publishing Company, Inc., 1984.

Dyson, James L. *The World of Ice*. New York: Knopf, 1962.

Eagleman, J. R. *Severe and Unusual Weather*. New York: Van Nostrand Reinhold, 1983.

Eating to Lower Your High Blood Cholesterol, (pamphlet). Washington, DC: U.S. Department of Health and Human Services, 1989.

Edelson, Edward. *Sports Medicine*. New York: Chelsea House, 1988.

Edmunds, Robert A. *The Prentice-Hall Encyclopedia of Information Technology*. Englewood Cliffs, NJ: Prentice-Hall, Inc., 1989.

Egg Science and Technology, 3rd ed. Westport, CT: AVI, 1986.

Elkort, Martin. *The Secret Life of Food*. Los Angeles, CA: Jeremy P. Tarcher, 1991.

Ellis, Keith. *Thomas Telford*. Duluth, MN: Priory Press, 1974.

Emaniol, Mary, ed. *Encyclopedia of Endangered Species*. Detroit, MI: Gale Research, Inc., 1994.

Emiliani, Cesare. *The Scientific Companion*. New York: John Wiley & Sons, Inc., 1988.

Encyclopedia Americana, International ed. vol. 4. Danbury, CT: Grolier, 1988.

Encyclopedia Americana, International Edition. vol. 18. Danbury, CT: Grolier, 1990.

Encyclopedia Americana. 30 vols. Danbury, CT: Grolier, 1990.

Encyclopedia of Associations, 27th ed., vol. 1, part 1. Detroit, MI: Gale Research, Inc., 1993.

Encyclopedia of Aviation. New York: Scribners, 1977.

Encyclopedia of Chemical Technology, 4th ed., vol. 2. New York: Wiley, 1992.

Encyclopedia of Chemical Technology, 4th ed., vol. 5. New York: Wiley, 1992.

Encyclopedia of Chemical Technology, 4th ed., vol. 15. New York: Wiley, 1992.

Encyclopedia of Chemical Technology, 4th ed., vol. 23. New York: Wiley, 1992.

Encyclopedic Dictionary of Science. New York: Facts On File, 1988.

Endangered Species Technical Bulletin, Reprint vol. 21. (January-February 1996)

Engelbert, Phillis. *Astronomy and Space: From the Big Bang to the Big Crunch*. 3 vols. Detroit, MI: UXL, 1996.

Engelbert, Phillis. *The Complete Weather Resource*. 3 vols. Detroit, MI: UXL, 1997.

Engineering and the Advancement of Human Welfare. Washington, DC: National Academy Press, 1989.

Everett, Thomas H. *Living Trees of the World*. New York: Doubleday, 1968.

The Facts on File Dictionary of Astronomy, 3rd ed. New York: Facts On File, 1994.

The Facts on File Dictionary of Chemistry, Rev. and enl. ed. New York: Facts On File, 1988.

Famighetti, Robert, ed. *The World Almanac and Book of Facts 1992*. New York: World Almanac Books, 1991.

Famighetti, Robert, ed. *The World Almanac and Book of Facts 1995*. New York: World Almanac Books, 1994.

Famighetti, Robert, ed. *The World Almanac and Book of Facts 1996*. New York: World Almanac Books, 1995.

Famighetti, Robert, ed. *World Almanac and Book of Facts 1997*. New York: World Almanac Books, 1996.

Farber, Edward. *Nobel Prize Winners in Chemistry 1901-1961*, Rev. ed. New York: Ablard-Schuman, 1963.

Farb, Peter. *The Insects*. Alexandria, VA: Time-Life Books, 1977.

FDA Consumer Special Report: Focus on Food Labeling. U. S. Food and Drug Administration.

Fejer, Eva, and Cecilia Fitzsimons. *An Instant Guide to Rocks and Minerals*. Stamford, CT: Longmeadow Press, 1988.

Feldman, David. *Do Penguins Have Knees?* New York: Harper Perennial, 1991.

Feldman, David. *When Do Fish Sleep? And Other Imponderables of Everyday Life*. New York: Harper & Row, 1989.

Feldman, David. *Why Do Clocks Run Clockwise? And Other Imponderables*. New York: Perennial Library, 1988.

Feltwell, John. *The Natural History of Butterflies*. New York: Facts On File, 1986.

Fenton, Carroll L. *The Fossil Book*. New York: Doubleday, 1989.

Field, Gary C. *Color and Its Reproduction*. Pittsburgh, PA: Graphic Arts Technical Foundation, 1988.

Field, Leslie. *The Queen's Jewels*. New York: Harry N. Abrams, 1987.

Fields, Alan. *Partly Sunny: The Weather Junkie's Guide to Outsmarting the Weather*. Boulder, CO: Windsor Peak Press, 1995.

50 Simple Things You Can Do to Save the Earth. Berkely, CA: Earth Works Press, 1989.

Findling, John E. *Historical Dictionary of World's Fairs and Expositions, 1851-1988*. Westport, CT: Greenwood, 1990.

Finniston, Monty, ed. *Oxford Illustrated Encyclopedia of Invention and Technology*. vol.6. Oxford, Eng.: Oxford University Press, 1992.

First Aid Book. Washington, DC: U.S. Mine Safety & Health Administration, 1991.

Fisher, Arthur. *The Healthy Heart*. New York: Time-Life Books, 1981.

Flakus, Greg. *Living with Killer Bees*. Oakland, CA: Quick Trading, Co., 1993.

Flaste, Richard, ed. *The New York Times Book of Science Literacy: What Everyone Needs to Know From Newton to Knuckleball*. New York: Times Books, Random, 1991.

Flatow, Ira. *Rainbows, Curve Balls, and Other Wonders of the Natural World Explained*. New York: Harper & Row Publishers, 1988.

Fogle, Bruce. *Know Your Cat: An Owner's Guide to Cat Behavior*. New York: Dorling Kindersley, Inc., 1991.

Foods and Nutrition Encyclopedia, 2nd ed., vol. 2. Boca Raton, FL: CRC Press, 1994.

Forrester, Frank H. *1001 Questions Answered About the Weather*. New York: Grosset & Dunlap, 1957.

Fox, Michael W. *The Animal Doctor's Answer Book*. New York: Newmarket, 1984.

Franck, Irene. *The Green Encyclopedia*. New York: Prentice-Hall, 1992.

Frankel, Edward. *Poison Ivy, Poison Oak, Poison Sumac, and Their Relatives*. Pacific Grove, CA: Boxwood Press, 1991.

Freedman, Alan. *The Computer Glossary*, 6th ed. New York: AMACOM, 1993.

Freiberger, Paul, and Michale Swaine. *Fire in the Valley: The Making of the Personal Computer*. Berkeley, CA: Osborne/McGraw-Hill, 1984.

Frew, Timothy. *Salmon*. New York: Mallard Press, 1991.

Freydberg, Nicholas. *The Food Additives Book*. New York: Bantam, 1982.

Fritts, Harold C. *Tree Rings and Climate*. New York: Academic Press, 1976.

Fruits and Vegetables: 1001 Gardening Questions Answered. Pownal, VT: Storey Communications, Inc., 1990.

Funk, Charles E. *Horse Feathers and Other Curious Words*. New York: Harper, 1958.

Gale Book of Averages. Detroit, MI: Gale Research, Inc., 1994.

Gardiner, Mary S. *The Biology of Invertebrates*. New York: McGraw-Hill, 1972.

Garrison, Ervan G. *A History of Engineering and Technology: Artful Methods*. Boca Raton, FL: CRC Press, 1991.

Garrison, Webb. *How It Started*. Nashville, TN: Abingdon Press, 1972.

Gatland, Kenneth. *The Illustrated Encyclopedia of Space Technology*. New York: Orion Books, 1989.

Gay, Kathlyn. *The Greenhouse Effect*. New York: Franklin Watts, 1986.

Gay, Kathlyn. *Ozone*. New York: Franklin Watts, 1989.

Gibson, Carol. *The Facts On File Dictionary of Mathematics*, Rev. ed. New York: Facts On File, Inc., 1988.

Giscard d'Estaing, Valerie-Anne, ed. *Inventions and Discoveries 1993: What's Happened, What's Coming, What's That*. New York: Facts On File, 1993.

Giscard d'Estaing, Valerie-Anne. *The Second World Almanac Book of Inventions*. New York: World Almanac, 1986.

Giscard d'Estaing, Valerie-Anne. *The World Almanac Book of Inventions*. New York: World Almanac Publications, 1985.

Giwojna, Pete. *Marine Hermit Crabs*. Hong Kong: T. F. H. Publications, 1978.

G. K. Hall Encyclopedia of Modern Technology. Boston, MA: Equinox, 1987.

Godish, Thad. *Indoor Air Pollution Control*. Chelsea, MI: Lewis Publications, 1989.

Golob, Richard. *Almanac of Science and Technology: What's New and What's Known*. San Diego, CA: Harcourt Brace Jovanovich, 1990.

Gong, Victor. *AIDS: Facts and Issues*. Brunswich, NJ: Rutgers University Press, 1980.

Good Housekeeping editors. *The Good Housekeeping Family Health and Medical Guide*. Hearst Books, 1988.

Gousha 1996 Road Atlas, 19th ed. Comfort, TX: The H. M. Gousha Company, 1996.

Gray, Peter. *The Encyclopedia of the Biological Sciences*. New York: Van Nostrand Reinhold, 1970.

Great Britain Meteorological Office. *Meteorological Glossary*. New York: Chemical Publishing, 1972.

Great Engineers and Pioneers in Technology. vol. 1. New York: St. Martin's Press, 1981.

The Great Scientists. vol. 3. Danbury, CT: Grolier, 1989.

The Great Scientists. vol. 7. Danbury, CT: Grolier, 1989.

The Great Scientists. vol. 8. Danbury, CT: Grolier, 1989.

Green, James Harry. *The Dow Jones-Irwin Handbook of Telecommunications*. Homewood, IL: Dow Jones-Irwin, 1986.

Griesbach, Ellen, and Jerry Taylor, *Prentice-Hall Encyclopedia of Mathematics*. Englewood Cliffs, NJ: Prentice-Hall, 1982.

Griffith, H. Winter. *Complete Guide to Vitamins, Minerals and Supplements*. Tucson, AZ: Fisher Books, 1988.

Grimm, William C. *The Illustrated Book of Trees*. Harrisburgh, PA: Stackpole, 1983.

Groves, Don. *The Ocean Book*. New York: Wiley, 1989.

Grzimek, Bernhard. *Grzimek's Animal Life Encyclopedia*. vol. 11. New York: Van Nostrand Reinhold Company, 1974.

Grzimek, Bernhard. *Grzimek's Encyclopedia of Mammals*, 2nd ed., vol. 4. New York: McGraw-Hill, 1990.

Guiley, Rosemary E. *Moonscapes*. Englewood Cliffs, NJ: Prentice-Hall, 1991.

Guinness Book of Answers, 8th ed. Enfield, Eng.: Guinness Publishing, 1991.

Guinness Book of Records 1992. New York: Bantam Books, 1991.

Guinness Book of Records 1994. New York: Bantam Books, 1993.

Guinness Book of Records 1995. New York: Bantam Books, 1994.

Guinness Book of Records 1996. New York: Bantam Books, 1995.

Guinness Book of Records 1997. New York: Bantam Books, 1996.

Gurney, Gene. *Space Shuttle Log*. Blue Ridge Summit, PA: TAB, 1988.

Guyton, Arthur C. *Textbook of Medical Physiology*, 8th ed. Philadelphia, PA: Saunders, 1991.

Haber, Louis. *Odyssey Black Pioneers of Science and Invention*. San Diego, CA: An Odyssey Book, Harcourt Brace Jovanovich Publishers, 1970.

Hale, Mason E., Jr. *The Biology of Lichens*, 2nd ed. London: Edward Arnold, Ltd., 1974.

Halliday, Tim R., ed. *The Encyclopedia of Reptiles and Amphibians*. New York: Facts On File, 1986.

Halliday, William R. *Depths of the Earth*. New York: Harper, 1976.

Hamilton, William R. *The Henry Holt Guide to Minerals, Rocks, and Fossils*. New York: Henry Holt, 1989.

Hanson, M. J. *The Boomerang Book*. Harmondsworth, Meddlesex: Puffin Books, 1974.

Harding, Anthony. *The Guinness Book of the Car* London: Guinness Superlatives, 1987.

Harris, Ben. *Make Use of Garden Plants*. New York: Barre, 1978.

Harris, Harry. *Good Old-Fashioned Yankee Ingenuity*. Chelsea, MI: Scarborough House, 1990.

Harrison, C. William. *Conservation*. New York: Julian Messner, 1973.

Harte, John. *Toxics A to Z*. Berkeley, CA: University of California Press, 1991.

Hartmann, William, and Ron Miller. *Cycles of Fire*. New York: Workman Publishing, 1987.

Hathaway, Nancy. *The Friendly Guide to the Universe*. New York: Penguin Books, 1994.

Hawkes, Nigel. *Structures*. New York: Macmillan, 1990.

Hawley's Condensed Chemical Dictionary, 12th ed. New York: Van Nostrand Reinhold, 1993.

Hawthorne, Douglas B. *Men and Women of Space*. San Diego, CA: Univolt, 1992.

Haygreen, John G. *Forest Products and Wood Science*, 2nd ed. Ames, IA: Iowa State University Press, 1989.

Hazen, Robert M., and James Trefil. *Science Matters: Achieving Scientific Literacy*. New York: Anchor Books, 1991.

Headstrom, Richard. *Spiders of the United States*. Stamford, CT: A. S. Barnes, 1973.

Heloise. *Heloise: Hints for a Healthy Planet*. New York: Perigee, 1990.

Henrickson, Charles H. *Chemistry for the Health Professions*. New York: Van Nostrand, 1980.

Heraud, Daniel P. *Chilton's Road Report*. Radnor, PA: Chilton, 1994.

Herbst, Sharon T. *The New Food Lover's Companion: Comprehensive Definitions of Over 4000 Food, Wine, and Culinary Terms*. Hauppauge, NY: Barron, 1995.

Hershey, David R. *Plant Biology Science Projects*. New York: John Wiley, 1995.

Hillman, Howard. *Kitchen Science*, Rev. ed. Boston, MA: Houghton Mifflin Company, 1989.

Hiscox, Gardner D. *Henley's Twentieth Century Book of Formulas, Processes, and Trade Secrets*. New York: NY Books, Inc., 1963.

Hofstadter, Douglas R. *Gödel, Escher, Bach: An Eternal Golden Braid*. New York: Vintage Books, 1979.

Holmes, Gwendolyn, Louise Theodore, and Ben Singh. *Handbook of Environmental Management and Technology*. New York: Wiley, 1993.

Hooper, Meredith. *More Everyday Inventions* London: Angus and Robertson, 1974.

Hopkins, Jeanne. *Glossary of Astronomy and Astrophysics*. Chicago, IL: University of Chicago Press, 1976.

Hopkins, Nigel J., John W. Mayne, and John R. Hudson. *The Numbers You Need*. Detroit, MI: Gale Research, 1992.

Horton, Edward. *The Illustrated History of the Submarine*. London: Sidgwick & Jackson, 1974.

Howes, F. N. *A Dictionary of Useful and Everyday Plants and Their Common Names*. Cambridge, Eng.: Cambridge University Press, 1974.

How in the World?: A Fascinating Journey Through the World of Human Ingenuity. Pleasantville, NY: The Reader's Digest Association, 1990.

How Products Are Made. Detroit, MI: Gale Research, 1994.

How Things Work in Your Home. New York: Holt, Rinehart, and Winston, 1985.

How to Do Just About Anything. Pleasantville, NY: The Reader's Digest Association, 1986.

Hoyle, Russ. *Gale Environmental Almanac*. Detroit, MI: Gale Research, 1993.

Hudgeons, Marc. *The Official Investors Guide: Buying, Selling, Gold, Silver, and Diamonds*. Orlando, FL: House of Collectables, 1981.

The Human Brain. Englewood Cliffs, NJ: Prentice-Hall, 1977.

Hunter, Linda Mason. *The Healthy Home*. New York: Pocket Books, 1989.

Hunt, V. Daniel. *The Gasohol Handbook*. New York: Industrial Press, 1981.

Huxley, Thomas H. *The Crayfish*. Cambridge, MA: MIT Press, 1974.

Hyne, Norman J. *Dictionary of Petroleum Exploration, Drilling and Production*. Tulsa, OK: PennWell, 1991.

Illingworth, Valerie. *The Facts on File Dictionary of Astronomy*, 3rd ed. New York: Facts On File, Inc., 1994.

Illustrated Encyclopedia of Wildlife. vol. 4. Lakeville, CT: Grey Castle Press, 1991.

Illustrated Encyclopedia of Wildlife. vol. 9. Lakeville, CT: Grey Castle Press, 1991.

The Illustrated Science and Invention Encyclopedia, International ed. vol. 2. Westport, CT: H. S. Stuttman Publishers, 1983, 23 vols.

The Illustrated Science and Invention Encyclopedia, International ed. vol. 3. Westport, CT: H. S. Stuttman Publishers, 1983. 23 vols.

Inglis, Andrew F. *Behind the Tube: A History of Broadcasting Technology and Business*. London: Focal Press, 1990.

Inventive Genius. New York: Time-Life Books, 1991.

The IUCN Amphibia-Reptilia Red Data Book. International Union for the Conservation of Nature & Natural Resources.

Iver, David F. *Dictionary of Astronomy, Space, and Atmospheric Phenomena.* New York: Van Nostrand Reinhold Co., 1979.

Jackson, Donald C. *Great American Bridges and Dams.* Washington, DC: The Preservation Press, 1988.

James, Glenn. *Mathematics Dictionary,* 4th ed. New York: Van Nostrand Reinhold, 1976.

James, Peter, and Nick Thorpe. *Ancient Inventions.* New York: Ballentine Books, 1994.

James, Robert C. *Mathematics Dictionary,* 5th ed. New York: Van Nostrand Reinhold, 1992.

Jerrard, H. G. *A Dictionary of Scientific Units,* 4th ed. New York: Chapman and Hall, 1980.

Jespersen, James. *RAMS, ROMS, and Robots.* New York: Atheneum, 1984.

Jones, Julia, and Barbara Deere. *Royal Pleasures and Pastimes.* Devon, Eng.: David and Charles, 1990.

Kane, Joseph N. *Famous First Facts,* 4th ed. New York: Wilson, 1981.

Kaplan, Eugene H. *Field Guide to Coral Reefs.* Boston, MA: Houghton Mifflin Co., 1982.

Karush, William. *Webster's New World Dictionary of Mathematics.* Englewood Cliffs, NJ: Webster's New World, 1989.

Kaufman, Peter B., et al. *Practical Botany.* New York: Prentice-Hall, 1983.

Keeler, Harriet L. *Our Early Wild Flowers.* New York: Charles Scribner's Sons, 1916.

Kemp, Peter. *Encyclopedia of Ships and Sailing.* Dobbs Ferry, NY: Stanford Maritime, 1989.

Kendig, Frank, and Richard Hutton. *Life-Spans.* New York: Holt, Rinehart, and Winston, 1979.

Kidder, Frank. *Architects' and Builders' Handbook.* New York: Wiley, 1931.

Knappman, Edward W., ed. *Great American Trials.* Detroit, MI: Gale Research, 1994.

Labatut, Jean, and J. L. Wheaton. *Highways in Our National Life.* Princeton, NJ: Princeton University Press, 1950.

Lafferty, Peter, and Julian Rowe, eds. *The Dictionary of Science.* New York: Simon & Schuster, 1994.

Lambert, David. *The Field Guide to Early Man.* New York: Facts On File, 1987.

Larijani, L. Casey. *The Virtual Reality Primer.* New York: McGraw-Hill, 1994.

Larson, David E., ed. *Mayo Clinic Family Health Book: The Ultimate Home Medical Reference.* New York: Marrow, 1990.

Lawrence, Eleanor. *Henderson's Dictionary of Biological Terms,* 10th ed. New York: John Wiley and Sons, 1989.

Lean, Geoffrey, et al. *WWF Atlas of the Environment.* Boston, MA: Willard Grant Press, 1991.

Lean, Geoffrey, et al. *WWF Atlas of the World.* Boston, MA: Willard Grant Press, 1991.

Lederberg, Joshua *Encyclopedia of Microbiology.* vol. 2. San Diego, CA: Academic Press, 1992.

Lee, Sally. *Predicting Violent Storms.* New York: Franklin Watts, 1989.

Leet, L. Don, and Sheldon Judson. *Physical Geology,* 4th ed. Englewood Cliffs, NJ: Prentice-Hall, 1971.

Leff, Jonathan. *Consumer Reports Health Answer Book.* Yonkers, NY: Consumer Reports Books, 1993.

Leggett, Jeremy. *Global Warming.* Oxford: Oxford University Press, 1990.

Lennes, N. J. *New Practical Mathematics.* New York: Macmillan, 1939.

Leopold, Luna B. *Water.* New York: Time, 1966.

Leung, Albert Y. *Encyclopedia of Common Natural Ingredients.* New York: Wiley, 1980.

Levy, Richard C. *Inventing and Patenting Sourcebook.* Detroit, MI: Gale Research, 1990.

Levy, Richard C. *The Inventor's Desktop Companion.* Detroit, MI: Visible Ink Press, 1991.

Lewis, Richard J. Sr. *Hawley's Condensed Chemical Dictionary,* 12th ed. New York: Van Nostrand Reinhold, 1993.

Lincoln, John W. *Driving Without Gas.* Pownal, VT: Garden Way, 1980.

Lincoln, R. J. *A Dictionary of Ecology, Evolution, and Systematics.* New York: Cambridge University Press, 1982.

Longley, Dennis, and Michael Shain. *Van Nostrand Reinhold Dictionary of Information Technology,* 3rd ed. New York: Van Nostrand Reinhold, 1989.

Ludlum, David M. *The Audubon Society Field Guide to North American Weather.* New York: Knopf, 1991.

Macdonald, David W., ed. *The Encyclopedia of Mammals.* New York: Facts On File, 1984.

MacEachern, Diane. *Save Our Planet.* New York: Dell, 1990.

Mace, Alice E., ed. *The Birds Around Us.* San Ramon, CA: Ortho, 1986.

Maclean, Norman. *Dictionary of Genetics and Cell Biology.* New York: New York University Press, 1987.

The Macmillan Visual Dictionary. New York: Macmillan, 1992.

Magill, Frank N. *Great Events from History II: Science and Technology Series.* vol. 5. Englewood Cliffs, NJ: Salem Press, 1991.

Magill, Frank N. *Magill's Survey of Science: Earth Science Series.* vol. 1. Englewood Cliffs, NJ: Salem Press, 1990.

Magill, Frank N. *Magill's Survey of Science: Earth Science Series.* vol. 3. Englewood Cliffs, NJ: Salem Press, 1990.

Magill, Frank N. *Magill's Survey of Science: Life Science Series.* vol. 5. Englewood Cliffs, NJ: Salem Press, 1991.

Magill, Frank N. *Magill's Survey of Science: Space Exploration Series.* vol. 1. Englewood Cliffs, NJ: Salem Press, 1989.

Magill, Frank N. *Magill's Survey of Science: Space Exploration Series.* vol. 4. Englewood Cliffs, NJ: Salem Press, 1989.

Magill, Frank N. *Nobel Prize Winners: Physiology or Medicine.* vol. 2. Englewood Cliffs, NJ: Salem Press, 1991.

Magner, Lois N. *A History of the Life Sciences.* New York: Marcel Dekker, 1979.

Maniquet, Xavier. *The Jaws of Death.* Dobbs Ferry, NY: Sheridan House, 1991.

Manko, Howard H. *Solders and Soldering,* 2nd ed. New York: McGraw-Hill, 1979.

Marchok, Janice. *Oh No! Not My Electric Blanket, Too?* Latrobe, PA: Jetmarc Group, 1991.

Margulis, Lynn. *Five Kingdoms.* New York: W. H. Freeman and Company, 1988.

Mariani, John F. *The Dictionary of American Food and Drink.* New York: Ticknor & Fields, 1994.

Mark's Standard Handbook for Mechanical Engineers, 9th ed. New York: McGraw-Hill, 1987.

Marshall Cavendish Illustrated Encyclopedia of Family Health. 24 vols. London: Marshall Cavendish, 1984.

Marshall, John. *The Guinness Railway Book.* London: Guinness Books, 1989.

Marshall, John. *Rail: The Records.* London: Guinness Books, 1989.

Matthews, Rupert O. *The Atlas of Natural Wonders.* New York: Facts On File, 1988.

Mayhew, Susan, and Anne Penny. *The Concise Oxford Dictionary of Geography.* New York: Oxford University Press, 1992.

May, John. *The Greenpeace Book of Antarctica: A New View of the Seventh Continent,* 1st ed. New York: Doubleday, 1989.

May, John. *The Greenpeace Book of the Nuclear Age.* New York: Pantheon, 1989.

McAleer, Neil. *The Body Almanac.* New York: Doubleday, 1985.

McElroy, Thomas P. *The New Handbook of Attracting Birds.* New York: Knopf, 1960.

McEwan, W.A., and A. H. Lewis. *Encyclopedia of Nautical Knowledge.* Centreville, MD: Cornell Maritime Press, 1953.

McGee, Harold. *On Food and Cooking.* New York: Collier Books, 1988.

McGraw-Hill Dictionary of Earth Science. New York: McGraw-Hill.

The McGraw-Hill Dictionary of Scientific and Technical Terms, 5th ed. New York: McGraw-Hill, 1994.

McGraw-Hill Encyclopedia of Science and Technology, 7th ed. 20 vols. New York: McGraw-Hill, Inc., 1992.

McGraw-Hill Yearbook of Science and Technology 1991. New York: McGraw-Hill, 1990.

McKinnell, Robert G. *Cloning of Frogs, Mice, and Other Animals,* Rev. ed. Minneapolis MN: University of Minnesota Press, 1985.

McMurray, Emily J., and Donna Olendorf, eds. *Notable Twentieth Century Scientists.* 4vols. Detroit, MI: Gale Research, 1995.

McNeil, Ian. *An Encyclopedia of the History of Technology.* London: Routledge, 1990.

McNulty, Faith. *Wholly Cats.* New York: Bobbs-Merrill, 1962.

Medawar, P.B., and J.S. Medawar. *Aristotle to Zoos.* Cambridge MA: Harvard University Press, 1983.

Melaragno, Michele. *An Introduction to Shell Structures.* New York: Van Nostrand Reinhold, 1991.

Melonakos, K. *Saunders Pocket Reference for Nurses.* Philadelphia, PA: Saunders, 1990.

Menninger, Edwin. *Fantastic Trees.* New York: Viking, 1967.

Menzel, Donald H., and Jay M. Pasachoff. *A Field Guide to Stars and Planets,* 2nd ed. Boston, MA: Houghton Mifflin Co., 1990.

Merck Manual of Diagnosis and Therapy, 15th ed. West Point, PA: Merck, Shark, & Dohme, 1987.

Mery, Fernand. *The Life, History, and Magic of the Dog*. New York: Grosset & Dunlap, 1970.

Michard, Jean-Guy. *The Reign of the Dinosaurs*. New York: Harry N. Abrams, Incorporated, 1992.

Milestones of Aviation. Washington, DC: Smithsonian Institution, 1989.

Miller, E. Willard. *Environmental Hazards: Toxic Waste and Hazardous Material*. Santa Barbara, CA: ABC-CLIO, 1991.

Miller, E. Willard, and Ruby M. Miller. *Environmental Hazards: Air Pollution*. Santa Barbara, CA: ABC-CLIO, 1989.

Miller, Ron, and William K. Hartmann. *The Grand Tour: A Traveler's Guide to the Solar System*. New York: Workman Publishing, 1981.

Millichap, J. Gordon. *Dyslexia as the Neurologist and Educator Read It*. Springfield, IL: Thomas, 1986.

Milner, Richard. *The Encyclopedia of Evolution*. New York: Facts On File, 1990.

Minerals Yearbook 1993. Washington, DC: U.S. Bureau of Mines, 1995.

Mondey, David. *The Guinness Book of Aircraft*. London: Guinness, 1988.

Moorcroft, William H. *Sleep, Dreaming, and Sleep Disorders*. Lanham, MD: University Press of America, 1989.

Moore, John E. *Submarine Warfare*. Bethesda, MD: Alder & Alder, 1987.

Moore-Landecker, Elizabeth. *Fundamentals of the Fungi*, 3rd ed. Englewood Cliffs, NJ: Prentice Hall, 1990.

Moore, Laurence A. *Lightning Never Strikes Twice and Other False Facts*. New York: Avon Books, 1994.

Moore, Patrick. *Atlas of the Solar System*. New York: Crescent Books with the Royal Astronomical Society, 1990.

Moore, Patrick. *International Encyclopedia of Astronomy*. New York: Orion Books, 1987.

Morgan, George W. *Geodesic and Geodetic Domes and Space Structures*. Madison, WI: Sci-Tech Publications, 1985.

Morgans, W. M. *Outlines of Paint Technology*. New York: Halsted Press, 1990.

Morlan, Michael. *Kitty Hawk to NASA: A Guide to U.S. Air and Space Museums and Exhibits*. Shawnee Mission, KS: Bon a Tirer, 1991.

Morris, C., ed. *Academic Press Dictionary of Science and Technology*. Academic Press, 1992.

Mosby's Medical, Nursing and, Allied Health Dictionary, 3rd ed. St. Louis, MO: Mosby, 1990.

Motz, Lloyd, and Jefferson Hane Weaver. *Conquering Mathematics*. New York: Plenum Press, 1991.

Mount, Ellis, and Barbara A. List. *Milestones in Science and Technology: The Ready Reference Guide to Discoveries, Inventions, and Facts*. Phoenix, AZ: Oryx Press, 1987.

MVMA *Motor Vehicle Facts and Figures '91*. Detroit, MI: Motor Vehicle Manufacturers Association of the United States, 1991.

Naar, Jon. *Design for a Livable Planet*. Harper & Row, Publishers, 1990.

Nash, Jay R. *Darkest Hours: A Narrative Encyclopedia of Worldwide Disasters from Ancient Times to the Present*. Nelson-Hall, 1976.

The National Inventors Hall of Fame 1990. Washington, DC: U.S. Patent and Trademark Office, 1990.

Nayler, Joseph L. *Aviation: Its Technical Development*. Chester Springs, PA: Dufour Editions, 1965.

Neal, Valerie, et. al. *Spaceflight: A Smithsonian Guide*. New York: Macmillan, 1995.

Netboy, Anthony. *The Salmon*. Boston, MA: Houghton Mifflin, 1974.

The New Book of Popular Science. 6 vols. Danbury, CT: Grolier, 1989.

The New Dog Encyclopedia. Harrisburg, PA: Stackpole, 1970.

New Encyclopaedia Britannica, 15th ed. 29 vols. Chicago, IL: Encyclopaedia Britannica, 1990.

The New Encyclopaedia Britannica, Micropaedia. vol. 5. Chicago, IL: Encyclopaedia Britannica, 1990.

New Illustrated Science and Invention Encyclopedia. vol. 24. Westport, CT: Stuttman, 1988.

New York Public Library Staff. *The New York Public Library Desk Reference*. New York: Webster's New World, 1989.

The 1992 Information Please Environmental Almanac. Boston, MA: Houghton Mifflin Company, 1992.

The Nobel Prize Winners: Physics. 3 vols. Pasadena, CA: Salem Press, 1989.

The Nobel Prize Winners: Physiology or Medicine. vol. 2. Pasadena, CA: Salem Press, 1989.

Nock, O .S. *Encyclopedia of Railways*. London: Octopus Books, 1977.

Norman, David. *Dinosaur!* New York: Prentice-Hall, 1991.

Nowak, Ronald M. *Walker's Mammals of the World*, 5th ed. 2 vols. Baltimore, MD: The Johns Hopkins University Press, 1991.

The Nuclear Waste Primer. New York: Nick Lyons Books, 1985.

O'Brien, Tim. *Where the Animals Are*. Old Saybrook, CT: Globe Peuot Press, 1992.

Odum, Eugene. *Fundamentals of Ecology*, 3rd, ed. Philadelphia, PA: Saunders, 1971.

The Official World Wildlife Fund Guide to Endangered Species of North America. 3 vols. Washington, DC: Beacham Publishing, 1990-1991.

Oglesby, Clarkson H., and R. Gary Hicks. *Highway Engineering*. New York: John Wiley & Sons, 1982.

Ojakangas, Richard. *Schaum's Outline of Theory and Problems of Introductory Geology*. New York: McGraw-Hill, 1991.

101 Ways to Save Money and Save Our Planet. New Orleans, LA: Paper Chase Press, 1992.

Ortho's Complete Guide to Successful Gardening. San Ramon, CA: Ortho Books, 1983.

Otto, James H. *Modern Biology*. Fort Worth, TX: Holt, Rinehart, and Winston, 1981.

The Oxford Dictionary for Scientific Writers and Editors. Oxford, Eng.: Oxford University Press, 1991.

Oxford Illustrated Encyclopedia of Invention and Technology. Oxford, Eng.: Oxford University Press, 1992.

Palmer, Ephram Laurence. *Fieldbook of Natural History*, 2nd ed. New York: McGraw-Hill, 1974.

Palmer, Joan. *Dog Facts*. New York: Dorset Press, 1991.

Panati, Charles. *Panati's Browser's Book of Beginnings*. Boston, MA: Houghton Mifflin, 1984.

Parker, Sybil P. *McGraw-Hill Concise Encyclopedia of Science and Technology*, 5th ed. New York: McGraw-Hill, 1997.

Parkinson, Clair L. *Breakthroughs: A Chronology of Great Achievements in Science and Mathematics*. Boston, MA: G. K. Hall, 1985.

Partington, J. R. *A Short History of Chemistry*, 3rd ed. New York: Dover, 1989.

Pasachoff, Jay M. *Contemporary Astronomy*. Philadelphia, PA: W. B. Saunders, Co., 1977.

Passarin d'Entreves, P. *The Secret Life of Insects*. New York: Chartwell, 1976.

Passport to World Band Radio. Penn's Park, PA: International Broadcasting Services, 1992.

Pearl, Richard M. *1001 Questions Answered About the Mineral Kingdom*. New York: Dodd, Mead, 1959.

Pendergrast, Mark. *For God, Country, and Coca-Cola*. New York: Charles Scribner's Sons, 1993.

Pfadt, Robert E. *Fundamentals of Applied Entomology*, 3rd ed. New York: Macmillan, 1978.

Pickering, James S. *1001 Questions Answered About Astronomy*. New York: Dodd, Mead, 1958.

Plants: Their Biology and Importance. New York: Harper & Row, Publishers, 1989.

The Plastic Waste Primer. New York: Lyons and Burford, 1993.

Platt, Rutherford. *1001 Questions Answered About Trees*. New York: Dodd, Mead, 1959.

Pleasant, Barbara. *The Gardener's Bug Book*. Ponwal, VT: Storey Communications, 1994.

Plumridge, John H. *Hospital Ships and Ambulance Trains*. London: Seeley, 1975.

Porter, Roy, ed. *The Biographical Dictionary of Scientists*, 2nd ed. New York: Oxford University Press, 1994.

Press, Frank. *Earth*, 2nd ed. San Francisco, CA: W. H. Freeman, 1978.

Preston-Mafham, Rod. *The Book of Spiders and Scorpions*. New York: Crescent Books, 1991.

Prevention's Giant Book of Health Facts. Emmaus, PA: Rodale Press, 1991.

Professional Guide to Diseases, 4th ed. Springhouse, PA: Springhouse Corp., 1992.

The Public Health Consequences of Air Disasters 1989. Atlanta, GA: Centers for Disease Control, 1989.

Pugh, Anthony. *Polyhedra*. Berkeley, CA: university of California Press, 1976.

Purnell's Encyclopedia of Inventions. London: Purnell & Sons, Ltd., 1976.

Raven, Peter and George B. Johnson. *Biology*, 4th ed. Dubuque, IA: Wm C. Brown, Publishers, 1996.

Raymond, Eric S. *The New Hacker's Dictionary*. Cambridge, MA: The MIT Press, 1991.

Reader's Digest Editors. *Great Disasters: Dramatic True Stories of Nature's Awesome Powers*. New York: Reader's Digest Association, 1989.

Resh, Howard M. *Hydroponic Food Production*. Santa Barbara, CA: Woodbridge Press, 1995.

The Reston Encyclopedia of Biomedical Engineering Terms. Reston.

Rheingold, Howard. *Tools for Thought*. New York: Simon & Schuster, 1985.

Rhodes, Frank H. T. *Geology*. New York: Golden Press, 1972.

Rhodes, Richard. *The Making of the Atomic Bomb*. New York: Simon & Schuster, 1986.

Rickard, Teresa. *Barnes and Noble Thesaurus of Physics*. New York: Harper & Row, 1984.

Robertson, Patrick. *The Book of Firsts*. New York: Clarkson N. Potter, Inc., 1974.

Robinson, Andrew. *Earthshock*. Thames Hudson, 1993.

Rochester, Jack B. *The Naked Computer*. New York: Morrow, 1983.

Rodale's Illustrated Encyclopedia of Gardening and Landscaping Techniques. Emmaus, PA: Rodale Press, 1990.

Room, Adrian. *Dictionary of Trade Name Origins*. New York: Routledge, 1988.

Root, Waverly L. *Food*. New York: Simon & Schuster, 1980.

Rosenberg, Jerry M. *Dictionary of Computers, Data Processing, and Telecommunications*. New York: John Wiley & Sons, 1984.

Rosenfeld, Sam. *Science Experiments with Water*. Irvington-on-Hudson, NY: Harvey House, 1965.

Ross, Frank Xavier. *The Metric System—Measures for All Mankind*. New York: Phillips, 1974.

Roth, Charles E. *The Plant Observer's Guidebook*. Englewood Cliffs, NJ: Prentice-Hall, Inc., 1984.

Rovin, Jeff. *Laws of Order*. New York: Ballantine, 1992.

Rush to Burn: Solving America's Garbage Crisis. Washington, DC: Island Press, 1989.

Saari, Peggy, and Diane L. Dupuis, eds. *Cities of the United States: The West*. Detroit, MI: Gale Research, 1989.

The Safe Food Book. Washington, DC: U.S. Department of Agriculture, 1985.

Sagan, Carl, and Ann Druyan. *Comet*. New York: Random House, 1980.

Sammons, Vivian O. *Blacks in Science and Medicine*. New York: Hemisphere Publishing, 1990.

Sanders, Dennis. *The First of Everything*. New York: Delacorte, 1981.

Sanders, Ti. *Weather*. South Bend, IN: Icarus Press, 1985.

Savitskii, E.M. *Handbook of Precious Metals*. New York: Hemisphere Publishing Corp., 1989.

Schaefer, Vincent J., and John A. Day. *A Field Guide to the Atmosphere*. Boston, MA: Houghton Mifflin Company, 1981.

Schlager, Neal, ed. *When Technology Fails*. Detroit, MI: Gale Research, Inc., 1994.

Schmittroth, Linda, Mary Reilly McCall, and Bridget Travers, eds. *Eureka!: Scientific Discoveries and Inventions That Shaped the World*. vol 3. Detroit, MI: UXL, 1995.

Schneck, Marcus, and Jill Caravan. *Cat Facts*. New York: Dorset Press, 1990.

Schneider, Herman, *The Harper Dictionary of Science in Everyday Language*. New York: Harper & Row, 1988.

Schodek, Daniel L. *Landmarks in American Civil Engineering*. Cambridge, MA: MIT Press, 1987.

Schwartz, Herbert F. *Patent Law and Practice*, 2nd ed., Washington, DC: Federal Judicial Center, 1995.

Schweighauser, Charles A. *Astronomy from A to Z*. Springfield, IL: Illinois Issues, 1991.

Schweitzer, Glenn E. *Borrowed Earth, Borrowed Time*. New York: Plenum, 1991.

Science and Technology Illustrated. 28 vols. Chicago, IL: Encyclopaedia Britannica, Inc., 1984.

Scott, John S. *Dictionary of Civil Engineering*. New York: Halstead Press, 1981.

Seager, Spencer. *Introductory Chemistry for Today*, 2nd ed. St Paul, MN: West Publishing, 1994.

Selkurt, Ewald E. *Physiology*, 5th ed. Boston, MA: Little, Brown, 1984.

Shacket, Sheldon R. *The Complete Book of Electric Vehicles*. Northbrook, IL: Domus Books, 1979.

Shafritz, Jay M. *The Facts On File Dictionary of Military Science*. New York: Facts On File, 1989.

Shapiro, Max S. *Mathematics Encyclopedia*. New York: Doublday, 1977.

Shores, Christopher F. *Fighter Aces*. London: Hamly, 1975.

Silverman, Sharon H. *Going Underground*. Philadelphia, PA: Camino Books, 1991.

Simon, Andre L. and Robin Howe. *Dictionary of Gastronomy*, 2nd ed. Woodstock, NY: The Overlook Press, 1978.

Simon, Sheridan. *Stephen Hawking: Unlocking the Universe*. Silver Burdett Press, 1991.

Sinclair, Ian R. *The HarperCollins Dictionary of Computer Terms*. New York: HarperPerennial, 1991.

Skinner, Brian J. *The Dynamic Earth*. New York: John Wiley & Sons, 1989.

Smallwood, Charles A., et al. *The Cable Car Book*. Berkeley, CA: Celestial Arts, 1980.

Smith, Doris C., ed. *Physicians' Guide to Rare Diseases*. Montvale, NJ: Dowden, 1992.

Smith, Marcia. *Space Activities of the United States and Other Launching Countries/Organizations: 1957-1991*. Washington, DC: Library of Congress, Science Policy Research Division, 1992.

Smith, Michael D. *All About Bulbs*. San Ramon, CA: Ortho Books, 1986.

Smithsonian Institute. *Annual Report, 1939*. Washington, DC: U.S. Government Printing Office, 1940.

Soloman, Eldra Pearl, and Gloria A. Phillips. *Understanding Human Anatomy and Physiology*. Philadelphia, PA: W. B. Saunders Company, 1987.

Spangenburg, Ray, and Diane Moser. *Space People From A-Z*. New York: Facts On File, 1990.

Spar, Jerome. *The Way of the Weather*. Mankato, MN: Creative Educational Society, 1967.

Standard Handbook for Civil Engineers, 3rd ed. New York: McGraw-Hill, 1983.

Starr, Cecie, and Ralph Taggart. *Biology: The Unity and Diversity of Life*, 6th ed. Belmont, CA: Wadsworth Publishing, Company, 1992.

Stedman's Medical Dictionary, 25th ed. Baltimore, MD: Williams & Wilkins, 1990.

Stein, Edwin I. *Arithmetic for College Students*, Rev. ed. Needhame Heights, MA: Allyn and Bacon, 1961.

Stephens, John H. *The Guinness Book of Structures*. London: Guinness Superlatives, Ltd., 1976.

Stephenson, D. J. *Newnes Guide to Satellite TV*. London: Newnes, 1991.

Stewart, David. *The Earthquake America Forgot*. Marble Hill, MO: Gutenberg-Richter Publications, 1995.

Stewart, John. *Antarctica: An Encyclopedia*, 2 vols. McFarland & Company, 1990.

Stilwell, E. Joseph, et al. *Packaging for the Environment*. New York: AMACOM, 1991.

Stimpson, George. *Information Roundup*. New York: Harper, 1948.

Stokes, Donald. *The Complete Birdhouse Book*. Boston, MA: Little, Brown, 1991.

Stories Behind Everyday Things. Pleasantville, NY: Reader's Digest, 1980.

The Straight Dope. New York: Ballantine, 1986.

Sussman, Martin. *Total Health at the Computer*. Barrytown, NY: Station Hill, 1993.

Sutton, Caroline, and Duncan M. Anderson. *How Do They Do That?* New York: Quill, 1982.

Swank, James M. *History of the Manufacture of Iron in All Ages*. New York: Burt Franklin, 1965.

Taber, Robert W. *1001 Questions Answered About the Oceans and Oceanography*. New York: Dodd, Mead, 1972.

Taylor, David. *You and Your Cat*. New York: Alfred Knopf, 1988.

Taylor, Walter H. *Concrete Technology and Practice*. New York: McGraw-Hill, 1977.

Temple, Robert K.G. *The Genius of China*. New York: Simon and Schuster, 1986.

Terres, John K. *The Audubon Society Encyclopedia of North American Birds*. New York: Wings Book, 1991.

Thomas, Clayton L. *Taber's Cyclopedic Medical Dictionary*, 17th ed. Philadelphia, PA: Davis, 1993.

Thomas, David A. *Math Projects for Young Scientists*. New York: Franklin Watts, 1988.

Thrush, Paul W. *A Dictionary of Mining, Minerals, and Related Terms*. Washington, DC: U.S. Bureau of Mines, 1968.

Thygerson, Alton L. *First Aid Essentials*. Boston, MA: Jones and Bartlett, 1989.

Tidwell, William D. *Common Fossil Plants of Western North America*. Provo, UT: Brigham Young University Press, 1975.

Tilling, Robert I. *Eruptions of Mount St. Helens*, Rev. ed. Washington, DC: U.S. Department of the Interior, 1990.

The Timetable of Technology. San Diego, CA: Harvest Books, 1992.

Tortora, Gerard J. *Introduction to the Human Body*. New York: HarperCollins, 1991.

Tortora, Gerard J. *Principles of Anatomy and Physiology*, 4th ed., New York: Harper and Row, 1984.

Tortora, Gerard J. *Principles of Human Physiology*, 2nd ed. Reading, MA: Addison-Wesley Education, 1995.

Towle, Albert. *Modern Biology*. Austin, TX: Holt, Rinehart, and Winston, 1989.

Toxics in the Community. Washington, DC: U.S. Environmental Proctection Agency, 1990.

Traffic Engineering Handbook, 2nd ed. Washington, DC: Institute of Traffic Engineers, 1959.

Travers, Bridget, ed. *The Gale Encyclopedia of Science*. vol.1. Detroit, MI: Gale Research, 1996.

Travers, Bridget, ed. *The Gale Encyclopedia of Science*. vol. 5. Detroit, MI: Gale Research, 1996.

Travers, Bridget, ed. *World of Invention*. Detroit, MI: Gale Research, 1994.

Travers, Bridget, ed. *World of Scientific Discovery*. Detroit, MI: Gale Research, 1994.

Trefil, James. *1001 Things Everyone Should Know About Science*. New York: Doubleday, 1992.

Tufty, Barbara J. *1001 Questions Answered About Earthquakes, Avalanches, Floods, and Other Natural Disasters*. New York: Dover Publications, Inc., 1978.

Tufty, Barbara. *1001 Questions Answered About Hurricanes, Tornados, and Other Natural Air Disasters*. New York: Dover Publications, Inc., 1987.

Tunnell, James E. *Latest Intelligence*. Blue Ridge Summit, PA: TAB, 1990.

Tzimopoulos, Nicholas D., et al. *Modern Chemistry*. Fort Worth, TJX: Holt, Rinehart, and Winston, 1990.

Understanding Computers: Illustrated Chronology and Index. New York: Time-Life Books, 1989.

U.S. Department of Agriculture. *Farmers' Bulletin no. 1500*. Washington, DC: U.S. Department of Agriculture, 1926.

U.S. Department of Agriculture. *USDA's Food Guide Pyramid*. Washington, DC: U.S. Department of Agriculture.

U.S. Department of Commerce. Patent and Trademark Office. *Basic Facts About Registering a Trademark*. Washington, DC: U.S. Department of Commerce, 1994.

U.S. Department of Commerce. *Tornadoes…Nature's Most Violent Storms*. Washington, DC: U.S. Department of Commerce, 1992.

U.S. Department of Health and Human Services. *Marijuana*, (pamphlet). Washington, DC: U.S. Department of Health and Human Services, 1984.

U.S. Department of the Interior. *The Story of the Hoover Dam*. Washington, DC: U.S. Department of the Interior, 1971.

U. S. Department of the Navy. *Poisonous Snakes of the World*. New York: Dover, 1991.

Used Car Buying Guide 1994. Yonkers, NY: Consumers Union of United States, 1994.

U.S. Energy Information Administration. *International Energy Outlook 1994*, July 1994

U.S. General Accounting Office. *Highway Safety: Safety Belt Use Laws Save Lives and Reduce Costs to Society*, May 1992

U.S. Geological Survey. *Our Changing Continent*, (pamphlet). Washington, DC: U.S. Geological Survey, 1991.

U.S. National Oceanic and Atmospheric Administration.*Lightning Safety Rules* (C55.102:L62). Washington, DC: U.S. National Oceanic and Atmospheric Administration.

U.S. Patent and Trademark Office. *Basic Facts About Patents*. Washington, DC: U.S. Patent and Trademark Office, 1994.

Van Andel, Tjeerd H. *New Views On an Old Planet*. New York: Cambridge University Press, 1985.

Van der Leeden, Frits. *The Water Encyclopedia*, 2nd ed. Chelsea, MI: Lewis, 1990.

Van Nostrand Reinhold Encyclopedia of Chemistry, 4th ed. New York: Van Nostrand Reinhold, 1984.

Vengris, Jonas. *Lawns*, 3rd ed. Fresno, CA: Thomson Publications, 1982.

Vergara, William C. *Science in Everyday Life*. New York: Harper and Row, Publishers, 1980.

Vickery, Donald M., and James F. Fries. *Take Care of Yourself: Your Personal \Guide to Self-Care and Preventing Illness*, 5th ed. Reading, MA: Addison-Wesley Publihing Company, 1996.

Villee, Claude A. *Biology*, 2nd ed. New York: CBS College Publishing, 1985.

Voelker, William. *The Natural History of Living Mammals*. Medford, NJ: Plexus, 1986.

Wallace, Irving. *The Book of Lists #2*. New York: Morrow, 1980.

Wallechinsky, David. *The Book of Lists*. New York: Morrow, 1977.

Walters, Michael. *Birds' Eggs*. New York: Dorling Kindersly, 1994.

Ward, Jack A. *Biology Today and Tomorrow*. St. Paul, MN: West, 1980.

Webster's New Geographical Dictionary. Springfield, MA: Merriam-Webster, 1988.

Webster's Ninth New Collegiate Dictionary. Springfield, MA: Merriam-Webster, 1989.

The Wellness Encyclopedia of Food and Nutrition: How to Buy, Store, and Prepare Every Fresh Food. New York: Rebus, 1992.

Williams, Gene B. *Nuclear War, Nuclear Winter*. New York: Franklin Watts, 1987.

Williams, Jack. *The Weather Book*. New York: Vintage Books, 1992.

Williams, Robin. *Jargon*. Berkeley, CA: Peachpit Press, 1993.

Winkler, Connie. *Careers in High Tech*. Englewood Cliffs, NJ: Prentice Hall Press, 1987.

Wise, David Burgess. *The Motor Car*. New York: Putnam, 1979.

The Wise Garden Encyclopedia. New York: HarperCollins, 1990.

Wolke, Robert L. *Chemistry Explained*. Englewood Cliffs, NJ: Prentice-Hall, Inc., 1980.

Woman's Day Encyclopedia of Cookery. 12 vols. New York: Fawcett, 1966-67.

Wood, Gerald L. *The Guinness Book of Animal Facts and Feats*, 3rd ed., London: Guinness Superlatives, Ltd., 1982.

Wood, Gerald L. *The Guinness Book of Pet Records*. London: Guinness Books, 1984.

World Almanac 1996. New York: World Almanac, 1995.

World Book Encyclopedia. 22 vols. Chicago, IL: World Book, 1994.

Wright, John W., ed. *The Universal Almanac 1994*. Kansas City, MO: Andrews and McMeel, 1993.

Wright, John W. ed. *Universal Almanac 1996*. Kansas City, MO: Andrews & McMeel, 1995.

Wright, R. Thomas. *Understanding Technology*. South Holland, IL: Goodheart-Wilcox, 1989.

Wyatt, Allen L. *Computer Professional's Dictionary*. New York: McGraw-Hill, 1990.

Wyman, Donald. *Wyman's Gardening Encyclopedia*, 2nd ed. New York: Macmillan, 1986.

Wyngaarden, James B., and Lloyd H. Smith. *Cecil Textbook of Medicine*, 18th ed., Philadelphia, PA: Saunders, 1988.

Yearbook of Science and the Future 1991. Chicago, IL: Encyclopaedia Britannica, Inc., 1990.

Yearbook of Science and the Future 1993. Chicago, IL: Encyclopaedia Britannica, Inc., 1992.

Zahradnik, Jiri. *A Field Guide in Color to the Animal World*. London: Octopus, 1979.

Zim, Herbert S., and Paul Shaffer. *Rocks and Minerals*. New York: Golden Press, 1957.

Zimmerman, O. T. *Conversion Factors and Tables*, 3rd ed. Durham, NH: Industrial Research Services, 1961.

JOURNALS AND PERIODICALS

American Forests, March-April 1992.

American Scientist, May-June 1987.

American Heritage of Invention and Technology, Fall 1990.

American Transportation Builder, Winter 1981.

The Ann Arbor News, March 8, 1996; July 14, 1996; September 12, 1996; April 13, 1997; March 8, 1997.

Astronomy, November 1991; February 1996.

Audubon Magazine, March 1991; March-April 1992.

Aviation Week and Space Technology, February 20, 1995.

Biocycle, April 1995.

The Bulletin of the Atomic Scientists, September 1993.

Buzzworm: The Environmental Journal, November-December 1991; March-April 1992.

Chemical and Engineering News, April 27, 1992.

Chemical Marketing Reporter, June 26, 1995; October 7, 1996.

Compute, August 1991.

The Conservationist, 1994.

Country Journal, May 1988.

Current Health, April 1990; March 1991.

Detroit Free Press, July 13, 1993; December 21, 1993.

Discover, May 1985; January 1992; March 1992; January 1995.

The Economist, December 12, 1992.

Environment, November 1991.

EPA Journal, January-February 1990.

Facts On File News Digest with Index, August 1-7, 1945.

FDA Consumer, December 1987-January 1988; May 1993; June 1993.

Flower and Garden, May 1990.

The Futurist, January-February 1990.

Garbage, Summer 1994.

Good Housekeeping, September 1989.

Harrowsmith Country Life, May-June 1994; July-August 1994.

Health, July-August 1994.

Home and Garden Bulletin, 1992; 1993.

Horticulture, January 1981; April 1991.

Life, September 1992

MMWR: Morbidity and Mortality Weekly Report, December 23, 1994; February 1996.

Motor Trend, August 1970.

National Geographic, October 1987; July 1997.

National Wildlife, April-May 1992.

Natural History, December 1940; October 1957; January 1990.

Nature Magazine, 1945.

New Scientist, December 8, 1990; December 15, 1990; February 29, 1992; March 14, 1992.

Newsweek, April 23, 1990; September 7, 1992.

The New York Times, May 27, 1986.

The New York Times Magazine, December 3, 1995.

Nuclear News, March 1995.

Oil and Gas Journal, April 11, 1994; October 31, 1994.

Physics Today, April 1992.

Popular Mechanics, July 1994.

Popular Science, January 1994; May 1994.

Safety and Health, September 1991.

Scholastic Update, March 21, 1997.

Science, July 21, 1989; February 18, 1994; December 23, 1994.

Science Digest, February 1974; January 1984.

Science 80, September-October 1980.

Science 82, November 1982.

Science News, September 12, 1992; September 11, 1993; May 28, 1994.

Scientific American, April 1960; May 1989; March 1991; October 1991; December 1993; October 1995; December 1995.

Sky and Telescope, January 1993; May 1994.

Smithsonian, August 1989; April 1990; April 1992; May 1992; January 1994.

Status Report, October 6, 1990.

Technology Review, January 1994.

Time, April 23, 1990; July 9, 1990.

Traffic Safety, January-February 1995.

Vegetarian Times, April 1992.

Weatherwise, August 1983; December 1996-January 1997.

ONLINE SOURCES

Ailes, Christopher. HDTV: A Thing of the Past or the Future? [Online] Available http:www.emerson.edu/acadepts/mc/cnme/tool/hdtv/hdtv.html, July 16, 1997.

A Little "Lite" Reading. U.S. Food and Drug Administration. [Online] Available http://www.fda.gov/fdac/special/foodlabel/lite.html, July 30, 1997.

Arnett, Bill. Pluto. [Online] Available http://seds.lpl.arizona.edu/billa/tnp/pluto.html, March 14, 1996.

Beatty, J. Kelly. Life from Ancient Mars? Sky & Telescopes Weekly News Bulletin: Special Edition. [Online] Available http://www.skypub.com/news/marslife.html, August 8, 1996.

Biotechnology of Food. FDA Backgrounder. [Online] Available http://www.fda.gov/opacom/backgrounders/biotech.html, July 30, 1997.

The Bowie Knife and Its Inventor. [Online] Available. http://www.history.rochestor.edu/Scientific_American/vol2/001/p1c4.htm, August 20, 1997.

Chicago apparently defeated in Tall Building Wars—by Kuala Lumpur. [Online] Available http://www2.nandonet/newsroom/ntn/nation/041396/nation9_4440.html, July 23, 1997.

EPA Fact Sheet: Setting Environmental Standards for Yucca Mountain. [Online] Available http://www.epa.gov/radiation/yucca/factrev.htm, August 19, 1997.

Hamilton, Calvin J. Voyager Uranus Science Summary: December 21, 1988. [Online] Available http://bang.lanl.gov/solarsys/vgrur.htm, April 22, 1996.

Henahan, Sean. What's News: Giganotosaurus. [Online] Available http://www.gene.com/ae/WN/SU/gigant597.html, June 12, 1997.

Herzer, Jeff. The World's Tallest Buildings Page. [Online] Available http://www.dcircle.com/wtb/progress.html, July 23, 1997.

Hummves. [Online] Available http://www.sofcom.com.au/4WD/4WD.html, August 21, 1997.

Introduction to EVs. [Online] Available http://www.phy.syr.edu/courses/PHY106/Termprojects/Projects/Cars/index.html, July 18, 1997.

Legislate. News of the Day: Congress to Hold Hearings into Air Bag Safety for Children. [Online] Available http://www.legislate.com/n/news/961212.htm, July 18, 1997.

Lyndon B. Johnson Space Center. Biographical Data: Shannon W. Lucid. [Online] Available http://www.jsc.nasa.gov/Bios/htmlbios/lucid.html, May 9, 1996.

Mars Pathfinder Homepage. NASA. [Online] Available http://mpfwww.jpl.nasa/gov/default.html, August 17, 1997.

Michard, Jean-Guy. The Reign of the Dinosaur, p. 14; Skull Unveiled of Largest Predator Dinosaur. [Online] Available http://newscenter.delphi.com/item.cfm/2115575, June 12, 1997.

National Climatic Data Center. Billion Dollar U.S. Weather Disasters, 1980-1996. [Online] Available http://www.ncdc.noaa.gov/, November 19, 1996.

Petronas Twin Towers. [Online] Available http://www.satech.net.au/~ciaran/Towers.html, July 23, 1997.

Roller Coaster FAQ. [Online] Available http://faq.rollercoaster.com/index.html, July 23, 1997.

Rudd, Richard. Voyager Project Home Page. [Online] Available http://vraptor.jpl.nasa.gov/voyager/voyager.html, July 2, 1996.

Safety Agency Announces Proposal to Reduce Air Bag Risk to Children. [Online] Available http://nsi.org/library/safety/airbagrisk.html, July 18, 1997.

Sagar, Wayne. Spruce Goose. Flightline Magazine. [Online] Available http://www.flightlinemag.com/goose/goose.html, July 21, 1997.

Saturn EV1 Homepage. [Online] Available http://www.gmev.com/index.htm, July 28, 1997.

Savitskie, Jeffrey. Push is on to tighten state's seat belt law. The Detroit News, Jan. 2, 1996. [Online] Available http://detnews.com/menu/stories/30468.htm, July 17, 1997.

Schlumberger, M. Institut Gustave Roussy, Villejuif, France. Médecins et rayonnements ionisants (Physicians and ionizing radiation). [Online] Available http://www.edf.fr/html/en/mag/iode/evo.html, August 15, 1997.

Summary of Federal District Court's Ruling on FDA's Jurisdiction Over, and Regulation of, Cigarettes and Smokeless Tobacco. FDA Backgrounder. [Online] Available http://www.fda.gov/opacom/backgrounders/bg97-9.html, July 30, 1997.

U.S. Department of Energy. Annual Energy Review. [Online] Available http://www.eia.doe.gov/emeu/aer/aergs/aer2.html, August 14, 1997.

Waste Management. [Online] Available http://lep.cl.msu.edu/msue.me/htdoc/mod02/01500582.html, August 19, 1997.

Weiss, Michael J. You Shoulda Been There!: Zing went the spring. Discovery Channel Online. [Online] Available http://www.discovery.com/doc/1012/world/birthday/birthday10096/birthday.html, August 20, 1997.

What the Liggett Documents Reveal. Campaign for Tobacco-Free Kids. [Online] Available http://www.tobaccofreekids.org/html/liggett_documents_reveal.html, July 30, 1997.

WHD-TV Dedicated as Model HDTV Station Broadcasts First Live, On-Air Grand Alliance HDTV Signal. [Online] Available http:www.eia.org/cema/CESNEWS/FILES/pr0796/whd-tv.htm, July 16, 1997.

CD-ROMS

Encyclopaedia Britannica CD 97. Chicago: Encyclopaedia Britannica, Inc. 1997.

The 1996 Grolier Multimedia Encyclopedia. Danbury, CT: Grolier Electronic Publishing, Inc.

the EARTH

| CHARACTERISTICS

• What is the **mass of the Earth**?

Mass is the amount of matter in an object. The mass of the Earth is estimated to be 6 sextillion, 588 quintillion short tons (6.6 sextillion short tons) or 5.97×10^{24} kilograms. A short ton equals 2,000 pounds as opposed to a long ton, the unit used in Great Britain, which equals 2,240 pounds. The Earth has an average density of 5.52 grams per cubic centimeter, which is 5.52 times the average density of water (the standard).

The method for calculating the mass of the Earth was adopted by the International Astronomical Union in 1964 and recognized by the International Union of Geodesy and Geophysics in 1967.

Sources: Asimov, Isaac. *Asimov's Guide to the Earth and Space*, pp. 34-35; Emiliani, Cesare. *The Scientific Companion*, p. 167; Famighetti, Robert, ed. *The World Almanac and Book of Facts 1995*, p. 269.

• How much of the **Earth's surface** is **land** and how much is **water**?

Land covers 29.22 percent of the Earth's surface. This is about 57.5 million square miles (149×10^6 square kilometers). Water covers the other 70.78 percent of the Earth's surface. This is about 139.4 million square miles (361×10^6 square kilometers).

Source: Barnes-Svarney, Patricia. *The New York Public Library Science Desk Reference*, p. 372.

• What are the **highest and lowest points** on **Earth?**

The highest point on land is the peak of Mount Everest at 29,028 feet (8,848 meters) above sea level (the level of the ocean's surface), plus or minus 10 feet (3 meters) because of snow. Mount Everest is in the Himalaya mountain range, on the border of Nepal and Tibet.

This height of Mount Everest was established by the Surveyor General of India in 1954 and accepted by the National Geographic Society. Prior to that the height was measured at 29,002 feet (8,840 meters). Satellite measurements taken in 1987 indicated that Mount Everest is 29,864 feet (9,102 meters) above sea level; however, this figure has not been adopted by the National Geographic Society.

The lowest point on land is the Dead Sea at 1,312 feet (399 meters) below sea level. The Dead Sea lies between Israel and Jordan. The lowest point on the Earth's surface (including land and sea) is thought to be in the Mariana Trench in the western Pacific Ocean, extending from southeast of Guam to the east side of the Mariana Islands. The Mariana Trench reaches a depth of approximately 36,200 feet (11,034 meters) below sea level.

Sources: Famighetti, Robert, ed. *The World Almanac and Book of Facts 1995*, p. 546; Ojakangas, Richard. *Schaum's Outline of Theory and Problems of Introductory Geology*, p. 5.

• What are the **highest and lowest elevations** in the **United States?**

Mount McKinley, Alaska, at 20,320 feet (6,194 meters) above sea level (the level of the ocean's surface), is the highest point in the United States and North America. Located in central Alaska, it is part of the Alaska Range of mountains. McKinley's South Peak reaches a height of 20,320 feet (6,194 meters) and its North Peak reaches a height of 19,470 feet (5,931 meters).

Mount McKinley is named in honor of U.S. president William McKinley (1843–1901). It boasts one of the world's largest continuous precipices (very steep or vertical rock wall) and is the main scenic attraction at Denali National Park. Denali means "high one" or "great one" and is a Native American name sometimes used for Mount McKinley.

Mount Whitney, California, at 14,494 feet (4,421 meters), is the highest point in the continental United States (the United States with the exception of Alaska and Hawaii). Death Valley, California, at 282 feet (86

Most of the Earth is covered by water.

meters) below sea level, is the lowest point in the United States and in the Western Hemisphere.

Source: Famighetti, Robert, ed. *The World Almanac and Book of Facts 1995*, pp. 547, 556.

• Which **elements** are contained in the **Earth's crust**?

The most abundant elements in the Earth's crust are listed in the table below. In addition, nickel, copper, lead, zinc, tin, and silver account for less than 0.02 percent of the Earth's crust. All other elements together comprise 0.48 percent.

Element	Percentage
Oxygen	47.0
Silicon	28.0
Aluminum	8.0
Iron	4.5
Calcium	3.5
Magnesium	2.5

215

Element	Percentage
Sodium	2.5
Potassium	2.5
Titanium	0.4
Hydrogen	0.2
Carbon	0.2
Phosphorous	0.1
Sulfur	0.1

Source: Considine, Glenn D. *Van Nostrand's Scientific Encyclopedia,* 8th ed., vol. 1, p. 962.

• How does the **temperature of the Earth** change as one goes deeper underground?

The Earth's temperature increases with depth. Measurements taken in mines and drill-holes deep beneath the Earth's surface, however, indicate that the rate at which temperature increases varies from place to place. The increase in underground temperature ranges from 59° Fahrenheit to 167° Fahrenheit (15 to 75° Celsius) per kilometer in depth.

Actual temperature measurements cannot be made beyond the deepest drill-holes, which are a little more than 6.2 miles (10 kilometers) deep. Estimates suggest that the temperatures at the Earth's center can reach 7,200° Fahrenheit (4,000° Celsius) or higher.

Sources: Barnes-Svarney, Patricia. *The New York Public Library Science Desk Reference,* p. 377; Skinner, Brian J. *The Dynamic Earth,* p. 5.

• What is the **interior of the Earth** like?

The Earth is divided into three main layers: the crust, the mantle, and the core.

The outer layer is the crust, which contains about 0.6 percent of the Earth's volume. The depth of the crust varies from 3.5 to 5 miles (5 to 9 kilometers) beneath the oceans to 50 miles (80 kilometers) beneath some mountain ranges. The crust consists primarily of rocks such as granite and basalt.

The layer beneath the crust is the mantle. The boundary between the crust and the mantle is known as the Mohorovičić discontinuity (or Moho for short). The Moho is the dividing line between layers of differ-

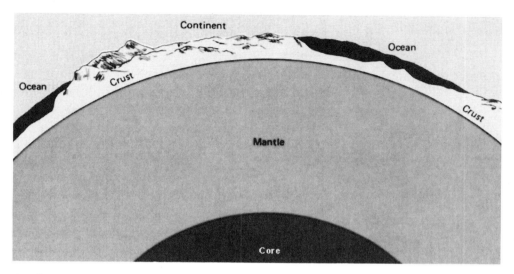

An illustration showing the structure of Earth's interior.

ent types of rock (crust and mantle), as well as the line at which the speed and direction of seismic waves (waves of motion within the Earth) shift. It is not a physical entity, but a boundary—much in the way that a boundary separates two nations or states. It is named for the Croatian seismologist (a scientist who studies earthquakes and the mechanical properties of the Earth), Andrija Mohorovičić (1857–1936), who discovered it in 1909.

Below the Moho is the mantle, which is about 1,800 miles (2,900 kilometers) thick and accounts for about 84 percent of the Earth's volume. The mantle is composed mostly of oxygen, iron, silicon, and magnesium. While most of the mantle is solid, its upper part, called the asthenosphere, is partially liquid.

Beneath the mantle lies the core. The core and mantle boundary is called the Gutenberg discontinuity. Like the Moho, it is not a physical entity but merely a dividing line. It's named for the German-American seismologist, Beno Gutenberg (1889–1960).

Made up primarily of iron and nickel, the core accounts for about 15 percent of the Earth's volume. The outer core is liquid and is about 1,400 miles (2,253 kilometers) thick. It extends from the base of the mantle to a depth of about 3,200 miles (5,155 kilometers) beneath the Earth's surface. The solid inner core is about 800 miles (1,287 kilometers) thick. It reaches

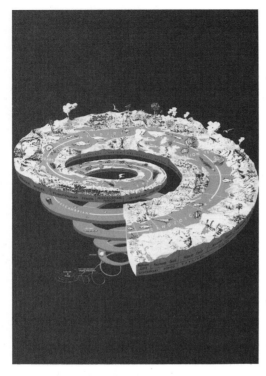

An illustration of geologic time.

from the bottom of the outer core to the center of the Earth, which is about 4,000 miles (6,440 kilometers) beneath the surface. The temperature of the inner core is estimated to be between 7,200 and 9,000° Fahrenheit (4,000 and 5,000° Celsius).

Sources: Barnes-Svarney, Patricia. *The New York Public Library Science Desk Reference*, pp. 377-78; *The Guinness Book of Answers*, 8th ed., p. 54; *How in the World?: A Fascinating Journey Through the World of Human Ingenuity*, p. 210.

• What are the major eras, periods, and epochs in geologic time?

Using modern dating techniques, scientists have constructed the following categorization of the various geologic time periods:

Era	Period	Epoch	(Est. millions of years)
Cenozoic	Quaternary	Holocene	10,000 years ago
		Pleistocene	1.9
	Tertiary	Pliocene	6
		Miocene	25
		Oligocene	38
		Eocene	55
		Paleocene	65
Mesozoic	Cretaceous		135
	Jurassic		200
	Triassic		250
Paleozoic	Permian		285
	Carboniferous (divided into Mississippian and Pennsylvanian periods by some in the U.S.)		350

Era	Period	Epoch	(Est. millions of years)
	Devonian		410
	Silurian		425
	Ordovician		500
	Cambrian		570
Precambrian	Proterozoic		2500
	Archaeozoic		3800
	Azoic		4600

Sources: *The Guinness Book of Answers*, 8th ed., p. 61; Lambert, David. *The Field Guide to Early Man*, p. 16.

| LAND

• Where are the **northernmost and southernmost points of land**?

By some accounts, the most northern point of land is Cape Morris K. Jesup on the northeastern tip of Greenland. It is 440 miles (708 kilometers) from the North Pole, at a latitude of 83 degrees, 39 minutes north (latitude is an imaginary line encircling Earth, parallel to the equator, which tells one's position north or south on the globe). However, *The Guinness Book of Records* reports that the tiny island of Oodaq, just 100 feet (30 meters) across, is situated the furthest north. Oodaq sits at 83 degrees, 40 minutes north latitude, just 438.9 miles (706 kilometers) from the North Pole.

Unlike the North Pole, which is covered by a frozen sea, the South Pole is covered by land. Therefore, the southernmost point of land is the South Pole itself, on the continent of Antarctica. The geographic South Pole is marked by a flag just a few meters from a U.S. research outpost.

In the United States, the northernmost point of land is Point Barrow, Alaska (71 degrees, 23 minutes north latitude), and the southernmost point of land is Ka Lae or South Cape (18 degrees, 55 minutes north latitude) on the island of Hawaii. In the continental United States (the U.S. minus Alaska and Hawaii), the northernmost point is Northwest Angle, Minnesota (49 degrees, 23 minutes north latitude); the southernmost point is Key West, Florida (24 degrees, 33 minutes north latitude).

Sources: Famighetti, Robert, ed. *The World Almanac and Book of Facts 1995*, p. 497; *The Guinness Book of Records 1996*, p. 56; Stimpson, George. *Information Roundup*, p. 416.

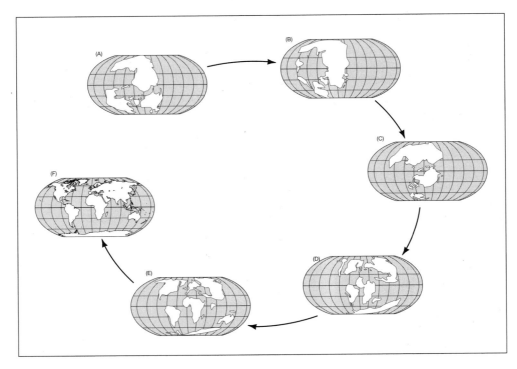

An illustration showing the phases of continental drift.

• Do the **continents** move?

Yes, the continents do move very slowly over time. The theory of continental drift was developed in 1912 by German geologist (a scientist who studies the origin, history, and structure of the Earth) Alfred Lothar Wegener (1880–1930). Wegener proposed that between 200 and 250 million years ago all land on Earth was joined together in one huge continent. The continent, called Pangaea (from the Greek word meaning "all-Earth"), was situated near present-day Antarctica. Wegener believed that forces deep within the Earth caused the land to break apart, first into two major continents called Laurasia and Gondwanaland, and eventually into the six continents in their current configuration.

While Wegener's theory was initially discounted, subsequent research showed that the continents do move—an estimated 0.75 inches (19 millimeters) annually. However, they do not "drift," as Wegener proposed, but move sideways by a process called plate tectonics. American geologists William Maurice Ewing (1906–1974) and Harry Hammond Hess

(1906–1969) proposed that the Earth's crust is not a solid mass, but is composed of eight major and seven minor plates. Those plates can collide, move away from, slide past, and override one another. Where the plates meet they create mountains, volcanoes, and the sites of earthquakes.

Even today the continents continue to move, although very slowly. If current predictions come true, in a few million years San Francisco and Tokyo will be connected.

Sources: Asimov, Isaac. *Isaac Asimov's Guide to Earth and Space*, pp. 42-43; Byrum, W.F., et al. *Dictionary of the History of Science*, p. 78; Emiliani, Cesare. *Scientific Companion*, pp. 177-93, 203-5; Engelbert, Phillis. *The Complete Weather Resource*, vol.3, pp. 486-88.

• What and where is the **Continental Divide** of **North America?**

The Continental Divide, also known as the "great divide," is a continuous ridge of peaks in the Rocky Mountains that marks the boundary between eastward flowing waters and westward flowing waters in North America. To the east of the Continental Divide, water flows eastward into the Hudson Bay or the Mississippi River before reaching the Atlantic Ocean. To the west of the Continental Divide, water generally flows westward through the Columbia River or the Colorado River on its way to the Pacific Ocean.

Sources: Famighetti, Robert, ed. *The World Almanac and Book of Facts, 1995*, p. 499; Press, Frank. *Earth*, p. 180.

• Are there **tides** in the solid part of the Earth as well as in its waters?

Yes, the gravitational pull of the moon and the sun does affect both the solid Earth and the oceans. The gravitational effect is stronger on the oceans, creating tides of up to several feet. The same force only pulls the solid Earth between 4.5 and 14 inches (11.4 and 35.6 centimeters).

Many people believe that tides are caused simply by water being pulled in the direction of the moon. However, if the process were this simple, only one high tide each day would take place. A high tide would occur only in water that had rotated to a position facing the moon. In reality, two cycles of high and low tides occur each day, roughly thirteen hours apart. High tides occur both where water is closest to the moon and on the opposite side of the Earth, where it is farthest from the moon. In the other places on Earth—which neither face nor oppose the moon—the water flows away from the shores. Those areas experience low tides.

The moon's gravity pulls most strongly on the water on the side of the Earth nearest the moon. This creates a high tide there. The moon's gravity also pulls, although not as strongly, at the solid Earth beneath the water. The pull is strong enough, however, to move the solid Earth away from the water on the opposite side of the planet. Therefore, a high tide is also experienced there.

The sun's gravitational field also influences the tides, but only about 33 to 46 percent as much as the moon's. During a new moon or a full moon, when the Earth, sun, and moon are in a straight line, the gravitational fields of the moon and the sun reinforce each other. This pattern creates the highest tides, called spring tides. During first quarter and last quarter moons, the sun and moon are at right angles to one another and their gravitational fields partially cancel each other out. This results in the lowest tides, called neap tides.

Relatively small bodies of water, such as lakes, do not experience tides because the gravity of the moon and sun raises the whole body of water at once, along with the land beneath it.

Sources: Asimov, Isaac. *Isaac Asimov's Guide to Earth and Space,* pp. 97-98; Engelbert, Phillis. *Astronomy and Space: From the Big Bang to the Big Crunch,* vol. 3, pp. 639-40; Feldman, David. *Do Penguins Have Knees?* pp. 138-39; Pickering, James S. *1001 Questions Answered About Astronomy,* p. 41.

• How does a **stalactite** differ from a **stalagmite**?

A stalactite is a conical or cylindrical formation that hangs like an icicle from the roof of a cave. Stalactites are most often made of calcium carbonate, which is a soft, chalklike, rocky material. These formations are created over a span of centuries by the seepage of mineral-rich water through the limestone rock above the cave. As the water evaporates, it leaves behind deposits of calcium carbonate.

A stalagmite is a stone formation, also made of calcium carbonate, which develops upward from the cave floor. It resembles an upside-down icicle. Stalagmites are formed by the seepage of mineral-rich water from the limestone walls and roof of the cave.

A stalagmite sometimes joins a stalactite to form a column, running from the floor to the roof of the cave.

Sources: Bates, Robert, and Julia A. Jackson. *Glossary of Geology,* 3rd ed., p. 640; Leet, L. Don, and Sheldon Judson. *Physical Geology,* 4th ed., pp. 269-70.

> ## What causes sinkholes?
>
> A sinkhole is a large depression in the Earth's surface, often shaped like a well or a funnel, that can be up to several miles in diameter. Sinkholes are most common in limestone regions. Underground layers of limestone can be dissolved by groundwater or by seepage from above-ground streams. A crack in underground limestone is often the first step in the formation of a sinkhole. A sinkhole may also be caused by a dramatic event, such as the collapse of a cave roof.
>
> **Sources:** *The Encyclopedia Americana*, International Edition, p. 843; Magill, Frank N. *Magill's Survey of Science*, vol. 3, pp. 1310-17.

• How is "speleothem" defined?

Speleothem is a term given to those cave features that form after a cave itself has formed. They are secondary mineral deposits that are left after the evaporation of mineral-rich water. These mineral deposits usually contain calcium carbonate ($CaCO_3$) or limestone, and sometimes contain gypsum or silica. Stalactites, stalagmites, soda straws, cave coral, boxwork, and cave pearls are all examples of speleothems.

Sources: Mayhew, Susan, and Anne Penny. *The Concise Oxford Dictionary of Geography*, p. 28; Silverman, Sharon H. *Going Underground*, pp. 14-25.

• What is the difference between spelunking and speleology?

Spelunking is the exploration of caves as a recreational activity. Speleology, on the other hand, is the scientific study of caves and cave-related phenomena.

One subject of tremendous interest to speleologists is the world's deepest cave, called Jean Bernard, in the French Alps. This cave has a total depth of 5,036 feet (1,535 meters). Another speology destination is the world's longest cave system, the joint Mammoth Cave and Flint Ridge Cave system in west-central Kentucky. These caves have a combined length of 329 miles (530 kilometers).

Sources: Halliday, William R. *Depths of the Earth*, p. 407; "Jean Bernard." *Encyclopaedia Britannica CD 97*; "Mammoth Cave National Park." *Encyclopaedia Britannica CD 97*.

• Where are the world's largest deserts?

A desert is an area that receives little precipitation (moisture that falls from the clouds) and has scarce plant cover. Many deserts exist in two bands that run roughly at latitudes of 30 degrees north and south of the equator. The reason for this pattern is that air from the equatorial region descends in this area. In the process, moisture within the air evaporates and produces clear skies.

The equator, in contrast, is a rainy zone. This is because surface winds, called trade winds, blowing from the north and the south converge at the equator and rise. As the air rises, moisture condenses and forms rain-bearing clouds. It is because of this process that tropical rain forests exist around the equator.

The world's largest desert, the Sahara Desert, is three times the size of the Mediterranean Sea. In the United States, the largest desert is the Mojave Desert in southern California, with an area of 15,000 square miles (38,900 square kilometers).

Desert	Location	Area Square miles	Square kilometers
Sahara	North Africa	3,500,000	9,065,000
Gobi	Mongolia-China	500,000	1,295,000
Kalahari	Southern Africa	225,000	582,800
Great Sandy	Australia	150,000	338,500
Great Victoria	Australia	150,000	338,500

Sources: Cazeau, Charles J. *Science Trivia*, p. 64; Diagram Group Staff. *Comparisons*, p. 82; Engelbert, Phillis. *The Complete Weather Resource*, vol 1., pp. 23-24; vol. 3, pp. 460-62; *The Universal Almanac 1992*, p. 303.

• How tall is a **sand dune?**

Sand dunes can range from 3 feet (1 meter) to greater than 650 feet (200 meters) in height. Star dunes, which have one central peaked mound with radiating ridges, can grow as high as 1,000 feet (300 meters).

The type of dune that most people are familiar with from photographs and motion pictures is the barchan dune. Barchan dunes are formed by winds blowing in a nearly constant direction and moderate speed across relatively flat land with only a shallow layer of sand. These dunes, when viewed from above, resemble crescent moons, with the tips of the crescent pointing downwind. They have convex (curved outward) backs and steep, concave (curved inward) faces. A barchan dune may grow as tall as a several-story building.

Sources: Engelbert, Phillis. *The Complete Weather Resource*, vol. 1, p. 144; *McGraw-Hill Encyclopedia of Science and Technology*, vol. 5, pp. 433-34.

Massive moving sand dunes engulf a forest in Nags Head, North Carolina.

- ## Which **natural attractions** in the **United States** are the most popular?

  1. The Grand Canyon, Arizona
  2. Yellowstone National Park, Wyoming
  3. Niagara Falls, New York
  4. Mount McKinley, Alaska
  5. California's "Big Trees": the sequoias and redwoods
  6. Hawaii's volcanoes
  7. Florida's Everglades

Source: Wallechinsky, David. *The Book of Lists*, p. 25.

- ## How long is the **Grand Canyon**?

The Grand Canyon, located in the northwest corner of Arizona, is the largest land gorge in the world. The Grand Canyon was carved out by the Colorado River over a period of 15 million years. It is 4 to 13 miles (6.4 to

225

Part of the Grand Canyon showing visible layers or sediment that turned to rock over two billion years ago.

21 kilometers) wide at its brim, 4,000 to 5,500 feet (1,219 to 1,676 meters) deep, and 217 miles (349 kilometers) long. It extends from the mouth of the Little Colorado River to the Grand Wash Cliffs. If one includes the adjacent Marble Canyon, the Grand Canyon is 277 miles (445 kilometers) long.

However, the Grand Canyon is not the deepest canyon in the United States. That distinction belongs to Kings Canyon, which runs through the Sierra and Sequoia National Forests near East Fresno, California. Kings Canyon reaches a maximum depth of 8,200 feet (2,500 meters).

Another deep canyon in the United States is Hell's Canyon, which runs along the Snake River (between Idaho and Oregon). Also called the Grand Canyon of the Snake, it plunges 7,900 feet (2,400 meters) down from Devil Mountain to the Snake River. Hell's Canyon is 125 miles long; for 40 of those miles it is more than one mile deep.

Sources: Famighetti, Robert, ed. *The World Almanac and Book of Facts 1995*, p. 57; *The Guinness Book of Records 1995*, p. 512; "Hell's Canyon." *Encyclopaedia Britannica CD 97*; *Webster's New Geographical Dictionary*, p. 455.

• From what type of stone was **Mount Rushmore National Monument** carved?

The Mount Rushmore National Monument is carved from granite. Located in the Black Hills of southwestern South Dakota, the monument depicts the faces of four U.S. presidents: George Washington, Thomas Jefferson, Abraham Lincoln, and Theodore Roosevelt. Each of the faces is 60 feet (18 meters) high.

> ## What is the composition of the Rock of Gibraltar?
>
> The Rock of Gibraltar is composed of gray limestone with a dark shale overlay on parts of its western slopes. The Rock of Gibraltar is a mountain located on a peninsula at the southern edge of Spain. It sits at the east end of the Strait of Gibraltar, the narrow passage between the Atlantic Ocean and the Mediterranean Sea. "The Rock" is 1,398 feet (425 meters) tall at its highest point.
>
> **Sources:** *Encyclopedia Americana*, vol. 12, p. 734; *Webster's New Geographical Dictionary*, p. 442.

Sculptor Gutzon Borglum (1867–1941) designed the monument but died before its completion. His son, Lincoln, finished the project. From 1927 to 1941, 360 people, mostly construction workers, drillers, and miners, "carved" the monument using dynamite.

Sources: Famighetti, Robert, ed. *The World Almanac and Book of Facts 1995*, p. 663; *How In the World?: A Fascinating Journey Through the World of Human Ingenuity*, pp. 362-64; Panati, Charles. *Panati's Extraordinary Origins of Everyday Things*, pp. 282-84.

• What are the LaBrea tar pits?

The LaBrea tar pits are located in Los Angeles, California, in Hancock Park (formerly known as Rancho LaBrea). This natural attraction features heavy, sticky tar which oozes out of the Earth and fills the pits (*la brea* is Spanish for "the tar"). The tar is actually the scum from underground petroleum reservoirs.

Throughout history, countless numbers of animals became trapped in the tar pits. In the absence of oxygen, the remains of those animals were perfectly preserved. Paleontologists (scientists who study prehistoric life) have excavated (uncovered) the fossilized bones and skulls of numerous prehistoric species, including the imperial mammoth, mastodon, sabretoothed cat, and giant ground sloth. Paleontologists have even found the remains of the western horse and the camel, both of which originated in North America, migrated to other parts of the world, and became extinct in North America at the end of the Ice Age (around 10,000 years ago).

The tar pits were first recognized as a fossil site in 1875. However, scientists did not systematically excavate the area until 1901. By comparing La Brea's fossil specimens with their nearest living relatives, paleontologists have gained a greater understanding of the climate, vegetation, and animal life that existed in that area during the Ice Age. Today many fossils, along with life-sized reconstructions of these prehistoric species, are displayed beside the tar pits in Hancock Park. Other fossils from the tar pits are on display at the Los Angeles Natural History Museum.

Sources: "LaBrea Tar Pits." *Encyclopaedia Britannica CD 97*; *Natural History*, vol. 46 (December 1940), p. 284; *Natural History*, vol. 99 (January 1990), pp. 72-75; Saari, Peggy, and Diane L. Dupuis, eds. *Cities of the United States: The West*, p. 66.

| WATER

• What is the **chemical composition** of the **ocean?**

The ocean contains every known naturally occurring element plus various gases, chemical compounds, and minerals. Below is a sampling of the most abundant chemicals.

Constituent	Concentration (parts per million)
Chloride	18,980
Sodium	10,560
Sulfate	2,560
Magnesium	1,272
Calcium	400
Potassium	380
Bicarbonate	142
Bromide	65
Strontium	13
Boron	4.6
Fluoride	1.4

Sources: Groves, Don. *The Ocean Book*, pp. 45-46; Van der Leeden, Frits. *The Water Encyclopedia*, 2nd ed., p. 283.

• What causes **waves** in the **ocean?**

The most common cause of surface ocean waves is air movement (the wind). Waves within the ocean can also be caused by tides, interactions between waves, submarine earthquakes or volcanic activity, and atmospheric disturbances (storms). Wave size depends on wind speed, wind duration, and

Where are the world's highest tides?

The Bay of Fundy (New Brunswick, Canada) has the world's highest tides. They average about 45 feet (14 meters) in the northern part of the bay, far surpassing the world average of 2.5 feet (0.8 meters).

Source: *World Book Encyclopedia,* vol. 14, p. 181.

the distance of water over which the wind blows. The longer the distance the wind travels over water, or the harder it blows, the higher the waves.

As the wind blows over the water, it tries to drag the surface of the water with it. The surface water cannot move as fast as air, so the water rises. After it rises, the water is pulled back down by gravity. The falling water's momentum is carried below the surface, and water pressure from below pushes this swell back up again. This tug of war between gravity and water pressure creates wave motion.

Capillary waves are small waves caused by breezes of less than 2 knots (1 knot equals 1.15 miles per hour). A wind speed of 13 knots produces waves that are so steep that they tip over, creating whitecaps. For a whitecap to form, the wave height must be at least one-seventh the distance between wave crests.

The largest waves are generated not by the wind, but by large submarine earthquakes. Waves produced in this fashion are called tsunamis [tsoo-NAH-meez], or tidal waves. A tsunami is set in motion by a vertical shift in the ocean floor, which pushes the water ahead of it.

Tsunamis start out small and grow larger as they near land. They travel at speeds of up to 500 miles per hour (800 kilometers per hour) and measure 100 to 200 miles (161 to 322 kilometers) in length. It is typical for a tsunami to measure 60 to 100 feet (18 to 30 meters) in height by the time it reaches land.

Tsunamis occur most often in the Pacific Ocean. Several tsunamis have affected Alaska and Hawaii. In 1958, a 200-foot- (60-meter-) tall tsunami, generated by a minor earthquake and resultant rockfall into the sea, crashed into Lituya Bay, Alaska. It destroyed great tracts of forestland as far as 1,700 feet (520 meters) above sea level.

Sources: Engelbert, Phillis. *The Complete Weather Resource,* vol.1, pp. 147-49; vol2., p. 308; Flatow, Ira. *Rainbows, Curve Balls, and Other Wonders of the Natural World Explained,* pp. 28-32; Groves, Don. *The Ocean Book,* p. 29; Lee, Sally. *Predicting Violent Storms,* pp. 99-100.

• How **deep** is the **ocean?**

The average depth of the ocean floor is 13,124 feet (4,000 meters). The average depth of the four major oceans is given below:

Ocean	Average Depth	
	Feet	Meters
Pacific	13,740	4,188
Atlantic	12,254	3,735
Indian	12,740	3,872
Arctic	3,407	1,038
Average overall	13,124	4,000

There are great variations in ocean depth because the ocean floor is often very rugged. The deepest points are found in narrow depressions known as trenches, located along the margins of the continental plates.

The deepest point on the ocean floor—approximately 36,200 feet (11,034 meters) below the surface—is found in the Mariana Trench. The Mariana Trench is in the western Pacific Ocean and extends from southeast of Guam to the east side of the Mariana Islands. It was measured in January 1960 by French oceanographer (a scientist who explores and studies the oceans) Jacques Piccard and U.S. Navy Lieutenant David Walsh, who took the bathyscaphe (submersible, spherical vehicle used to explore ocean depths) *Trieste* to the bottom of the Mariana Trench.

Ocean	Deepest Point	Depth	
		Feet	Meters
Pacific	Mariana Trench	36,200	11,034
Atlantic	Puerto Rico Trench	28,374	8,648
Indian	Java Trench	25,344	7,725
Arctic	Eurasia Basin	17,881	5,450

Sources: Considine, Glenn D. *Van Nostrand's Scientific Encyclopedia*, 8th ed., vol. 2, pp. 2044-45; *The New Book of Popular Science*, vol. 2, p. 268.

• Why is the **sea blue?**

There is no single cause for the appearance of colors of the sea. The colors depend on the brightness of the sky, the concentration of particles suspended in the water, and the position of the observer.

The color of seawater is largely produced by the absorption and reflection of light of various wavelengths—by the water itself and by matter suspended in the water. Central to this concept is the fact that white light is actually the combination of wavelengths of light from the entire visible light spectrum. Each color of the rainbow occupies a different wavelength of light, with red and orange being the longest and blue, green, and violet being the shortest.

When sunlight hits seawater, some of the color components of white light are absorbed, while other colors collide with water molecules and are scattered. When a color is scattered, it is reflected in all directions—including up to the observer's eye.

In clear water, red and infrared wavelengths of light are mostly absorbed, while blue and green wavelengths are mostly reflected. This reflection accounts for the blue-green color of water. For this scattering effect to occur, the water must be a minimum of 10 feet (3 meters) deep.

Sources: Bohren, Craig F. *Clouds in a Glass of Beer*, p. 155; Engelbert, Phillis. *The Complete Weather Resource*, vol.2, pp. 317-19; Feldman, David. *Why Do Clocks Run Clockwise and Other Imponderables*, p. 213.

• How **salty** is **seawater?**

Seawater is, on average, 3.3 to 3.7 percent salt. The amount of salt in seawater varies from place to place. In areas where large quantities of fresh water are supplied by melting ice, rivers, or rainfall, such as the Arctic and Antarctic, the level of salinity (saltiness) is lower. In other areas, such as the Persian Gulf and the Red Sea, salt concentrations exceed 4.2 percent.

If all the salt in the seas could be extracted and dried, it would form a mass of solid salt the size of Africa. Most of salt in the seas has been dissolved from the solid Earth—a process occurring over hundreds of millions of years. Sea salt also comes from salty volcanic rock. This rock flows up from a giant rift which runs through every ocean basin.

Sources: Considine, Glenn D. *Van Nostrand's Scientific Encyclopedia*, 8th ed., vol. 2, p. 2047; Feldman, David. *Do Penguins Have Knees?* p. 149; Groves, Don. *The Ocean Book*, pp. 46-48.

• What is the difference between an **ocean** and a **sea**?

Although the terms "ocean" and "sea" are often used interchangeably, a sea is generally considered to be smaller than an ocean. One definition of "ocean" is: a great body of interconnecting salt water that covers 71 percent of the Earth's surface. There are four major oceans—Arctic, Atlantic, Indian, and Pacific. However, some sources do not include the Arctic Ocean, calling it a marginal sea. The term "sea" is often assigned to saltwater areas on the margins of oceans, such as the Mediterranean Sea situated beside the Atlantic Ocean.

Sources: Mayhew, Susan, and Anne Penny. *The Concise Oxford Dictionary of Geography*, p. 164; *The Guinness Book of Answers*, 8th ed., pp. 62-65; *The Universal Almanac 1992*, p. 296.

• Where is the **world's deepest lake**?

The deepest lake in the world is Lake Baikal, located in southeast Siberia, Russia. Lake Baikal is approximately 5,371 feet (1,638 meters) deep at its deepest point, the Olkhon Crevice. The second-deepest lake is Lake Tanganyika, on the border of Tanzania and Zaire (now called the Congo), with a depth of 4,708 feet (1,435 meters).

Source: Matthews, Rupert O. *The Atlas of Natural Wonders*, p. 96.

• Where are the five **largest lakes in the world** located?

Although Lake Huron, one of the Great Lakes, is ranked as the fifth largest lake by square miles, it is considerably deeper than both Lake Victoria in Africa and Lake Aral in Asia.

Location	Area		Length		Depth	
	Square miles	Square km[a]	Miles	Km[a]	Feet	Meters
Caspian Sea[b], Asia-Europe	143,244	370,922	760	1,225	3,363	1,025
Superior, North America	31,700	82,103	350	560	1,330	406
Victoria, Africa	26,828	69,464	250	360	270	85
Aral, Asia	24,904	64,501	280	450	220	67
Huron, North America	23,010	59,600	206	330	750	229

[a] Kilometers

[b] Saltwater lake

Sources: Famighetti, Robert, ed. *The World Almanac and Book of Facts 1995*, p. 555; *The Guinness Book of Answers*, 8th ed., p. 89; *The Universal Almanac 1992*, p. 296.

the EARTH

Who invented the **ancient Chinese Earthquake detector?**

The ancient Chinese Earthquake detector was invented by Zhang Heng (A.D. 78–139) around A.D.132. The instrument was a copper-domed urn with dragons' heads circling the outside. Each dragon head contained a bronze ball. A pendulum hung from the top of the dome, which would swing when the Earth shook. The swinging pendulum would knock a ball from the mouth of a dragon into the waiting open mouth of a bronze toad below.

The ball made a loud noise and signaled the occurrence of an earthquake. By observing which ball had been released, one could determine the direction of the earthquake's epicenter (the point on the Earth's surface directly above the quake's point of origin).

Sources: Temple, Robert K. G. *The Genius of China*, pp. 162-63; Tufty, Barbara. *1001 Questions About Earthquakes, Avalanches, Floods, and Other Natural Disasters*, pp. 44-45.

• What are the **longest rivers in the world?**

The two longest rivers in the world are the Nile, in Africa, and the Amazon, in South America. It's difficult to determine which of these two rivers is longer, for a couple of reasons.

First, the Amazon has several mouths that widen toward the South Atlantic, so the exact point where the river ends is uncertain. If the Pará estuary (the most distant mouth) is counted, its length is approximately 4,195 miles (6,750 kilometers). Second, the exact length of the Nile is a matter of debate. It was measured at 4,145 miles (6.670 kilometers); however, that was before the loss of a few miles of meanders (a bend or loop in the river) due to the formation of Lake Nasser behind the Aswan Dam.

River	Length	
	Miles	Kilometers
Nile (Africa)	4,145	6,670
Amazon (South America)*	4,000	6,404
Chang jiang-Yangtze (Asia)	3,964	6,378
Mississippi-Missouri river system (North America)	3,740	6,021
Yenises-Angara river system (Asia)	3,442	5,540

* excluding Pará estuary

Sources: Considine, Glenn D. *Van Nostrand's Scientific Encyclopedia*, 8th ed., vol. 1, p. 974; *The New Encyclopaedia Britannica*, 15th ed., vol. 17, p. 655; Rhodes, Frank H. T. *Geology*, pp. 126-27; Robinson, Andrew. *Earthshock*, pp. 52-56.

• When did the **most severe earthquake in American history** occur?

The New Madrid Earthquakes, a series of quakes beginning on December 16, 1811, and lasting until March 1812, is considered to be the most severe earthquake event in U.S. history. These earthquakes, located in New Madrid, Missouri, shook more than two-thirds of the United States and were felt in Canada. They changed the elevation of land by as much as 20 feet (6 meters) and altered the course of the Mississippi River. The New Madrid Earthquakes even created new lakes, such as Lake St. Francis west of the Mississippi and Reelfoot Lake in Tennessee.

Because the area was so sparsely populated, there were no deaths known to have occurred as a result of the earthquakes. Scientists agree that at least three, and possibly five, of the earthquakes had surface wave magnitudes of 8.0 or greater on the Richter scale. The largest was probably a magnitude of 8.8, which is larger than any earthquake yet experienced in California.

Sources: Stewart, David. *The Earthquake America Forgot,* p. 15; Tufty, Barbara J. *1001 Questions Answered About Earthquakes, Avalanches, Floods, and Other Natural Disasters,* pp. 9-10.

• Of what magnitude on the **Richter scale** was the **earthquake** that hit **San Francisco on April 18, 1906**?

The historic 1906 San Francisco earthquake registered 8.3 on the Richter scale and lasted 75 seconds. It took a mighty toll on the city and surrounding area. Over 700 people were killed; the newly constructed $6 million city hall was ruined; many poorly constructed buildings built on landfills were flattened; and almost all of the gas and water mains were destroyed. In addition, the Sonoma Wine Company collapsed, spilling 15 million gallons (57 million liters) of wine. Fires broke out shortly after the earthquake, incinerating 3,000 acres of the city, the equivalent of 520 blocks. Damage was estimated to be $500 million and many insurance agencies went bankrupt after paying out the claims.

On October 17, 1989, San Francisco was struck by another earthquake, this one measuring 7.1 on the Richter scale. It killed 67 people and caused billions of dollars worth of damage.

Sources: Nash, Jay R. *Darkest Hours: A Narrative Encyclopedia of Worldwide Disasters from Ancient Times to the Present,* pp. 490-507; *The Public Health Consequences of Disasters 1989,* p. 18; *The Universal Almanac 1994,* pp. 534.

• How many kinds of **volcanoes** are there?

Volcanoes are hills or mountains that are usually cone-shaped. A volcano is built around a vent that leads down to a reservoir of molten rock, or magma, below the surface of the Earth. When a volcano erupts, the molten rock is forced upward by gas pressure until it breaks through weak spots in the Earth's crust. The magma either emerges as a lava flow (when molten rock surfaces above ground it's called "lava") or shoots into the air as clouds of lava fragments, ash, and dust. The accumulation of debris from eruptions causes the volcano to grow in size. There are four kinds of volcanoes:

Cinder cones are made of lava fragments. They have slopes of 30 degrees to 40 degrees and seldom exceed 1,640 feet (500 meters) in height. Sunset Crater in Arizona and Paricutin in Mexico are examples of cinder cone volcanoes.

Composite cones are made of alternating layers of lava and ash. They are characterized by slopes of up to 30 degrees at the summit (top), tapering off to 5 degrees at the base. Mount Fuji in Japan and Mount St. Helens in Washington are examples of composite cone volcanoes.

Shield volcanoes are built primarily of lava flows. Their slopes are seldom more than 10 degrees at the summit and 2 degrees at the base. The Hawaiian Islands are comprised of clusters of shield volcanoes. Mauna Loa, a shield volcano, is the world's largest active volcano, rising 13,653 feet (4,161 meters) above sea level.

Lava domes are made of hardened, thick, pasty layers of lava that have been squeezed like toothpaste from a tube. Lava domes take on a variety of bizarre shapes. Examples of lava domes are Lassen Peak and Mono Dome in California.

Sources: Bair, Frank E. *The Weather Almanac*, 6th ed., pp. 200-204; Leet, L. Don, and Sheldon Judson. *Physical Geology*, 4th ed., pp. 74-75.

• Where is the **"Circle of Fire"**?

The "Circle of Fire" (also known as the "Ring of Fire") is the belt of volcanoes dotting the lands along the edges of the Pacific Ocean. It follows the west coast of the Americas from Chile to Alaska, through the Andes Mountains, Central America, Mexico, California, the Cascade Mountains, and the Aleutian Islands. It continues down the east coast of Asia from Siberia to New Zealand, through Kamchatka, the Kurile Islands, Japan, the

Philippines, Celebes, New Guinea, the Solomon Islands, and New Caledonia. Of the 850 active volcanoes in the world, more than 75 percent of them are part of the Circle of Fire.

The Earth's crust is composed of 15 pieces, called plates, which "float" on the partially molten layer below them. Most volcanoes, earthquakes, and mountain ranges occur along the unstable plate boundaries. The Circle of Fire marks the boundary between the plate underlying the Pacific Ocean and the surrounding plates.

Sources: *McGraw-Hill Encyclopedia of Science and Technology,* 7th ed., vol. 19, p. 279; Pearl, Richard M. *1001 Questions Answered About the Mineral Kingdom,* pp. 221-22.

• Which **volcanoes** have been the most destructive?

The five most destructive volcanic eruptions since 1700 are as follows:

Volcano	Date of eruption	Number killed	Cause of death
Mt. Tambora, Indonesia	April 5, 1815	92,000	12,000 directly by the volcano; 80,000 from starvation afterward
Karkatoa, Indonesia	Aug. 26, 1883	36,417	90% killed by a tsunami
Mt. Pelee, Martinique	Aug. 30, 1902	29,025	Pyroclastic flows
Nevada del Ruiz, Colombia	Nov. 13, 1985	23,000	Mud flow
Unzen, Japan	1792	14,300	70% killed by cone collapse; 30% by a tsunami

Sources: *The Guinness Book of Answers,* 8th ed., p. 72; *The Public Health Consequences of Disasters 1989,* p. 26.

• When did **Mount St. Helens** erupt?

Mount St. Helens, located in southwestern Washington state in the Cascade mountain range, erupted on May 18, 1980. Sixty-one people died as a result of the eruption. This was the first known volcanic eruption in the 48 contiguous United States (excluding Alaska and Hawaii) to claim a human life. Mount St. Helens is classified as a composite volcano (a steep-sided, often symmetrical cone constructed of alternating layers of lava flows, ash, and other volcanic debris). Composite volcanoes tend to erupt explosively.

Mount St. Helens and the other active volcanoes in the Cascade Mountains are a part of the "Circle of Fire," a ring of active volcanoes that dot the lands bordering the Pacific Ocean.

The eruption of Mount Saint Helens.

There are active volcanoes in three other U.S. states besides Washington; they are California, Alaska, and Hawaii. Lassen Peak in California is one of several volcanoes in the Cascade Range. It last erupted in 1921. Mount Katmai in Alaska erupted in 1912. The flood of hot ash from that eruption formed the Valley of Ten Thousand Smokes, 15 miles (24 kilometers) away. And the world's largest volcano, Mauna Loa, is in Hawaii. Mauna Loa is 60 miles (97 kilometers) wide at its base.

Sources: Reader's Digest Editors. *Great Disasters: Dramatic True Stories of Nature's Awesome Powers,* p. 272; Tilling, Robert I. *Eruptions of Mount St. Helens,* Rev. ed., p. 3.

| ICE AND ICE AGES

• How much of the **Earth's surface** is covered with **ice**?

About 10.4 percent of the world's land surface, or approximately 6,020,000 square miles (15,600,000 square kilometers), is glaciated. Glaciated means permanently covered with ice. That ice takes the form of glaciers, ice sheets, or ice caps.

237

What is a *moraine*?

A moraine is a land formation, such as mound or ridge, that was created by the movement of a glacier. Moraines are made of material that was deposited by a glacier, such as gravel, clay, or sand.

Sources: Bates, Robert, and Julia A. Jackson. *Glossary of Geology*, 3rd ed., pp. 432-33; Parker, Sybil P., ed. *McGraw-Hill Dictionary of Earth Science*, p. 228.

A glacier is a large mass of land ice that flows, under the force of gravity, at a rate of 10 to 1,000 feet (3 to 300 meters) per year. Glaciers on steep slopes may flow faster. For example, the Quarayoq Glacier in Greenland moves an average of 65 to 80 feet (20 to 24 meters) per day.

An ice sheet is a thick glacier that's larger than 19,000 square miles (50,000 square kilometers). An ice sheet blankets an area of land, completely covering its mountains and valleys, flowing outward in all directions. An ice cap is a sheet of ice and snow that continuously covers an area of land, but is smaller than an ice sheet.

The areas of glaciation in various parts of the world are:

Place	Area	
	Square miles	Square kilometers
Antarctica	5,250,000	12,588,000
North Polar Regions (Greenland, Northern Canada, Arctic Ocean islands)	799,000	2,070,000
Asia	44,000	115,800
Alaska & Rocky Mountains	29,700	76,900
South America	10,200	26,500
Iceland	4,699	12,170
Alpine Europe	3,580	9,280
New Zealand	391	1,015
Africa	5	12

Sources: *The Guinness Book of Answers*, 8th ed., pp. 92-93; Van der Leeden, Frits. *The Water Encyclopedia*, p. 203.

• How much of the **Earth's surface** is **permanently frozen?**

About one-fifth of the Earth's land contains permafrost, an underground layer that remains frozen year-round. The permanently frozen layer may be bedrock, sod, ice, sand, gravel, or any other type of material that has been frozen for at least two years. Nearly all permafrost is thousands of years old and is located in the polar and subpolar regions of the Earth.

Sources: Considine, Glenn D. *Van Nostrand's Scientific Encyclopedia*, 8th ed., vol. 1, p. 363; Dyson, James L. *The World of Ice*, p. 149; *World Book Encyclopedia*, vol. 15, p. 289.

• How thick is the ice that covers **Antarctica**?

The ice that covers Antarctica reaches a maximum thickness of 15,700 feet (4,785 meters), nearly 3 miles. This is about ten times taller than the Sears Tower in Chicago, the tallest building in the United States. The average thickness of ice in Antarctica is 7,100 feet (2,164 meters), about 1⅓ miles.

Source: *World Book Encyclopedia*, vol. 1, pp. 530, 532.

• Who was the **first person** on **Antarctica**?

Historians are unsure who first set foot on Antarctica. Antarctica is the fifth largest continent, covering 10 percent of the Earth's surface with its area of 5.4 million square miles (14 million square kilometers).

Between 1773 and 1775 British captain James Cook (1728–1779) sailed around the circumference (boundary) of the continent. American explorer Nathaniel Palmer (1799–1877) discovered Palmer Peninsula in 1820, without realizing that it was attached to the Antarctic continent. In the same year Fabian Gottlieb von Bellingshausen (1779–1852) sighted the Antarctic continent.

American sealer John Davis went ashore at Hughes Bay on February 7, 1821. In 1823, sealer James Weddell (1787–1834) traveled the farthest south across Antarctica (74 degrees south) than anyone had until that time and entered what is now called the Weddell Sea. In 1840, American Charles Wilkes (1798–1877), who followed the coast for 1,500 miles, announced the existence of Antarctica as a continent.

In 1841, Sir James Clark Ross (1800–1862) discovered Victoria Land, Ross Island, Mount Erebus, and the Ross Ice Shelf. In 1895, the whaler Henryk Bull landed on the Antarctic continent. Norwegian explorer Roald Amundsen (1872–1928) was the first leader to reach the South Pole, on December 14, 1911. Thirty-four days later, Amundsen's rival, the British captain Robert Falcon Scott (1868–1912), stood at the South Pole, the second leader to do so. However, Scott and his companions froze to death during their return trip.

Sources: Famighetti, Robert, ed. *The World Almanac and Book of Facts 1995,* pp. 544-45; May, John. *The Greenpeace Book of Antarctica: A New View of the Seventh Continent,* 1st ed., pp. 16, 110-13; Stewart, John. *Antarctica: An Encyclopedia,* pp. 110-13; *World Book Encyclopedia,* vol. 1, pp. 530, 536.

• When was the **Ice Age**?

Throughout Earth's history, there have been times when conditions have been alternately warmer and colder than they are today. There have also been several periods, called ice ages, during which large portions of the planet's surface have been covered with ice. Ice ages, or glacial periods, have occurred at irregular intervals for more than 2.3 billion years.

The Precambrian period (from 4.6 billion years ago to 570 million years ago) had four ice ages. The first occurred somewhere between 2.7 billion and 2.3 billion years ago. Then the Earth warmed up and was free of ice for almost a billion years. The second ice age occurred between 950 and 890 million years ago; the third between 820 and 730 million years ago; and the fourth between 640 and 580 million years ago. In each case, some area of the Earth was iced over for about 100 million years.

The Mesozoic Era (225 to 65 million years ago) experienced a number of temperature swings, ending in an ice age. This resulted in the extinction of about 70 percent of the living species on Earth, including the dinosaurs. That ice age may have been a result of a collision between an asteroid with the Earth, which created a dust cloud that blocked out the sun.

From 2.4 million years ago to 11,000 years ago, the period known as the "Great Ice Age" (which most people think of as *the* ice age), there were two dozen times when the global temperature has plummeted. And for seven different intervals over the last 1.6 million years, up to 32 percent of the Earth's surface has been covered with ice. Scientists estimate that throughout this time period, new ice ages have started about every 100,000 years and have been separated by warmer, interglacial periods, each lasting at least 10,000 years.

The most recent glacial period peaked between 22,000 and 18,000 years ago. At its height, about 27 percent of the world's present land area was covered by ice (compared with 10.4 percent today). There were glaciers up to 10,000 feet (3,050 meters) thick over most of North America, northern Europe, and northern Asia, as well as the southern portions of South America, Australia, and Africa. In North America, the ice covered Canada and moved southward to New Jersey; in the Midwest, it reached as far south as St. Louis. Small glaciers and ice caps also covered the western mountains.

The large ice sheets locked up a lot of water. The sea level fell about 450 feet (137 meters) below what it is today and exposed large areas of land that are currently submerged, such as the Bering land bridge, which connected the eastern tip of Siberia with the western tip of Alaska.

The glaciers' effect on the United States can still be seen. The drainage of the Ohio River and the position of the Great Lakes were shaped by the glaciers. The rich soil of the Midwest is mostly glacial in origin. Rainfall in areas south of the glaciers formed large lakes in Utah, Nevada, and California, such as Utah's Great Salt Lake.

This ice age was followed by a warm period, beginning 14,000 years ago. By 8,000 years ago most of the ice had melted, and between 7,000 and 5,000 years ago the world was 3 to 6° Fahrenheit warmer than it is today.

Some believe that the Great Ice Age is not over yet, but that we are merely in a time of retreating glaciers. The reason for this argument is that in a typical ice age, glaciers advance and retreat many times.

Sources: Ahrens, C. Donald. *Meteorology Today: An Introduction to Weather, Climate, and the Environment*, 5th ed., pp. 480-81; Engelbert, Phillis. *The Complete Weather Resource*, vol. 3, pp. 479-85, 505; Leet, L. Don, and Sheldon Judson. *Physical Geology*, 4th ed., pp. 304-5; U.S. Geological Survey. *Our Changing Continent* (pamphlet), p. 11.

MAPPING THE EARTH

• Who is regarded as the founder of **U.S. geology?**

Born in Scotland, the American William Maclure (1763–1840) is considered the founder of geology in the United States. Geology is the science concerned with the structure, origin, and history of the physical Earth.

From 1803 to 1807 Maclure was a member of a commission set up to settle land disputes between the United States and France. In 1809, Maclure made a geographical chart of the United States in which the land areas were categorized by rock types. He revised and enlarged this map in 1817. Maclure also wrote the first English-language articles and books on United States geology.

Sources: *Dictionary of Scientific Biography*, vol. 8, pp. 615-17; *Encyclopedic Dictionary of Science*, p. 155.

• What is the **prime meridian?**

A meridian is an imaginary circle that runs in a north-south direction around the Earth, connecting the North Pole and the South Pole. The word "meridian" is Latin for "midday" or "noon." When it is noon at one location on a meridian, it is also noon at every other point along that meridian.

Meridians are used to measure longitude, or how far east or west a given place is on the globe. Each degree of longitude is spaced 69 miles (111 kilometers) apart at the equator. A degree of longitude becomes progressively narrower as it approaches a pole; degrees of longitude come together at a single point at each pole.

The prime meridian is the meridian of 0 degrees longitude, which runs through Greenwich, England. The prime meridian is used as the origin for measurement of longitude. On maps of the world, locations west of the prime meridian are designated "longitude west of Greenwich" and locations east of the prime meridian are designated "longitude east of Greenwich."

The lines running east-west on a map are called parallels. Unlike meridians, they are parallel to one other. These east-west lines measure latitude, or how far north or south on the globe a particular place is located.

> ### Which direction does a compass needle point at the **north magnetic pole**?
>
> The compass needle would be attracted by the ground and point straight down.
>
> **Source:** *Science and Technology Illustrated*, vol. 7, p. 791.

There are 180 parallels encircling the Earth, one for each degree of latitude. The North Pole is at a latitude of 90 degrees north, the South Pole is 90 degrees south, and the equator is 0 degrees. Degrees of latitude and longitude are each divided into 60 minutes; each minute is further divided into 60 seconds.

Sources: Blocksma, Mary. *Reading the Numbers*, p. 107; *The McGraw-Hill Dictionary of Scientific and Technical Terms*, p. 1492.

• What is **Mercator's projection** for **maps**?

The Mercator projection is a technique used by cartographers (mapmakers) to transfer the spherical properties of the Earth to the flat surface of a map. It was created by Flemish cartographer Gerardus Mercator in 1569. The Mercator projection is most useful for navigation, since compass directions appear as straight lines.

To present land and sea in their correct proportions, the east-west parallels, or lines of latitude, are spaced at increasingly large distances toward the poles. This results in a severe exaggeration of size in the polar regions. In a Mercator projection Greenland, for example, appears five times larger than it actually is.

Sources: *Chambers Science and Technology Dictionary*, p. 564; *Encyclopedia Americana*, International Edition, vol. 18, pp. 283-84.

• What is **Foucault's pendulum**?

Foucault's pendulum was an instrument devised by French physicist (a scientist who studies matter and energy and the interactions between the two) Jean Bernard Léon Foucault (1819–1868) in 1851 to prove that the Earth rotates on its axis. Prior to Foucault's experiment, there was no proof that the Earth rotated. Many people believed that the Earth was still while the sun and stars moved around it.

Foucault's pendulum consisted of a large, swinging, iron ball suspended from a ceiling by a 200-foot-long wire. There was a pointer attached to the bottom of the ball, which etched the ball's path in the sand below. When the ball was first released, it would scratch a straight line in the sand. However, over the course of a day, that line would shift again and again until it came full circle. Since the pendulum did not change course, the only other explanation was that the Earth was rotating beneath it.

A reconstruction of Foucault's experiment is located in the convention center at Portland, Oregon. It swings from a cable 90 feet (27.4 meters) long—the longest pendulum in the world today.

Sources: *The Cambridge Dictionary of Science and Technology*, pp. 362, 812; Daintith, John. *The Facts On File Dictionary of Physics*, p. 78; Engelbert, Phillis. *Astronomy and Space: From the Big Bang to the Big Crunch*, vol. 1, pp. 163-64; *The Guinness Book of Records 1996*, p. 79.

• Who was the first person to map the **Gulf Stream?**

Benjamin Franklin (1706–1790) first mapped the Gulf Stream in 1770. Franklin, who was a diplomat, made regular sea voyages between America and France. He noticed that the boat ride took longer from France to America than vice-versa, and studied the ships' reports to determine the reason. He discovered that there was a current of warm water coming from the Gulf of Mexico, which crossed the North Atlantic Ocean in the direction of Europe.

Franklin believed that the current started in the Gulf of Mexico. However, the Gulf Stream actually originates in the western Caribbean Sea and moves through the Gulf of Mexico, the Straits of Florida, then north along the East Coast of the United States. Once it reaches Cape Hatteras in North Carolina, the Gulf Stream turns to the northeast.

The Gulf Stream eventually breaks up near Newfoundland, Canada, to form smaller currents, or eddies. Some of these eddies blow toward the British Isles and Norway, causing the climate of these regions to be milder than other areas of northwestern Europe.

Source: Asimov, Isaac. *Asimov's Chronology of Science and Discovery*, pp. 215-16.

ENERGY

CONSUMPTION AND CONSERVATION

● Does the **United States** currently produce enough **energy** to meet its consumption needs?

No. Since 1958 the United States has been consuming more energy than it has been producing. Imported energy makes up the difference.

In 1996, the United States produced 72.610 quadrillion BTUs of energy. (BTU stands for British thermal unit: the quantity of heat needed to raise the temperature of one pound of water by 1° Fahrenheit .) The energy produced in that year was divided among the following sources (in quadrillions of BTUs): coal (22.614); natural gas (19.532); crude oil (13.737); natural gas plant liquids, (2.531); nuclear power (7.168); hydro-electric power (3.591); geothermal energy (heat from the interior of the Earth [.341]); biomass fuel (energy derived from burning plant matter [3.017]); solar energy (.075); and wind energy (.036). Of that energy, 4.69 quadrillion BTUs were exported.

The United States' total energy consumption in 1996 was 93.81 quadrillion BTUs (33.88 in residential and commercial; 35.43 in industrial; and 24.43 in transportation). Therefore, the United States had to import 25.81 quadrillion BTUs, mostly in crude oil, to meet its energy needs. By

subtracting the energy exported, we find that the United States had a net
energy import of 21.2 quadrillion BTUs.

Source: U.S. Department of Energy. _Annual Energy Review_. [Online] Available. http://www.
eia.doe.gov/emeu/aer/aergs/aer2.html, August 14, 1997.

• Which countries consume the **most energy**?

One study projects that by the year 2010, the largest consumers are still expected to be the United States, the former Soviet Union, and China. It
predicts that between 1990 and 2012, China will increase its average annual energy consumption at twice the rate of the rest of the world. BTU
stands for British thermal unit: the quantity of heat needed to raise the
temperature of one pound of water by 1° Fahrenheit.

Top Energy-Consuming Countries

Country	1992 percentage of world total fuel consumed	1992 fuel consumption in quadrillion BTUs	2000 projected fuel consumption in quadrillion BTUs
United States	24.6%	85.8	95.1
Former Soviet Union	14.7%	51.2	48.0
China	8.4%	29.2	43.9
Japan	5.4%	19.0	23.0
Germany	4.0%	14.1	15.8
Canada	3.1%	11.0	14.0
United Kingdom	2.8%	9.7	11.5
France	2.8%	9.7	10.8
India	2.6% (1993)	9.1 (1993)	13.3
Italy	2.0%	7.0	7.8

Sources: International Energy Outlook 1995—Tables. [Online] Available http://www.eia.doe.gov/
oiaf/ieo95/tbls.html, Sept. 11, 1997; World Energy Consumption, Oil Production, and Carbon Emissions Tables. [Online] Available http://www.eia.doe.gov/oiaf/ieo96/front.html, Sept. 11, 1997.

> ### What does the term *"cooling degree day"* mean?
>
> "Cooling degree day" is a unit used to estimate the energy needed to cool a building. One unit is given for each degree Fahrenheit above the daily mean (average) temperature when the mean temperature exceeds 75°F (24°C). For example, a day on which the temperature is 85°F (29°C) would be rated as ten cooling degree days. The greater the number of cooling degree days, the more fuel is needed to maintain a comfortable indoor temperature.
>
> **Source:** *The McGraw-Hill Dictionary of Scientific and Technical Terms*, p. 431.

• How much **water** does an average person use each day?

An average person uses about 123 gallons (466 liters) of water daily. Some individual household activities and the amount of water they consume are listed below:

Activity	Water used
Shower	15-30 gallons (57-114 liters)
Brushing teeth (water running)	1-2 gallons (3.75-7.51 liters)
Shaving (water running)	10-15 gallons (38-57 liters)
Washing dishes by hand	20 gallons (75 liters)
Washing dishes in dishwasher	9-12 gallons (34-45 liters)
Flushing toilet	5-7 gallons (19-26 liters)

Sources: Famighetti, Robert, ed.*The World Almanac Book of Facts 1995*, p. 192; *Gale Book of Averages*, pp. 91-94.

• How long, at the present rate of consumption, will current major **energy reserves** last, in the world and in the **United States**?

The best estimates indicate there will be enough oil to provide energy to the world for another 50 years. The current supply of natural gas, at gradually increased rates of consumption, will last almost 60 years. Coal supplies should last anywhere from a few hundred to one thousand years (only 2.5 percent of the world's coal has thus far been consumed).

Energy reserves in the United States are expected to last: 32.5 years for oil; 58.7 years for natural gas; and 226 years for coal. These estimates are based on 1986 production rates.

Sources: "Conservation of Natural Resources." *Encyclopaedia Britannica CD 97*; "Fossil Fuels." *Encyclopaedia Britannica CD 97*; *Handy Science Answer Book*, p. 153; Hoyle, Russ. *Gale Environmental Almanac*, p. 572.

• How much energy is saved by **recycling** one **aluminum can**?

By some accounts, the energy saved by recycling one aluminum can equals the amount of energy it takes to run a TV set for four hours. This is the energy equivalent of 0.5 gallon (1.9 liters) of gasoline.

It takes nearly 9,000 pounds (4,086 kilograms) of bauxite (aluminum ore) and 1,020 pounds (463 kilograms) of petroleum coke (fuel) to manufacture one ton of aluminum. Using recycled aluminum to produce aluminum reduces raw material requirements by 95 percent and energy requirements by 90 percent.

Sources: Heloise. *Heloise: Hints for a Healthy Planet*, p. 56; *101 Ways to Save Money and Save Our Planet*, p. 122.

• What is the advantage of switching from **incandescent** to **fluorescent light bulbs**?

One 18-watt fluorescent bulb provides the light of a 75-watt incandescent bulb and lasts ten times as long. (A fluorescent light is tubular and its shine is produced by a chemical reaction; an incandescent light is bulbous and its shine is produced by heat.)

Even though the purchase price is higher, a fluorescent bulb is more economical over an extended period of time. An 18-watt fluorescent light bulb, over its lifetime, uses far less electricity than a 75-watt incandescent bulb. In fact, the use of a fluorescent bulb saves 80 pounds (36 kilograms) of coal (coal is used to produce electricity). This translates into 250 fewer pounds (113 kilograms) of carbon dioxide released into the Earth's atmosphere.

Source: MacEachern, Diane. *Save Our Planet*, p. 34.

> ### How is a "heating degree day" defined?
>
> Early in the twentieth century, engineers developed the concept of heating degree days as a useful index of heating fuel requirements. They found that when the daily mean (average) temperature is lower than 65° Fahrenheit (18° Celsius), most buildings require heat to maintain a 70° Fahrenheit (21° Celsius) temperature. Each degree of mean temperature below 65° Fahrenheit (18° Celsius) is counted as "one heating degree day."
>
> For every additional heating degree day, more fuel is needed to maintain a 70° Fahrenheit (21° Celsius) indoor temperature. For example, a day with a mean temperature of 35° Fahrenheit (1.5° Celsius) would be rated as 30 heating degree days and would require twice as much fuel as a day with a mean temperature of 50° Fahrenheit (10° Celsius ; 15 heating degree days).
>
> **Source:** Bair, Frank E. *The Weather Almanac,* 6th ed., p. 148.

| FOSSIL FUELS

• Why are **coal, oil, and natural gas** called **fossil fuels?**

Coal, oil, and natural gas are composed of fossils—that is, the remains of organisms that lived as long ago as 500 million years. Oil and gas originated as organisms in the oceans, such as phytoplankton, that over time became incorporated into the sediments on the ocean floor.

Coal is the fossilized remains of trees and other plants that were buried in the Earth. Over millions of years, these remains were subjected to pressure, temperature, and chemical processes to become transformed into coal.

Source: Ojakangas, Richard. *Schaum's Outline of Theory and Problems of Introductory Geology,* p. 78.

• How and when was **coal** formed?

Coal was formed from the remains of plants that have been buried in the Earth for millions of years. The dead plants were first converted into peat, a highly organic soil, which was then buried. Over millions of years, the peat deposits were subjected to high pressure and temperatures as the Earth's crust buckled and folded. The peat was compressed into lignite, a material with a woody texture, and eventually into coal.

249

The Carboniferous Period, during which coal was produced, occurred between 286 and 360 million years ago. Geologists (scientist specializing in the study of the origin, history, and structure of the Earth) in the United States sometimes divide this period into the Pennsylvanian (286 to 300 million years ago) and Mississippian (300 to 360 million years ago) periods. Most of the high-grade coal deposits were formed during the Pennsylvanian period.

Sources: Barnes-Svarney, Patricia. *The New York Public Library Science Desk Reference*, p. 388; *The New Book of Popular Science*, vol. 2, pp. 320-21.

• What types of **coal** are there?

There are four types of coal, each of which are produced by pressure, temperature, and chemical processes that occur over long periods of time.

The early stages of coal formation yield lignite, a dark brown, woody-textured substance. With increased pressure, lignite is converted into a harder, blacker substance called sub-bituminous coal. Under still greater pressure, a somewhat harder coal called bituminous coal ("soft coal") is produced. Intense pressure changes bituminous coal into anthracite, the hardest of all coals.

Sources: Brady, George S. *Materials Handbook*, 13th ed., p. 207; *World Book Encyclopedia*, vol. 4, pp. 716-17.

• How is underground **coal mined**?

There are two basic types of underground mining methods: the first is called "room and pillar" and the second is called "longwall." In room and pillar mines,

An offshore oil rig located in the Gulf of Mexico.

coal is removed by cutting rooms, or large tunnels, in the solid coal. Pillars of coal are left standing to support the roof. In longwall mining, miners remove successive slices of coal from the entire length of a long working face, or wall.

In the United States, almost all of the coal recovered by underground mining is by room and pillar method. In other parts of the world, such as Great Britain, the longwall method is more popular.

The thickness of coal deposits in the United States ranges from a thin film to over 50 feet (15 meters). The thickest coalbeds are in the western states, ranging from 10 feet (3 meters) in Utah and New Mexico to 50 feet (15 meters) in Wyoming.

Source: Cuff, David J. *The United States Energy Atlas*, p. 21.

• When was the first **oil well** in the **United States** drilled?

The first oil well in the United States was the Drake well at Titusville, Pennsylvania. It was completed on August 28, 1859 (some sources list the date as August 27). The well was owned by Edwin L. Drake (1819–1880) and drilled by William "Uncle Billy" Smith to a depth of 69.5 feet (21 meters) underground. Within 15 years, Pennsylvania oil fields were yielding more than 10 million barrels of oil a year (a barrel holds 42 gallons).

Sources: Hyne, Norman J. *Dictionary of Petroleum Exploration, Drilling and Production*, p. 585; Kane, Joseph N. *Famous First Facts*, 4th ed., p. 439; McNeil, Ian. *An Encyclopedia of the History of Technology*, p. 211.

• Why was **lead** added to **gasoline** and why is lead-free gasoline used in new cars?

Tetraethyl lead (a colorless, oily, poisonous liquid), commonly called "lead," was used as a gasoline additive for automobiles made between the mid-1940s and the end of the 1970s. There were several reasons for adding lead to gasoline. First, lead improved the way that gasoline burned. Second, it reduced or eliminated the "knocking" sound caused by premature ignition in high-performance large engines and in smaller, high-compression engines. Lead also provided lubrication, which prevented the close-fitting parts of the engine from chafing against one another.

New cars (cars made between the 1980s to the present), however, require the use of lead-free gasoline. This is because new cars come with pollution control devices called catalytic converters, and lead destroys the substance used as the catalyst.

Source: *Mark's Standard Handbook for Mechanical Engineers*, pp. 7-16.

• When did **gasoline stations** open?

The first service station (or garage) was opened in Bordeaux, France, in December 1895 by A. Barol. It provided overnight parking and repair service, and sold motor oil and "motor spirit" (fuel). In April 1897 a parking and refueling establishment—Brighton Cycle and Motor Company—opened in Brighton, England.

The first gasoline pump was devised by Sylanus Bowser of Fort Wayne, Indiana, in September 1885. However, this pump was originally used to dispense kerosene. Twenty years later Bowser manufactured the first self-regulating gasoline pump.

In 1912, a Standard Oil of Louisiana superstation opened in Memphis, Tennessee. It featured 13 gas pumps, a ladies' rest room, and a maid who served ice water to waiting customers. On December 1, 1913, in Pittsburgh,

The exhaust from motor vehicles is one of the main components of smog.

Pennsylvania, the Gulf Refining Company opened the first 24-hour drive-in gas station. The station sold only 30 gallons (114 liters) of gasoline on its first day of business.

Sources: Harris, Harry. *Good Old-Fashioned Yankee Ingenuity,* pp. 136-37; Kane, Joseph N. *Famous First Facts,* 4th ed., p. 598.

• What are the main components of **motor vehicle exhaust**?

The main components of motor vehicle exhaust are nitrogen, carbon dioxide, and water. Smaller amounts of nitrogen oxides, carbon monoxide, hydrocarbons, aldehydes, and other products of incomplete combustion (burning) are also present. The worst air pollutants, in order of amount produced, are carbon monoxide, nitrogen oxides, and hydrocarbons.

Source: *Concise Encyclopedia of Chemistry,* p. 394.

• How is **gasohol** made?

Gasohol is a mixture of 90 percent unleaded gasoline and 10 percent ethyl alcohol (ethanol). Its performance as a motor vehicle fuel is comparable to

253

that of 100 percent unleaded gasoline, with the added benefit of superior antiknock properties (no premature fuel ignition). No engine modifications are needed for the use of gasohol, which has in recent years gained some acceptance as an alternative to pure gasoline.

Corn is most often used to produce ethanol in the United States, since it is the nation's most abundant grain crop. However, ethanol can be made from a wide range of organic (living) raw materials, such as oats, barley, wheat, milo, sugar beets, and sugar cane. Potatoes, cassava (a starchy plant), and cellulose (material taken from the cell walls of plants) are other possible sources.

The first step in making ethanol from corn is to grind and cool the corn starch. In the process, the starch is converted into a sugar. The sugar is then converted into alcohol by adding yeast. Finally, the water is then boiled off, leaving behind pure alcohol.

While one acre of corn yields 250 gallons (946 liters) of ethanol, other plants are more efficient ethanol producers (for instance, an acre of sugar beets yields 350 gallons [1,325 liters] of ethanol). In the future, it's possible that motor fuel will be produced almost exclusively from organic material. At present, the process of converting organic material to ethanol is prohibitively expensive.

Sources: Hunt, V. Daniel. *The Gasohol Handbook*, pp. 1, 4; Lincoln, John W. *Driving Without Gas*, p. 7; Sutton, Caroline, and Duncan M. Anderson. *How Do They Do That?*, pp. 210-11.

• What are the advantages and disadvantages of the **alternatives to gasoline** to power **automobiles**?

Because the emissions produced by the burning of gasoline are a major source of air pollution, alternatives to gasoline are currently being developed. None of the alternatives (listed below) delivers as much energy con-

These dried corn stalks will be used to make ethanol.

tent as gasoline. Therefore, it takes greater quantities of each of these fuels, than it does gasoline, to drive an equal number of miles.

The most viable alternative to gasoline is called "flexible fuel," a combination of methanol and gasoline. The use of flexible fuel, however, would require an expensive fuel sensor and a longer fuel tank, adding at least $300 to the price of a car.

Alternative	Advantages	Disadvantages
Electricity from batteries	No vehicle emissions, good for stop and go driving	Short-lived bulky batteries; limited trip range
Ethanol from corn, biomass, etc.	Relatively clean fuel	Costs, corrosive damage
Hydrogen from electrolysis, etc.	Plentiful supply; nontoxic emissions	High cost; highly flammable
Methanol from methanol gas, coal, biomass, wood	Cleaner combustion; less volatile emissions	Corrosive; some irritant
Natural gas from hydrocarbons and petroleum deposits	Cheaper on energy basis; relatively clean	Cost to adapt vehicle, bulky storage; sluggish performance

Source: Brennan, Richard. *Dictionary of Scientific Literacy*, pp. 113-14.

| ALTERNATIVE ENERGY

• What is **alternative energy**?

Alternative energy is a general term that includes sources of energy other than those that are most commonly used in society. Coal, oil, and natural gas—and nuclear and hydroelectric power to a lesser extent—are considered dominant or "conventional" forms of energy. The dominant forms, collectively, account for between 85 percent and 97 percent of all energy consumption on Earth (the exact percentage is not known because information is not available from many remote areas).

The most familiar types of "alternative energy" are solar power, wind power, tidal power (power derived from ocean tides), geothermal power (heat from the interior of the Earth), and biomass energy (derived from burning plant matter).

The use of alternative energy sources has increased in recent years, as the world's supply of fossil fuels (coal, oil, and natural gas) dwindles. Another attractive aspect of alternative fuels is that, unlike fossil fuels, they do not contribute to air pollution.

Sources: "Energy Conversion: Exploiting Renewable Energy Sources." *Encyclopaedia Britannica CD 97*; Naseri, Muthena, and Douglas Smith. "Alternative Energy Sources." *Environmental Encyclopedia*, pp. 30-31.

• There are three types of primary **energy** that flow continuously on or to the **surface of the Earth**. What are they?

Geothermal energy is heat contained beneath the Earth's crust and brought to the surface in the form of steam or hot water. The five main sources of geothermal energy are: steam fields below the Earth's surface, which provide dry, super-heated steam; geysers and hot springs, which provide hot water and wet steam; dry rocks into which cold water is pumped to create steam; pressurized fields of hot water and natural gas beneath ocean beds; and magma (molten rock) in or near volcanoes and 5 to 30 miles (8 to 48 kilometers) below the Earth's crust.

Geothermal sources contribute to such things as the production of electric power, industrial processing, and space heating. The first geothermal power station was built in 1904 at Larderello, Italy. Currently, the California Geysers project is the world's largest geothermal electric generating complex, with 200 steam wells that provide some 1,300 megawatts (one million watts) of power. Most buildings in Iceland are currently heated by geothermal energy, and a few communities in the United States, such as Boise, Idaho, use geothermal home heating.

Solar radiation, the energy of the sun, is the second type of energy that is continuously supplied on the surface of the Earth. The ability to harness solar energy, however, depends both on the frequency of sunny (versus cloudy) days in a given location and the ability to store solar energy for night use.

Solar radiation can be used directly for heating and lighting or can be harnessed and used to generate electricity. Although many of the large-scale applications of solar energy are still in the planning stages, small-scale applications are already in use in many parts of the world, particularly where sunshine is plentiful. For instance, in some areas solar heat-absorbers produce hot water for residential use. And photovoltaic cells, which contain semiconductor (material such as silicon that amplifies and controls electrical currents) crystals, are placed on sides of buildings, where they convert sunlight to electricity.

A solar thermal facility (LUZ International Solar Thermal Plant) in the Mojave Desert currently produces 274 megawatts and is used to supplement power needs of the Los Angeles utilities companies. Japan has 4 million solar panels installed on roofs. In Israel, two-thirds of the houses have solar panels, as do 90 percent of the homes in Cyprus.

Another arena of solar power is space. Virtually every spacecraft and satellite since 1958 has received all or part of its power through the conversion of sunlight by solar panels.

Tidal and wave energy is a third form of continuous, free-flowing energy. The first tidal-powered mill was built in England in 1100. A second mill, built in Woodbridge, England, in 1170, has functioned for more than 800 years.

The Rance River Power Station in France, in operation since 1966, was the first large tidal electric generator plant, producing 160 megawatts. A tidal station works like a hydropower dam, with its turbines (machines that convert the kinetic energy of moving fluids to mechanical power) spinning as the tide flows through them.

A solar energy system at the National Renewable Energy Laboratory in Colorado.

Ocean wave energy can also be made to drive electrical generators. Unfortunately, the 13.5-hour interval between high tides makes it difficult to integrate the times of peak power production and peak consumption.

Sources: Cone, Robert J. *How the New Technology Works*, p. 23; Cunningham, William P., and Barbara Woodhouse Saigo. *Environmental Science: A Global Concern*, pp. 392-95; Engelbert, Phillis. *The Complete Weather Resource*, vol. 3, pp. 517-20; *How in the World?: A Fascinating Journey Through the World of Human Ingenuity*, pp. 125-28.

• What is the difference between **passive solar energy systems** and **active solar energy systems**?

Passive solar energy systems use the architectural design, natural materials, or absorptive structures of a building as an energy-saving system. The building itself serves as a solar collector and storage device. An example would be thick-walled stone and adobe dwellings that slowly collect heat during the day and gradually release it at night. Another example of a passive solar energy system is a greenhouse. Passive systems require little or no investment of external equipment.

Active solar energy systems require a solar collector (a device used to store energy) and controls linked to pumps or fans that draw heat from storage as necessary. Active solar systems generally pump a heat-absorbing fluid (air, water, or an antifreeze solution) through a collector. Collectors, such as insulated water tanks, vary in size, depending on the number of sunny or cloudy days in a locale. Heat storage systems use eutectic (phase-changing) chemicals to store a large amount of energy in a small volume.

Source: Cunningham, William P., and Barbara Woodhouse Saigo. *Environmental Science: A Global Concern,* p. 377.

• What is **biomass energy?**

Biomass energy is energy produced by burning biomass. Biomass is a broad category of material encompassing all the living matter in an area. Wood, crops and crop waste, and wastes of plant, mineral, and animal matter comprise much of an area's biomass. Much of this material is considered "garbage" and ends up in landfills.

It has been estimated that 90 percent of U.S. waste products could be burned, thereby providing the equivalent energy of 100 million tons of coal (20 percent of waste products will not burn though they can be recycled). In Western Europe, there are more than 200 power plants that burn rubbish (garbage) to produce electricity.

Biomass can also be converted into energy-providing biofuels, such as biogas, methane, methanol, and ethanol. However, the biofuel production process is more expensive than the conventional fossil fuel processes.

Rubbish buried in the ground naturally yields methane gas during anaerobic decomposition (the decaying of organic matter in the absence of oxygen). One ton of refuse can produce 8,000 cu feet (227 cu meters) of methane. Worldwide, there are 140 methane-collecting operations that tap into underground rubbish.

Some crops, such as sugar cane, sorghum, ocean kelp, water hyacinth, and various species of trees, are grown specifically to be burned for biomass energy.

Sources: Cunningham, William, and Barbara Woodhouse Saigo. *Environmental Science: A Global Concern,* pp. 384-86; *How in the World?: A Fascinating Journey Through the World of Human Ingenuity,* pp. 118-19; Wright, R. Thomas. *Understanding Technology,* p. 72.

| NUCLEAR ENERGY

• What is **nuclear energy?**

Nuclear energy is energy derived from a type of nuclear reaction called fission. Fission occurs when neutrons strike and split the nuclei of certain isotopes of uranium, for instance uranium-235 (isotopes are defined by the total number of protons and neutrons in an atom). When a uranium nucleus is split, it releases the following: neutrons, two or more lighter nuclei, and a large amount of energy. Neutrons are involved in both sides of the fission equation—they are used to initiate fission and are by-products of fission. This recycling of neutrons creates what is known as a "chain-reaction" and drives the fission reaction until the uranium runs out.

Nuclear power plants, in use since 1957, are facilities where the energy released by fission is harnessed. This energy is used to boil water, which creates steam. The steam, in turn, spins a turbine (a machine that converts the kinetic energy of moving fluids into mechanical power) and generates electricity.

The central feature of a nuclear power plant is the reactor core, which consists of three main elements. The first is the fuel rods, which are narrow tubes of fissionable uranium. The second is the moderator, generally made of graphite (pure carbon) or water. The moderator slows down the fast-moving neutrons released by fission. This is necessary because only slow-moving neutrons will initiate fission. The third component is the control rods—rods made of neutron-absorbing material such as cadmium or boron. The control rods absorb excess neutrons in the core, keeping the number of neutrons released by fission equal to the number of neutrons needed to keep the reaction going.

Nuclear power was once viewed as a promising solution to the United States' energy crisis. However, a series of accidents has soured that promise. Varying amounts of radiation have been accidentally released at nuclear reactor sites in Idaho Falls, Idaho; Liverpool, England; Three Mile Island in Harrisburg, Pennsylvania; and Chernobyl near Kiev, Ukraine.

Another problem with nuclear energy is the lack of permanent storage for nuclear wastes. At present, all nuclear waste is placed in short-term storage, such as water-filled pools at the individual plant sites and in shallow landfills. It has been proposed that a permanent, high-level nuclear waste repository be constructed at Yucca Mountain, located at the edge of the Nevada Test Site in southeastern Nevada. This repository, which still faces significant local opposition, is not due to open until sometime early in the next century.

Sources: Cunningham, William P., et al. *Environmental Encyclopedia*, pp. 572-73; "Energy Conversion: Waste Disposal." *Encyclopaedia Britannica CD 97*.

• How many **nuclear power plants** are there worldwide?

As of 1994, 432 nuclear reactors were operational, with 48 more under construction.

Country	Number of Units
Argentina	2
Belgium	7
Brazil	1
Bulgaria	6
Canada	22
China	3
Czech Republic	4
Finland	4
France	56
Germany	21
Hungary	4
India	9
Japan	49
Kazakhstan	1
Korea, South	10
Lithuania	2
Mexico	2
Netherlands	2
Pakistan	1
Russia	29
South Africa	2
Slovakia	4
Slovenia	1
Spain	9
Sweden	12
Switzerland	5
Taiwan	6
Ukraine	15
United Kingdom	34
United States	109

As of May 1995, the United States had 109 reactors in operation, with one under construction. The plants generated 640,440 million net kilowatt hours or 22 percent of domestic electricity in 1994.

Sources: Famighetti, Robert, ed. *The World Almanac and Book of Facts 1996*, p. 205; *Nuclear News*, vol. 38 (March 1995), p. 42.

• What is the difference between **nuclear fission** and **nuclear fusion?**

Nuclear fission is the process used in the production of nuclear power. Fission involves splitting the nucleus of a heavy atom, such as uranium. This yields two or more lighter nuclei and a large amount of energy.

Fusion, on the other hand, is the combination of two hydrogen nuclei into one helium nucleus, under conditions of extreme heat and pressure. Fusion is the process by which energy is created in the sun.

While the hydrogen bomb relies on fusion, fusion has not yet been used in the production of nuclear power. The latter fact is primarily because it is extremely expensive to create the conditions necessary to begin a fusion reaction. A process called "cold fusion," which does not require heat, is currently in the experimental stages.

Sources: Barnes-Svarney, Patricia. *The New York Public Library Science Desk Reference*, pp. 300, 486; "The Technology of War: Nuclear Power Plants." *Encyclopaedia Britannica CD 97*.

• What is the **Rasmussen Report?**

Norman C. Rasmussen of the Massachusetts Institute of Technology (MIT) conducted a study of nuclear reactor safety for the United States Atomic Energy Commission in the early 1970s. (A nuclear reactor is any device used for controlling the release of nuclear power so that it can be used for constructive purposes.) The study, called the "Reactor Safety Study," better known as the "Rasmussen Report," cost four million dollars and took three years to complete. It concluded that the odds against a worst-case nuclear accident occurring were astronomically large: ten million to one.

The report predicted that a worst-case accident would result in about 3,000 early deaths and 14 billion dollars in property damage due to contamination. In addition, about 1,500 people per year would contract cancer following the accident. The study concluded that the safety features engineered into a plant are very likely to prevent serious accidents from occurring.

Some groups criticized the Rasmussen Report, claiming that the estimates of risk were too low. In light of the Chernobyl nuclear disaster in 1986, many scientists now estimate that a major nuclear accident might, in fact, happen every decade. The partial meltdown of the core at Chernobyl nuclear power plant in Ukraine (part of the former Soviet Union) was the worst nuclear power accident in history. The accident began as one of the plant's four reactors rapidly overheated, which led to explosions and a fire. This caused the lid to blow off the reactor, releasing as much radioactive material (material containing radiation) in the air as ten atomic bombs like the one that was dropped on Hiroshima, Japan, in August 1945.

Sources: Lean, Geoffrey, et al. *WWF Atlas of the Environment,* p. 119; ReVelle, Penelope. *The Environment,* pp. 317-18.

• What is a **meltdown?**

A meltdown is an accident in a nuclear reactor (any device used for controlling the release of nuclear power so that it can be used for constructive purposes) in which the fuel core melts, resulting in the release of dangerous amounts of radiation (energy in the form of waves or particles). In most cases the large containment structure that houses a nuclear reactor would prevent the radioactivity from escaping. However, there is a small possibility that the molten core could become hot enough to burn through the floor of the containment structure and go deep into the Earth. All reactors are equipped with emergency systems to prevent such an accident from occurring. Between 1957 and 1986, however, there have been four accidents in which major core damage has resulted.

Sources: Blair, Ian. *Taming the Atom,* pp. 170-71; *The Macmillan Visual Dictionary,* p. 765; *World Book Encyclopedia,* vol. 14, p. 587.

• Where did the expression **"China Syndrome"** originate?

The expression "China Syndrome" was first coined during a discussion of the potential consequences of a nuclear reactor (any device used for controlling the release of nuclear power so that it can be used for constructive purposes) meltdown. (A meltdown is when the fuel core of a nuclear reactor melts and releases dangerous amounts of radiation.) One scientist commented that the molten reactor core could bore a hole straight through the Earth to China (assuming the reactor was in the United States). This worst-case scenario was thus nicknamed the "China Syndrome."

Although the scientist was grossly exaggerating, some people took him seriously. In fact, a molten core would bore a hole only about 30 feet (10 meters) into the Earth. This, however, would still have grave consequences for the surrounding area.

Source: Blair, Ian. *Taming the Atom,* p. 171.

• Which **nuclear reactors** have had **accidents**?

Nuclear power was once viewed as a promising solution to the United States' energy crisis. However, a series of accidents has soured that promise. Varying amounts of radiation have been released in a series of accidents, spanning the years from 1955 to 1986. Since the 1979 Three Mile Island accident in Harrisburgh, Pennsylvania, no new nuclear power plants have been developed in the United States. The plans to construct 65 new plants were canceled.

Incidents with core damage in nuclear reactors

Description of incident	Site	Date	Adult thyroid dose (in rems)
Minor core damage (no release of radiologic material)	Chalk River, Ontario, Canada	1952	not applicable
	Breeder Reactor, Idaho	1955	not applicable
	Westinghouse Test Reactor	1960	not applicable
	Detroit Edison Fermi, Michigan	1966	not applicable
Major core damage (radioiodine released)			
Noncommercial	Windscale, England	1957	16
	Idaho Falls SL-1, Idaho	1961	0.035
Commercial	Three Mile Island, Pennsylvania	1979	0.005
	Chernobyl, Soviet Union	1986	100 (est.)

Source: Famighetti, Robert, ed. *The World Almanac and Book of Facts 1995*, p. 571.

• What caused the **Chernobyl accident**?

The Chernobyl nuclear power plant in Ukraine (part of the former Soviet Union) is the site of the worst nuclear power accident in history. Human error and design features (such as the use of graphite in construction and lack of a containment building) are generally cited as the causes of the accident.

On April 25, 1986, operators at the Chernobyl plant began conducting unauthorized experiments. They deliberately circumvented (bypassed) safety systems in order to learn more about the plant's operation. Then, at 1:24 a.m. on April 26, one of the four reactors rapidly overheated and its water coolant "flashed" into steam. ("Flashed" refers to a sudden, temporary, radical increase in radioactivity within a substance.) The hydrogen formed from the steam reacted with the graphite moderator, causing two major explosions and a fire. The core underwent a partial meltdown.

The explosions blew apart the 1,000-ton (907-metric ton) lid of the reactor, and released radioactive debris high into the atmosphere. It is estimated that 50 tons of the reactor's fuel and 10 percent of the graphite reactor itself were emitted into the atmosphere. The radioactive material released into the atmosphere was equal to that of ten atomic bombs like the one that was dropped on Hiroshima, Japan, in August 1945. In addition, 70 tons of fuel and 700 tons of radioactive graphite settled on the ground near the reactor.

According to Soviet government accounts, there were 31 deaths initially of those who were trying to put out the fire. More than 240 others fell victim to severe radiation sickness; some have since died and the rest suffer from long-term illnesses. Within eight days of the explosion, 150,000 people living near the reactor were relocated and some may never be allowed to return home. Hundreds of thousands of other people continue to live in contaminated areas.

Fallout from the explosions, containing the radioactive isotope (a form of an element that gives off radiation and changes into another isotope; isotopes are defined by the number of protons and neutrons in an atom) cesium 137, was carried by the winds westward across Europe. Cesium 137 is produced when uranium undergoes fission (the splitting of the nucleus of a heavy atom) in a nuclear reactor or in nuclear weapons. Cesium 137 is known to cause cancer and genetic mutations in humans.

The Chernobyl disaster created overwhelming problems, some of which continue today. Beginning in 1990, an increase was found in the rate of thyroid cancers among children in Belarus, the country directly north of Ukraine (see table below). There has also been a significant decline in the overall health of children in Gomel and Mogilëv, the heaviest hit areas of Belarus.

Cases of Thyroid Cancer in Children 14 Years and Younger

	1986-88	1989	1990	1991	1992	1993	1994
Belarus	2-5	7	29	59	66	79	82
Ukraine	4-9	11	26	22	47	42	

It is estimated that the Chernobyl disaster will affect, in one way or another, 20 percent of the population of Ukraine (2.2 million people). The Chernobyl accident has raised serious questions about the safety of nuclear power plants everywhere, and has cast doubt on the future of nuclear power.

Sources: *The Bulletin of the Atomic Scientists*, vol. 49 (September 1993), pp. 38-43; "Chernobyl Accident." *Encyclopaedia Britannica CD 97*; Cunningham, William P., et al. *Environmental Encyclopedia*, pp. 137, 142-43; Finniston, Monty, ed. *Oxford Illustrated Encyclopedia of Invention and Technology*, p. 72; Magill, Frank N. *Great Events from History II: Science and Technology Series*, vol. 5, pp. 2321-23; May, John. *The Greenpeace Book of the Nuclear Age*, pp. 215-28; *Physicians and Ionizing Radiation*, [Online] Available http://www.edf.fr/html/en/mag/iode/evo.html, August 15, 1997.

• What was the distribution of **radioactive fallout** after the **Chernobyl accident?**

Radioactive fallout is the term used to describe radioactive debris that is emitted into the air in the wake of a nuclear reactor explosion and settles back to the ground.

The radioactive fallout from the Chernobyl disaster, which contained the isotope cesium 137, was extremely uneven because of the shifting wind patterns. It extended 1,200 to 1,300 miles (1,930 to 2,090 kilometers) from the point of the accident. Roughly 50 tons of the reactor fuel, containing 50 to 100 million curies, was released. (A curie is a unit of radioactivity based on a standard rate of decay of a radioactive element.)

Nuclear contamination covered an enormous area of western Asia and Europe, including Ukraine, Belarus, Latvia, and Lithuania (the central portion of the former Soviet Union); the Scandinavian countries; and Poland, Austria, Czechoslovakia, Germany, Switzerland, northern Italy, eastern France, Romania, Bulgaria, Greece, Yugoslavia, the Netherlands, and the United Kingdom.

The anticipated effects of this fallout are that 28,000-100,000 deaths will occur due to cancer and genetic defects over the next 50 years. In addition, since the accident many livestock throughout the region have been born with deformities.

Sources: "Chernobyl Accident." *Encyclopaedia Brittanica CD 97*; Cunningham, William P., and Barbara Woodhouse Saigo. *Environmental Science: A Global Concern*, pp. 354-55; Cunningham, William P., et al. *Environmental Encyclopedia*, pp. 137, 142-43; Finniston, Monty, ed. *Oxford Illustrated Encyclopedia of Invention and Technology*, p. 72; Miller, E. Willard, and Ruby M. Miller. *Environmental Hazards: Air Pollution*, pp. 67-68.

A photograph showing the four cooling towers of Three Mile Island Nuclear Power Plant.

• What actually happened at **Three Mile Island**?

On March 28, 1979, the Three Mile Island nuclear power plant in Harrisburg, Pennsylvania, experienced a partial meltdown of its reactor core. (A meltdown is when the fuel core of a nuclear reactor melts and releases dangerous amounts of radioactivity.) Radioactive steam escaped into the atmosphere and radioactive water leaked from the plant into the Susquehanna River.

The accident occurred just after 4:00 a.m., when a water pump in the secondary cooling system of the Unit 2 pressurized water reactor failed. A relief valve jammed open, flooding the containment vessel with radioactive water. A backup system for pumping water was shut down for maintenance. Temperatures inside the reactor core rose and fuel rods ruptured. A partial (52 percent) meltdown of the radioactive uranium core occurred because the core was almost entirely uncovered by coolant for 40 minutes.

The thick steel-reinforced containment building prevented nearly all the radiation from escaping. As a result, the amount of radiation released into the atmosphere was only one-millionth of that at Chernobyl. However, had the coolant not been replaced, the molten fuel would have bored

267

A pile of radioactive waste covered only by a tarp in Cleveland, Ohio.

down through the reactor containment vessel. Then the fuel would have come into contact with the water, causing a steam explosion and a breaching (rupture) of the reactor dome. That would have produced a radiation leak similar to that which occurred in Chernobyl.

No one died as a direct result of the Three Mile Island accident. However, many people were exposed to dangerous levels of radiation. It's too soon to know what the long-term consequences will be to the health of area residents or their offspring.

Sources: Brennan, Richard P. *Dictionary of Scientific Literacy*, pp. 297-98; Cunningham, William P., et al. *Environmental Encyclopedia*, pp. 830-31; May, John. *The Greenpeace Book of the Nuclear Age*, pp. 215-28.

• How is **nuclear waste stored**?

There are various types of wastes created in the production of nuclear power. The two main categories are fission products and transuranic elements. Fission products, the more radioactive (the tendency of an element to break down spontaneously into one or more elements) of the two, are formed by fission, the splitting of atoms of uranium, cesium, strontium, or krypton. Transuranic elements, which remain radioactive far longer than fission products (hundreds of thousands of years), form when uranium atoms absorb free neutrons.

These wastes exist in three forms: 12 feet- (4 meter-) long spent fuel rods; high-level radioactive waste in liquid or sludge; and low-level radioactive waste in such things as reactor hardware, piping, toxic resins, or water from the fuel pool.

The U.S. government agency charged with the storage and disposal of nuclear waste is called the Office of Civilian Radioactive Waste Management, a division of the Department of Energy. This agency is involved in both the short-term storage of nuclear wastes and the development of a long-term storage site. At present, all nuclear waste is placed in short-term storage.

It has been proposed that a permanent, high-level nuclear waste repository be constructed at Yucca Mountain, located at the edge of the Nevada Test Site in southeastern Nevada. The Nevada Test Site is one of two locations where most the U.S. nuclear weapons testing took place. Despite opposition from Nevada residents, the repository—which has not yet under construction—is slated for completion early in the twenty-first century. The Nuclear Waste Policy Act of 1982, however, mandated that a method of permanent disposal of nuclear waste be established by 1998.

In the United States, most of the spent nuclear fuel rods have been sitting for ten years or more in water-filled pools at the individual plant sites. Most low-level radioactive waste has been stored in steel drums in shallow landfills at six nuclear dump sites and at the Hanford Nuclear Reservation in the state of Washington. Most high-level nuclear waste has been stored in double-walled stainless-steel tanks surrounded by 3 feet (1 meter) of concrete.

The best-known storage method, developed by the French in 1978, is to incorporate the waste into a special molten glass mixture, then enclose it in a steel container. All countries that operate nuclear power plants agree that the treated nuclear waste should then be buried in rock layers, far underground. After the waste is inserted in the ground, the pits would be filled and sealed.

An estimated 8,000 to 9,000 metric tons (8,816 to 9,918 tons) of high-level nuclear waste, from both nuclear power and nuclear weapon production, is created in the United States each year. The safe disposal of nuclear wastes is one of the greatest challenges to nuclear power and nuclear weapons producers. And as nuclear waste continues to pile up, the potential consequences to the environment and human health also continue to grow.

Sources: Cunningham, William P., et al. *Environmental Encyclopedia*, pp. 558, 583-84; "Energy Conversion: Waste Disposal." *Encyclopaedia Britannica CD 97; EPA Fact Sheet: Setting Environmental Standards for Yucca Mountain*, [Online] Available http://www.eap.gov/radiation/yucca/factrev.htm., April 1, 1996; *How in the World?: A Fascinating Journey Through the World of Human Ingenuity*, pp. 122-23; Naar, Jon. *Design for a Livable Planet*, pp. 161-63.

the ENVIRONMENT

| ECOLOGY

• What is **ecology**?

Ecology is the scientific study of the way that living organisms interact with their environment. "Ecology" comes from the Greek words *oikos*, meaning "house," and *logos*, meaning "logic" or "knowledge." The term was coined by German zoologist (scientist who studies animals) Ernst Haeckel in 1870.

While many people confuse the work of an "ecologist" with that of an "environmentalist," there are significant differences between the two occupations. Environmentalists seek to preserve natural systems. Ecologists, while they may share the ideals of environmentalists, are mainly involved with gathering information about the communities of animals and plants, as well as the physical elements (such as rocks and soil) present in a given geographical area.

Sources: Barnes-Svarney, Patricia. *The New York Public Library Science Desk Reference*, p. 458; Cunningham, William P., et al. *Environmental Encyclopedia*, pp. 248-50.

• How does a **food chain** work?

A food chain is the transfer of food energy from one organism to another. It begins with a plant, which is eaten by an animal. It continues with a second animal, which eats the first, and so on. There are usually four or five steps

271

or "links" in a sequence. The concept of food chains was introduced by German zoologist (scientist who studies animals) Karl Semper in 1891.

The links in a food chain are called trophic levels. Each trophic level is occupied by a group of organisms that obtain their food in the same way. The first trophic level is occupied by plants. The second level is occupied by herbivores, animals (such as rabbits) that eat plants. The third level consists of primary carnivores, which are animals that eat herbivores. An example of a primary carnivore is a fox. The final link in a food chain is occupied by a "top predator," a carnivore which is not hunted by other animals, such as a killer whale.

Sources: Cunningham, William P., et al. *Environmental Encyclopedia*, pp. 344-46; Odum, Eugene. *Fundamentals of Ecology*, 3rd ed., p. 63; Otto, James H. *Modern Biology*, p. 666; Trefil, James. *1001 Things Everyone Should Know About Science*, p. 43.

• What is a **food web**?

A food web is a series of interwoven food chains. Food chains overlap within an ecosystem (a community of plants and animals and their physical surroundings) because many organisms eat a variety foods rather than a single species of animal or plant.

For example, squirrels and mice eat several species of plants, as well as insects. The predatory broad-winged hawk feeds on insects, mice, and small reptiles. And foxes hunt a variety of creatures from worms to rabbits.

Animals that eat a variety of plant and/or animal species have a greater chance of survival than those that have a single food source. Complex food webs provide greater stability to an ecosystem.

Sources: Barrett, James A. *Biology*, pp. 937-38; Cunningham, William P., et al. *Environmental Encyclopedia*, pp. 344-46; Ward, Jack A. *Biology Today and Tomorrow*, pp. 421-22.

• What is a **biome**?

A biome is a large geographical area characterized by certain types of plants and animals. A biome is defined by the complex interactions of plants and animals with the climate, geology (rock formations), soil types, water resources, and latitude (position north or south on the globe) of an area.

One example of a biome is a desert. Deserts are the world's driest regions. Most of the vegetation there takes the form of drought-resistant plants such as cacti (plural form of cactus), which store water in their stems and have waxy coverings, and scrubby plants like the creosote bush, that have extensive root systems.

The animals that live in the desert are able to survive with little or no water. The camel, for instance, stores water and fat in its hump. And the kangaroo rat gets all the moisture it needs from solid food; it can go its entire life without drinking a drop of water.

Other examples of important biomes include tundra (bitterly cold regions with little plant growth), coniferous (evergreen) forests, deciduous (trees that usually lose their leaves in the fall) forests, grasslands, and tropical rain forests.

Sources: Engelbert, Phillis. *The Complete Weather Resource*, vol. 3, pp. 461-62; Lean, Geoffrey, et al. *WWF Atlas of the Environment*, p. 11; *World Book Encyclopedia*, vol. 2, pp. 322-24.

• Why is **El Niño** harmful?

Near the end of each calender year, along the west coast of South America, a warm current of nutrient-poor tropical water moves southward, replacing the cold, nutrient-rich surface waters off the coast of Peru. Because this condition frequently occurs around Christmas, local residents call it El Niño (Spanish for child), referring to the Christ child. In most years the warming lasts for only a few weeks. Occasionally—usually once every three to seven years—the warm waters don't leave. When they last for a year or two, it's called a major El Niño event.

During a major El Niño event, large numbers of fish and marine plants may die. Decomposition of the dead material depletes the water's oxygen supply, which leads to the bacterial production of huge amounts of smelly hydrogen sulfide. A greatly reduced fish (especially anchovy) harvest affects the world's fishmeal supply, leading to higher prices for poultry and other animals which normally eat fishmeal.

Studies reveal that El Niño is not an isolated occurrence, but is part of a pattern of change in the global circulation of the oceans and atmosphere. Specifically, the warming of the waters off the coast of Peru causes a decrease in air pressure over the eastern Pacific Ocean. As a result, the air pressure in the western Pacific rises (usually air pressure is higher over the eastern Pacific, near South America, and lower over the western Pacific, near Australia). This phenomenon of shifting air pressure across the Pacific is called the Southern Oscillation.

In "normal" years, when a major El Niño event and the Southern Oscillation do not occur, the difference in air pressure across the Pacific drives the trade winds (winds that blow throughout the tropics) westward, toward the

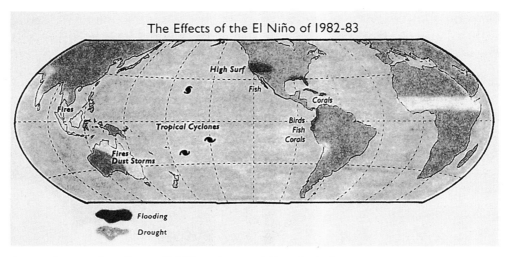

The Effects of the El Niño of 1982-83

High Surf · Fish · Corals · Birds Fish Corals · Tropical Cyclones · Fires · Fires Dust Storms

Flooding

Drought

A map showing the effects of El Niño during 1982 and 1983.

equator. The trade winds influence surface water circulations and the sea level throughout the world. However, when the pressure differential fluctuates, the course of the trade winds is altered. As a result, weather patterns are disrupted throughout the Pacific region of the Southern Hemisphere, as well as into the Northern Hemisphere as far north as Alaska and northern Canada.

The 1982 to 1983 El Niño was one of the most severe climatic events of the twentieth century. It brought about devastating droughts, floods, and storms in many parts of the world. Australia was hit with its worst drought ever. Hawaii, Mexico, southern Africa, the Philippines, and Indonesia also experienced droughts. Meanwhile, extensive flooding was experienced in Louisiana, Florida, Cuba, Ecuador, Peru, and Bolivia.

The 1986 to 1987 El Niño may have contributed to making 1987 the warmest year in the last century.

Sources: Ahrens, C. Donald. *Meteorology Today: An Introduction to Weather, Climate, and the Environment,* 5th ed., p. 311; Engelbert, Phillis. *The Complete Weather Resource,* vol. 1, pp.72-74; Golob, Richard. *Almanac of Science and Technology: What's New and What's Known,* pp. 296-302.

• How does **ozone** benefit life on Earth?

The ozone layer is important to humans and other living organisms because it absorbs most of the sun's harmful ultraviolet rays. Ozone is a type of oxygen molecule that has three atoms instead of the usual two. Ozone molecules are thinly spread within a belt that exists between 15 and 30 miles above the Earth's surface, in the atmospheric layer called the stratosphere. If all molecules of stratospheric ozone were settled onto the Earth's surface, they would form a layer that is only about ⅛-inch thick.

The depletion of the ozone layer, in recent years, has been linked to a number of human health problems. The most serious problem is a rise in cases of skin cancer. In fact, it is estimated that every 1 percent reduction in the ozone layer results in a 2 to 5 percent rise in the incidence of skin cancer. Other human consequences of the loss of protective ozone may include an increase in sunburns and eye cataracts, as well as the suppression of the immune system. Scientists also predict that depletion of the ozone layer could lead to the disruption of sensitive terrestrial (land) and aquatic ecosystems.

While ozone is beneficial in the stratosphere, when it is present near the ground it is a pollutant that contributes to the formation of photochemical smog and acid rain.

Sources: Engelbert, Phillis. *The Complete Weather Resource*, vol. 3, pp. 509, 513-16; Lean, Geoffrey, et al. *WWF Atlas of the Environment*, pp. 97-98; Schweitzer, Glenn E. *Borrowed Earth, Borrowed Time*, pp. 214, 218.

• What is **red tide** and what causes it?

Red tide is a term used to describe the brownish or reddish coloration of waters that sometimes occurs in oceans, rivers, or lakes. It is caused by algal blooms—the rapid reproduction of a variety of toxic, single-celled organisms. These organisms include dinoflagellates and diatoms, mostly of the genera (plural form of genus, a category or classification made up of species sharing similar characteristics) *Gymnodidium* and *Gonyaulax*, which contain a red pigment called peridinin.

In some cases red tides are harmless. However, during intense algal blooms, dangerous levels of toxins are released into the water. These toxins kill fish (millions of fish may die in a red tide) and accumulate in the fatty tissues of shellfish. Humans and other animals that eat contaminated shellfish may become paralyzed or even die.

Scientists do not fully understand why red tides occur. However, there seems to be a connection between the warm waters of the El Niño current and algal blooms.

Sources: Ashworth, William. *The Encyclopedia of Environmental Studies*, pp. 324-25; Cunningham, William P., et al. *Environmental Encyclopedia*, pp. 689-90; *Science Digest*, vol. 75 (February 1974), pp. 64-69.

ENVIRONMENTAL DEGRADATION

• How rapidly is **deforestation** occurring?

Deforestation is the removal of the entire ecosystem (the plants, animals, and microorganisms) of a forest. It involves not just removing trees and other plants, but transforming the land to serve another purpose. An example of deforestation is clearing a forest, then plowing the ground and planting crops. If one were to cut down the trees and then just leave the soil alone and let new trees grow, this would not be considered deforestation.

In the 1990 figures listed below, the annual amount of deforestation is given in square kilometers, and the annual rate of deforestation is given in the percentage of forested land being destroyed.

Country	Deforestation (square kilometers)	Percent
Brazil	13,820	0.4
Colombia	6,000	1.3
Mexico	7,000	1.5
Indonesia	10,000	0.9
Peru	2,700	0.4
Malaysia	3,100	1.5
Ecuador	3,400	2.4
India	10,000	2.7
Democratic Republic of Congo	4,000	0.4
Madagascar	1,500	1.5

Source: *American Forests*, vol. 98, nos. 3 and 4 (March-April 1992), p. 38.

• How many acres of **tropical forest** does the world lose annually?

Using data from satellite observations, it is estimated that between 16.4 and 20.4 million hectares of tropical forest are being destroyed each year (a hectare equals 107,639.1 square feet [10,000 square meters]). Only 50 percent of the world's mature tropical forests remain; 750 to 800 million hectares of the original 1.5 to 1.6 billion hectares of tropical forest have been destroyed.

There are two types of tropical forest: wet and dry. The greatest loss has occurred in wet forests, commonly called "rain forests." In Latin America

The deforestation of a tropical rainforest in Malaysia.

37 percent of tropical rain forests have been cleared; in Asia that figure is 42 percent, and in Africa, 52 percent. Most of the deforestation occurs as the result of logging, cutting trees for firewood, or the clearing of forests to create agricultural lands.

Attempts to grow crops on former rain forest land, however, are largely unsuccessful. This is because most of the nutrients in a tropical rain forest exist within the plants themselves; the soil is very nutrient-poor. When the plants are stripped away, the exposed soil is rapidly eroded by torrential rains. After the rain ceases, the sun bakes the ground into a hard crust, rendering the soil incapable of supporting vegetation.

Sources: Lean, Geoffrey, et al. *WWF Atlas of the Environment*, pp. 65-68; *National Wildlife*, vol. 30, no. 3 (April-May 1992), p. 16.

• What products come from **tropical forests?**

As the table shows, there are many products that come from tropical forests. Besides the products listed, many plants in tropical forests have medicinal value.

Products from Tropical Forests

Woods	Houseplants	Spices	Foods
Balsa	*Anthurium*	Allspice	Avocado
Mahogany	Croton	Black pepper	Banana
Rosewood	*Dieffenbachia*	Cardamom	Coconut
Sandalwood	*Dracaena*	Cayenne	Grapefruit
Teak	Fiddle-leaf fig	Chili	Lemon
	Mother-in-law's tongue	Cinnamon	Lime
Fibers	Parlor ivy	Cloves	Mango
Bamboo	Philodendron	Ginger	Orange
Jute/Kenaf	Rubber tree plant	Mace	Papaya
Kapok	Schefflera	Nutmeg	Passion fruit
Raffia	Silver vase bromeliad	Paprika	Pineapple
Ramie	*Spathiphyllum*	Sesame seeds	Plantain
Rattan	Swiss cheese plant	Turmeric	Tangerine
	Zebra plant	Vanilla bean	Brazil nuts
Gums, resins			Cane sugar
Chicle latex	**Oils, etc.**		Cashew nuts
Copaiba	Camphor oil		Chocolate
Copal	Cascarilla oil		Coffee
Gutta percha	Coconut oil		Cucumber
Rubber latex	Eucalyptus oil		Hearts of palm
Tung oil	Oil of star anise		Macadamia nuts
	Palm oil		Manioc/tapioca
	Patchouli oil		Okra
	Rosewood oil		Peanuts

A comparison illustration showing an atmosphere with natural levels of greenhouse gases (left) and an atmosphere of increased greenhouse effect (right).

Oils, etc.	Foods
Tolu balsam oil	Peppers
Annatto	Cola beans
Curare	Tea
Diosgenin	
Quinine	
Reserpine	
Strophanthus	
Strychnine	
Yang-Yang	

Source: *The 1992 Information Please Environmental Almanac,* p. 284.

• How long will it be before all **tropical forests** have been destroyed, if present rates of destruction continue?

If deforestation continues at present rates, all tropical forests will be cleared in about 170 years. These forests contain 155,000 of the 250,000 known plant species and innumerable insect and animal species. Half of all medicines prescribed worldwide are derived from plants found in tropical forests. In addition, the United States National Cancer Institute has identified more than two thousand tropical rain forest plants with the potential to fight cancer.

Sources: Lean, Geoffrey, et al. *WWF Atlas of the Environment,* pp. 65-68; *National Wildlife,* vol. 30, no. 3 (April-May 1991), p. 16.

• What is the **greenhouse effect**?

The greenhouse effect is a natural process by which the Earth's lower atmosphere is warmed. The term "greenhouse effect" has a negative connotation because of its association with air pollution and global warming. However, it is only because of the greenhouse effect that the Earth's surface is warm enough to sustain life. In the absence of the greenhouse effect, Earth's average surface temperature would be the same as its outer atmosphere, about 0° Fahrenheit (-18° Celsius)—a far cry from our actual average surface temperature of 59° Fahrenheit (33° Celsius)!

"Greenhouse gases" in the atmosphere— primarily water vapor and carbon dioxide and secondarily methane, nitrous oxide, and chlorofluorocarbons (CFCs)—trap heat in the same way as the glass of a greenhouse. Specifically, solar radiation enters the atmosphere in the form of visible light, is absorbed by the Earth's surface, and is converted to heat. Some of that heat radiates upward and is absorbed by greenhouse gases in the atmosphere. The gases reradiate heat outward in all directions, including back toward the surface. In this way the Earth's lower atmosphere is heated continuously, even at night when there is no incoming sunlight.

Since the Industrial Revolution (in the mid-1700s), levels of carbon dioxide and other greenhouse gases in the atmosphere have been increasing. This is primarily due to the burning of coal, oil, gas, and wood. The increase of greenhouse gases means that more heat is being trapped and returned to Earth, creating a condition known as "global warming."

Sources: Engelbert, Phillis. *The Complete Weather Resource*, vol. 3, pp. 500-4; Gay, Kathlyn. *The Greenhouse Effect*, pp. 2, 122-25; *McGraw-Hill Encyclopedia of Science and Technology*, 7th ed., vol. 8, pp. 225-26.

• What are the components of **smog**?

Photochemical air pollution, or photochemical smog, is the result of a number of complex chemical reactions. Nitrogen oxides and hydrocarbons, pollutants released in car exhaust fumes, are the raw materials for photochemical (based on the chemical action of light) reactions. In the presence of oxygen, these pollutants react with strong sunlight to produce a surface layer of ozone.

Whereas it's difficult to see photochemical smog at ground level, when looking down from above it appears as a whitish or brownish haze. Photo-

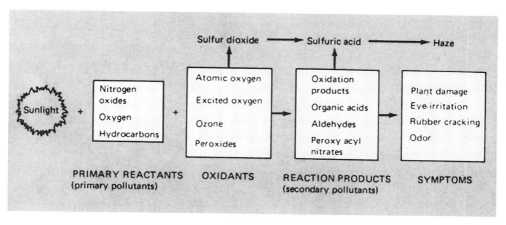

The chemistry of photochemical smog.

chemical smog is irritating to the eyes and throat and is a growing summertime problem in urban areas.

Photochemical smog is different from the pea-soup-type smog of London, which is a combination of sulfurous smoke and fog.

Sources: Engelbert, Phillis. *The Complete Weather Resource*, vol. 3, p. 509; Miller, E. Willard, and Ruby M. Miller. *Environmental Hazards: Air Pollution*, p. 77.

• How do **chlorofluorocarbons** affect the Earth's **ozone layer**?

Chlorofluorocarbons (CFCs) are hydrocarbons, such as freon, in which some or all of the hydrogen atoms have been replaced by fluorine atoms. CFCs can be liquids or gases, are nonflammable and heat-stable, and are used as refrigerants, aerosol propellants (such as in deodorant, whipped cream, and air fresheners), and solvents.

When released into the air, CFCs slowly rise through the Earth's lower atmosphere, and up to the stratosphere (second atmospheric layer, located about 7 to 30 miles [11 and 48 kilometers] above the Earth's surface). There they are converted by the sun's ultraviolet rays into chlorine compounds. The chlorine compounds react with stratospheric ozone molecules (O_3), converting them into ordinary oxygen molecules (O_2).

The release of CFCs into the atmosphere depletes the beneficial ozone layer faster than it can be recharged by natural processes. (The ozone layer is the atmospheric layer located approximately 15 to 30 miles above Earth's surface that protects the lower atmosphere from harmful radiation.) The

What are flue gas "scrubbers"?

The scrubbing of flue (chimney) gases refers to the removal of sulfur dioxide (SO_2) and nitric oxide (NO), which are major components of air pollution, from exhaust gas in industrial processes. There are two types of scrubbers: wet and dry. Wet scrubbers use a chemical solvent—lime, limestone, sodium alkali, or diluted sulfuric acid—to remove the SO_2 formed during chemical reactions. In dry scrubbing, either a lime/limestone mixture or ammonia is sprayed into the flue gases.

Source: Miller, E. Willard, and Ruby M. Miller. *Environmental Hazards: Air Pollution,* pp. 44-45.

loss of stratospheric ozone has been linked to a number of human health problems, including skin cancer, sunburns, eye cataracts, and suppression of the immune system.

In 1977, the U.S. government banned the use of all nonessential fluorocarbon aerosols, and in 1987 an international treaty banning CFCs was drafted. Chemical industries are mandated to reduce the levels of CFCs they manufacture by 50 percent by the year 2000. In addition, international treaties have restricted the manufacture and use of CFCs in other parts of the world.

Since 1988 there has been a substantial decline in the atmospheric buildup of CFCs. Experts suggest that concentrations of CFCs will peak before the year 2000, allowing the ozone layer to begin the slow process of repairing itself. However, a CFC molecule survives in the atmosphere for 50 to 100 years. And as long as CFCs persist, they will continue to destroy ozone.

Sources: Gay, Kathlyn. *Ozone*, pp. 50, 56-57; Hazen, Robert M., and James Trefil. *Science Matters: Achieving Scientific Literacy*, pp. 268-69; *Science News*, vol. 144 (September 11, 1993), p. 172.

• What is **acid rain**?

Rain is naturally slightly acidic. Rain that is made more acidic by sulfuric and/or nitric acid is called "acid rain." Sulfur dioxide and nitrogen dioxide are both gases emitted by car exhaust and industrial smokestacks. These gases react with moisture in the air to form sulfuric acid and nitric acid, respectively. The term "acid rain" was coined by British chemist Robert

The damage done to this building is the result of acid rain.

Angus Smith (1817–1884) who, in 1872, published *Air and Rain: The Beginnings of a Chemical Climatology.*

Acid rain causes various types of ecological damage. For one, it raises the acidity of lakes and rivers, making them inhospitable to many species of animals. Hundreds of highly acidic lakes in North America (especially northeastern United States and Canada) and in Scandinavia can no longer support fish. Acid rain also gradually eats away the surfaces of objects it encounters. Acid rain makes plants more susceptible to frost, insect infestation, and disease. In some areas where acid rain is a serious problem, entire forests have been wiped out. In Europe, where so many living trees have been stunted or killed, a new word, *Waldsterben* (forest death), has been coined.

In 1990, amendments to the (United States) Clean Air Act contained provisions to control emissions that cause acid rain. These include the reduction of sulfur dioxide emissions from 19 million tons to 9.1 million tons annually and the reduction of industrial nitrogen oxide emissions from 6 to 4 million tons annually, both by the year 2000. Also specified were the elimination of 90 percent of industrial benzene, mercury, and dioxin emissions; 60 percent of automotive nitrogen oxide emissions; and 40 percent hydrocarbon emissions by year 1997.

Sources: Adler, Bill. *The Whole Earth Quiz Book: How Well Do You Know the Planet*, p. 135; Bair, Frank E. *The Weather Almanac*, 6th ed., pp. 264-67; Engelbert, Phillis. *The Complete Weather Resource*, vol. 3, pp. 512-13; Hazen, Robert M., and James Trefil. *Science Matters: Achieving Scientific Literacy*, pp. 269-70.

• How acidic is **acid rain?**

Acidity and alkalinity are measured on a scale known as the pH (potential for Hydrogen) scale. It runs from 0 to 14. Since it is logarithmic, a change in one unit equals a tenfold increase or decrease of acidity/alkalinity. Therefore a solution of pH 2 is 10 times more acidic than a solution of pH 3 and 100 times as acidic as a solution of pH 4. Zero is extremely acid, 7 is neutral, and 14 is extremely alkaline.

Any rain below pH 5.0 is considered acid rain, although some scientists set the limit at 5.6. Normal rain and snow containing dissolved carbon dioxide (a weak acid) measure about pH 5.6.

The acidity of rain varies according to geographical area. Eastern Europe and parts of Scandinavia have rain with a pH of 4.3 to 4.5; in the rest of Europe the rain is pH 4.5 to 5.1; in the eastern United States and Canada it ranges from 4.2 to 4.6; and in the Mississippi Valley it's 4.6 to 4.8. The most acidic rain in North America, having a pH of 4.2, is centered around Lake Erie and Lake Ontario.

By way of comparison, some common items and their pH values are listed below:

Concentrated sulfuric acid	1.0
Lemon juice	2.3
Vinegar	3.3
Acid rain	4.3
Normal rain	5.0 to 5.6
Normal lakes and rivers	5.6 to 8.0
Distilled water	7.0
Human blood	7.35 to 7.45
Seawater	7.6 to 8.4

Sources: *How in the World?: A Fascinating Journey Through the World of Human Ingenuity*, p. 126; Lean, Geoffrey, et al. *WWF Atlas of the World*, p. 86; Wolke, Robert L. *Chemistry Explained*, pp. 386-93.

> ## Where are the *radioactive waste* disposal sites in the *United States*?
>
> The sites of low-level commercial and military radioactive waste disposal are Idaho Falls, Idaho; Livermore, California; Albuquerque and Los Alamos, New Mexico; Amarillo, Texas; Weldon Springs, Missouri; West Valley and Niagara Falls, New York; Sheffield, Illinois; Massey Flats and Paducah, Kentucky; Oak Ridge, Tennessee; Aiken and Barnwell, South Carolina; Beatty and Las Vegas, Nevada; Richland, Washington; and Fernald and Piketon, Ohio.
>
> **Source:** Cunningham, William P., et al. *Environmental Encyclopedia*, p. 674.

• What are **PCBs**?

Polychlorinated biphenyls (PCBs) are a group of compounds that were manufactured in the United States from 1929 until 1977. They were widely used in the electrical industry as a coolant for transformers and in capacitors and other electrical devices. PCBs do not break down in nature and spread through the water, soil, and air.

In the mid 1970s, PCBs were found to cause a variety of health and environmental problems. They have been linked to cancer and reproductive disorders and have been shown to cause liver function abnormalities. The U.S. government banned PCBs in 1977. Since that time, the manufacture and use of PCBs has been restricted throughout most of the world.

Sources: *Encyclopedia of Chemical Technology*, 4th ed., vol. 5, p. 844; Schweitzer, Glenn E. *Borrowed Earth, Borrowed Time*, pp. 9-10.

• What is **eutrophication**?

Eutrophication is a process by which plant growth increases in a lake or pond. In time, eutrophication may cause plants to completely fill in the area where a lake or pond once stood. The word "eutrophic" is of Greek origin, meaning "truly nourished."

The accelerated growth and overcrowding of plants is due to either natural fertilizing agents that are washed from the soil, or the runoff of chemical fertilizers applied to agricultural lands. Eutrophication may also be brought about by the drainage of sewage, industrial wastes, or detergents into a body of water.

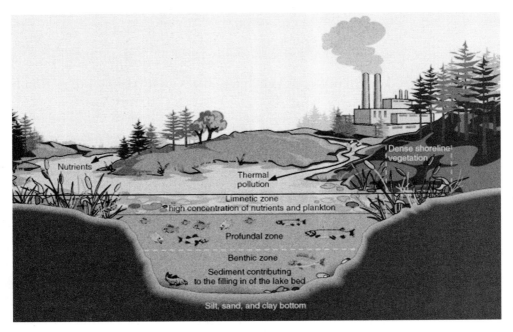

An illustration showing the structure of an eutrophic lake.

As the overcrowded plants die off, the dead and decaying vegetation depletes the lake's oxygen supply. This, in turn, leads to the death of fish in the lake. The accumulated dead plant and animal material eventually changes a deep lake to a shallow one. The shallow lake then becomes a swamp, and finally it becomes dry land.

Sources: Cunningham, William P., et al. *Environmental Encyclopedia*, p. 205; Schneider, Herman. *The Harper Dictionary of Science in Everyday Language*, p. 113.

• How much **oil** is dumped into the **seas**?

Every year, well over 3 million metric tons of oil contaminate the seas. (One metric ton equals .91 short tons; one short ton equals 2,000 pounds.) Half of this oil comes from ships, with the rest coming from land-based pollution. Only 33 percent of the oil is spilled by accident. More than 1.1 million metric tons of oil are deliberately discharged from the washing out of tankers.

Source of oil	Percent of total
Tankers operational discharge	22
Municipal wastes	22

Source of oil	Percent of total
Tanker accidents	12.5
Atmospheric rainout (oil released by industry and cars)	9.5
Bilge and fuel oils	9.0
Natural seeps	7.5
Non-refining industrial waste	6.0
Urban runoff	3.5
Coastal oil refineries	3.0
Offshore production	1.5
River runoff	1.0
Others	2.5

Source: Lean, Geoffrey, et al. *WWF Atlas of the Environment*, pp. 175-76.

• Where did the first major **oil spill** occur?

The first major oil spill occurred during World War II (1939–45), between January and June of 1942. German U-boat attacks on tankers off the East Coast of the United States spilled 590,000 tons of oil.

The first major commercial oil spill occurred on March 18, 1967, when the tanker *Torrey Canyon* ran aground on the Seven Stones Shoal off the coast of Cornwall, England. The tanker spilled 830,000 barrels (119,000 tons) of Kuwaiti oil into the sea.

On January 25, 1991, during the Gulf War, almost 1.5 million tons of oil was deliberately dumped from Sea Island into the Persian Gulf. Another major spill occurred in Russia in October 1994, in the Komi region of the Arctic. The size of that spill was reported to be as much as 2 million barrels (286,000 tons).

Spills such as the aforementioned were far larger than the much-publicized *Exxon Valdez* spill in 1989. That spill, caused by the grounding of a tanker on the coast of Alaska, released 35,000 tons of oil into the sea and was the largest oil spill in U.S. history.

Date	Cause	Thousands tons spilled
1/42-6/42	German U-boat attacks on tankers off the East Coast of U.S. during World War II.	590
3/18/67	Tanker *Torrey Canyon* grounds off Land's End in the English Channel.	119

The containment of an oil spill.

Date	Cause	Thousands tons spilled
3/20/70	Tanker *Othello* collides with another ship in Tralhavet Bay, Sweden.	60–100
12/19/72	Tanker *Sea Star* collides with another ship in Gulf of Oman.	115
5/12/76	*Urquiola* grounds at La Coruna, Spain	100
3/16/78	Tanker *Amoco Cadiz* grounds off Northwest France.	223
6/3/79	Itox I oil well blows in southern Gulf of Mexico.	600
7/79	Tankers *Atlantic Express* and *Aegean Captain* collide off Trinidad and Tobago.	300
2/19/83	Blowout in Norwuz oil field in the Persian Gulf.	600
8/6/83	Fire aboard *Castillo de Beliver* off Cape Town, South Africa.	250
1/25/91	Iraq begins deliberately dumping oil into Persian Gulf from Sea Island, Kuwait.	1,450

Sources: Franck, Irene. *The Green Encyclopedia*, pp. 220-21; Miller, E. Willard, and Ruby M. Miller. *Environmental Hazards: Toxic Waste and Hazardous Material*, p. 96; *Oil and Gas Journal*, vol. 92 (April 11, 1994), pp. 107-8; vol. 92 (October 31, 1994), p. 23 *The Universal Almanac 1992*, p. 537.

• Which **pollutants** lead to indoor **air pollution**?

Indoor air pollution, also known as "tight building syndrome," affects modern, high-energy efficiency buildings. This condition results when there is limited outside air exchange (inadequate ventilation), chemical contamination, and/or microbial (microorganism) contamination. Indoor air pollution can produce various symptoms in a building's inhabitants, such as headaches, nausea, and irritations of the eyes, nose, and throat.

Indoor air pollution may affect houses, where it emanates from consumer and building products and from tobacco smoke. Below are listed some pollutants found in houses:

Pollutant	Sources	Effects
Asbestos	Old or damaged insulation, fireproofing, or acoustical tiles.	Many years later, chest and abdominal cancers and lung diseases.
Biological pollutants	Bacteria, mold and mildew, viruses, animal dander and cat saliva, mites, cockroaches, and pollen.	Eye, nose, and throat irritation; shortness of breath; dizziness; lethargy; fever; digestive problems; asthma; influenza and other infectious diseases.
Carbon monoxide	Unvented kerosene and gas heaters; leaking chimneys and furnaces; wood stoves and fireplaces; gas stoves; automobile exhaust from attached garages; tobacco smoke.	At low levels, fatigue; at higher levels, impaired vision and coordination; headaches; dizziness; confusion; nausea. Fatal at very high concentrations.
Formaldehyde	Plywood, wall paneling, particle board, fiber-board; foam insulation; fire and tobacco smoke; textiles; and glues.	Eye, nose, and throat irritations; wheezing and coughing; fatigue; skin rash; severe allergic reactions; may cause cancer.
Lead	Automobile exhaust; sanding or burning of lead paint; soldering.	Impaired mental and physical development in children; decreased coordination and mental abilities; kidney, nervous system, and red blood cells damage.
Mercury	Some latex paints.	Vapors can cause kidney damage; long–term exposure can cause brain damage.

Pollutant	Sources	Effects
Nitrogen dioxide	Kerosene heaters, unvented gas stoves and heaters, tobacco smoke.	Eye, nose, and throat irritation; may impair lung function and increase respiratory infections in young children.
Organic gases	Paints, paint strippers, solvents, wood preservatives; aerosol sprays; cleansers and disinfectants; moth repellants; air fresheners; stored fuels; hobby supplies; dry-cleaned clothing.	Eye, nose, and throat irritation; headaches; loss of coordination; nausea; damage to liver, kidney, and nervous system; some organics cause cancer in animals and are suspected of causing cancer in humans.
Pesticides	Products used to kill household pests and products used on lawns or gardens that drift or are tracked inside the house.	Irritation to eye, nose, and throat; damage to nervous system and kidneys; cancer.
Radon	Earth and rock beneath home; well water; building materials.	No immediate symptoms; estimated to cause about 10 percent of lung cancer deaths; smokers at higher risk.

Sources: Cassens, B. *Preventive Medicine and Public Health*, p. 214; *The Guinness Book of Answers*, 8th ed., pp. 536-37.

• How much **solid waste** is generated annually in the **United States?**

The United States produces 4.543 million tons of solid waste annually.

Type of waste	Million tons	Percent
Agriculture	2,340	52
Mineral industries (mining and milling waste)	1,620	36
Industrial (nonhazardous)	225	5
Municipal (domestic)	180	4
Utility	90	2
Hazardous	45	2
Low-level radioactive	3	0.0007

Of the municipal solid wastes generated in 1993, paper waste accounted for the greatest proportion. (Municipal solid wastes are those wastes generated by households, businesses, and institutions.)

Municipal Solid Waste (1993)

Type of waste	Million of tons
Paper and paperboard	77.8
Plastics	19.3
Metals	17.1
Glass	13.7
Wood	13.7
Rubber, leather, and textiles	12.3
Other	3.3

Sources: Famighetti, Robert, ed. *The World Almanac and Book of Facts 1992*, p. 657; Miller, E. Willard, and Ruby M. Miller. *Environmental Hazards: Toxic Waste and Hazardous Material*, p. 4.

• How much **garbage** does the average American generate?

According to one study, each American produces about 230 million tons of refuse a year. That's 5.1 pounds (2.3 kilograms) per person a day or about 1,900 pounds (863 kilograms) per year. Another survey reported that a typical suburban family of three generated 40 pounds (18 kilograms) of garbage weekly, with the percentages of various components presented below:

Type of solid waste	Percent
Aluminum	1
Polystyrene meat trays, cups, egg cartons, and packing	3
Disposable diapers	3
Wood, textiles, old clothing	5
Metal cans and nails	5
Plastic soda bottles and bags	5
Glass	8
Miscellaneous	10
Food	11
Paper	21
Yard waste and grass clippings	23

In 1990, the U.S. Environmental Protection Agency (EPA) published an analysis of solid waste generated by individuals over a span of nearly three decades. In addition to reporting an increase of garbage generated per person over time, the EPA found that the content of garbage had changed.

Garbage in pounds per person per day

Waste materials	1960	1970	1980	1988
Total nonfood product wastes	1.65	2.26	2.57	2.94
Paper and paperboard	0.91	1.19	1.32	1.60
Glass	0.20	0.34	0.36	0.28
Metals	0.32	0.38	0.35	0.34
Plastics	0.01	0.08	0.19	0.32
Rubber and leather	0.06	0.09	0.10	0.10
Textiles	0.05	0.05	0.06	0.09
Wood	0.09	0.11	0.12	0.14
Other	0.00	0.02	0.07	0.07
Other wastes				
Food wastes	0.37	0.34	0.32	0.29
Yard wastes	0.61	0.62	0.66	0.70
Miscellaneous inorganic waste	0.04	0.05	0.05	0.06
Total waste generated	2.66	3.27	3.61	4.00

Sources: *Good Housekeeping*, vol. 209 (September 1989), p. 272; *The 1992 Information Please Environmental Almanac*, p. 108; *Rush to Burn: Solving America's Garbage Crisis*, pp. 21, 29.

• How much does **packaging** contribute to **municipal solid waste**?

Packaging accounted for 30.3 percent of municipal solid waste in 1990. (Municipal solid wastes are those generated by households, businesses, and institutions.) This figure includes the following materials, in the following proportions: paper (47.7 percent), glass (24.5 percent), plastic (14.5 percent), steel (6.5 percent), wood (4.5 percent), and aluminum (2.3 percent).

Source: Stilwell, E. Joseph, et al. *Packaging for the Environment*, p. 2.

• How critical is the problem of **landfilling** in the **United States**?

A landfill is a large area dug out of the ground (often a sand or gravel pit), or a valley, that is used for trash disposal. Some landfills are "secure," meaning they have a clay and plastic liner, while other landfills have no barrier between the waste and the ground.

There are more than 9,000 landfills in the United States. However, landfill capacity is rapidly dwindling in the most populous regions of the country. A 1995 study reported that the number of landfills accepting mu-

---

*How much waste paper does a **newspaper** generate?*

On average, a year's worth of newspaper (one paper per day) produces 550 pounds (250 kilograms) of waste paper. An average *New York Times* Sunday edition produces 8 million pounds (3.6 million kilograms) of waste paper.

Source: *Audubon Magazine,* vol. 92 (March 1990), p. 4.

---

nicipal solid waste has declined to 3,558. (Municipal solid wastes are those generated by households, businesses, and institutions.)

In 1960, 62 percent of all garbage was sent to landfills; in 1980 the figure was 81 percent; in 1988 it decreased to 73 percent; and in 1995 it further decreased to 67 percent. The decrease in percentage of municipal waste going to landfills has been largely due to recycling, reuse, and composting programs initiated throughout the United States. However, about 80 percent of *all* solid waste (including that from industry and agriculture) generated in the United States is still dumped in landfills.

There are numerous environmental problems associated with landfills, particularly due to leaking chemicals that contaminate the groundwater and surface water. These chemical leaks, plus the unsanitary conditions which exist at many landfills, are a threat to the health of humans, pets, and wildlife in the vicinity. Despite these problems, landfilling continues to be an essential component of waste management.

Sources: *Biocycle,* vol. 36 (April 1995), pp. 54-55; Cunningham, William P., et al. *Environmental Encyclopedia,* pp. 477-78; Stilwell, E. Joseph, et al. *Packaging for the Environment,* pp. 104-5; *The Universal Almanac 1992,* p. 538.

• What are **Operation Ranch Hand** and **Agent Orange**?

Operation Ranch Hand is the name of a U.S. military campaign undertaken during the Vietnam War (1961–75). The campaign involved spraying herbicides, from aircraft, on South Vietnam. Herbicides are chemicals that kill vegetation and defoliate trees (strip them of leaves). In all, approximately 19 million gallons (72 million liters) of herbicides were sprayed over 4 million acres (1.6 million hectares).

The specific herbicides used in Operation Ranch Hand were 2,4-D and 2,4,5-T, collectively known as Agent Orange. (The names 2,4-D and 2,4,5-

T refer to the chemical configurations of the molecules.) The name Agent Orange comes from the color-coded drums in which the herbicides were stored.

Operation Ranch Hand officially began in 1962 (although the spraying of Agent Orange, in limited amounts, started in 1961) and continued throughout most of the war. It peaked in the years 1965 to 1967; in 1967 the military was dumping the herbicides faster than manufacturers in the United States could produce them.

One purpose of Operation Ranch Hand was to kill the crops in areas that were inhabited by enemy troops (the Viet Cong), thus depriving them of food. Another was to destroy the dense jungle growth in which Viet Cong troops were hiding.

For the civilian populations of the affected areas, Operation Ranch Hand was nothing short of a campaign of terror. With their food crops destroyed, the villagers were forced to leave their homes. And many people who came into contact with the herbicide developed health problems. Despite repeated promises, the U.S. military never resupplied food to the affected civilian population.

Concerns about the health effects of Agent Orange were initially voiced in 1970 when it was revealed that Agent Orange contained dioxin, a potent carcinogen (cancer-causing agent). Thousands of the U.S. troops who served in Vietnam later developed cancer and many of their children were born with deformities.

There were few precautionary measures taken in the handling of Agent Orange during the Vietnam War. It is now suspected that most of the nearly 3 million U.S. troops who served in Vietnam were exposed to Agent Orange, either by breathing it in the air or eating and drinking contaminated food and water.

In 1993, a 16-member panel of experts reviewed the existing scientific evidence and found strong evidence of a statistical association between Agent Orange and soft-tissue sarcoma (a rare but varied group of tumors that arise in the muscles, connective tissue, inner layer of skin, bone, and other tissues), non-Hodgkin's lymphoma (cancer of the lymphatic system), Hodgkin's disease (cancer that affects the immune system), and chloracne (a skin rash resembling acne, caused by exposure to chlorine compounds). On the other hand, they concluded that no connection appeared to exist between exposure to Agent Orange and skin cancer, bladder cancer, brain tumors, or stomach cancer.

Sources: *Agent Orange and Its Associated Dioxin: Assessment of a Controversy*, p. 10; Cunningham, William P., et al. *Environmental Encyclopedia*, pp. 13-14; Miller, E. Willard, and Ruby M. Miller. *Environmental Hazards: Toxic Waste and Hazardous Material*, p. 13; *Science News*, vol. 144 (July 31, 1993), pp. 70-71.

ENDANGERED AND EXTINCT SPECIES

• Under what conditions is a **species** considered **"endangered"**?

An endangered species is defined as a species that's "in danger of extinction throughout all or a significant portion of its range [the geographic area in which a kind of animal or plant normally lives or grows]." The determination of which species are considered "endangered" is a complex process.

While the population size of a species is a factor, there is no set "number of living members" below which a species is defined as endangered. For instance, a species with a million living members, all of which are clustered in one small area, could be considered endangered; whereas another species having a smaller number of members, but spread across a broad area, might not be considered endangered. Another factor is a species' reproduction data, such as the frequency of reproduction, the average number of offspring, and their survival rate.

In the United States, the director of the Fish and Wildlife Service (within the Department of the Interior) determines which species are to be considered endangered. These designations are based on research and field data from biologists (scientists who study living organisms and life processes), botanists (scientists who specialize in the study of plants), and naturalists (scientists specializing in the study of plants and animals in their natural surroundings).

According to the Endangered Species Act of 1973, a species can be listed as endangered if it is threatened by any of the following:

1. The present or threatened destruction, modification, or curtailment of its habitat or range.

2. Utilization for commercial, sporting, scientific, or educational purposes at levels that detrimentally affect it [a species].

3. Disease or predation.

4. Absence of regulatory mechanisms adequate to prevent the decline of a species or degradation of its habitat.

5. Other natural or man-made factors affecting its continued existence.

Source: Sutton, Caroline, and Duncan M. Anderson. *How Do They Do That?* pp. 92-93.

• Which animal species have become extinct since the Endangered Species Act was passed in 1973?

Seven domestic species have been declared extinct: Florida's dusky seaside sparrow, the Santa Barbara song sparrow, the Tecopa pupfish, the Sampson's pearly mussel, and the following fish species—the blue pike, the longjaw cisco, and the Amistad gambusic.

A total of 13 species have been removed from the federal endangered and threatened species list since 1973. This number includes the seven extinct species listed above plus five species that are no longer endangered: bald eagle, peregrine falcon, alligator, gray whale, and grizzly bear.

Sources: *Buzzworm: The Environmental Journal*, vol. 3, no. 6 (November-December 1991), p. 33; *National Wildlife*, vol. 30, no. 3 (April-May 1992), p. 16; *Scholastic Update*, vol. 129, no. 12, March 21, 1997, p. 8.

• How many **species** of plants and animals are **threatened** in the United States?

According to the Endangered Species Act of 1973, there are two categories into which species may be placed: threatened and endangered. Threatened means "likely to become an endangered species within the foreseeable future throughout all or a significant portion of its range [the geographic area in which a kind of animal or plant normally lives or grows]." Endangered means "in danger of extinction throughout all or a significant portion of its range." Presently there are 206 threatened species (114 animals and 92 plants) and 754 endangered species (320 animals and 434 plants) in the United States.

Category	Threatened	Endangered	Threatened & Endangered
Mammals	9	55	64
Birds	16	74	90
Reptiles	19	14	33
Amphibians	5	7	12
Fishes	40	65	105
Snails	7	15	22
Clams	6	51	57
Crustaceans	3	14	17
Insects	9	20	29
Arachnids	0	5	5
Plants	92	434	526
TOTAL	206	754	960

Sources: Cunningham, William P., et al. *Environmental Encyclopedia*, pp. 266-68; *Endangered Species Technical Bulletin*, Reprint vol. 21, (January-February 1996), back cover.

• Are turtles endangered?

Some species of sea turtles are considered endangered. For example, Kemp's ridley sea turtle (*Lepidochelys kempii*) is believed to have a population of only a few hundred.

Worldwide turtle populations have declined due to several factors. Among these factors are: habitat destruction; hunting by humans (for turtle eggs, leather, and meat); and becoming accidentally ensnared in the nets of fishermen.

Sources: Cunningham, William P., et al. *Encyclopedia of Endangered Species*, pp. 765-66; *The IUCN Amphibia-Reptilia Red Data Book*, pp. iv-vii.

The endangered Kemp's ridley sea turtle.

• What is the status of the **African elephant?**

From 1979 to 1989, Africa lost half of its elephant population due to poaching (illegal hunting) and illegal ivory trade. Elephants are often killed for their tusks, which are made of ivory. The elephant population decreased from an estimated 1.3 million to 600,000. This led, in October 1989, to a change in the African elephant's status of "threatened" to "endangered," according to the Convention in International Trade in Endangered Species (CITES). Threatened means "likely to become an endangered species within the foreseeable future throughout all or a significant portion of its range [the geographic area in which a kind of animal or plant normally lives or grows]." Endangered means "in danger of extinction throughout all or a significant portion of its range."

An ivory ban took effect on January 18, 1990. However, six African countries (South Africa, Zimbabwe, Botswana, Namibia, Malawi, and Zambia) wish to resume the ivory trade and, to that end, are trying to return the elephants to a "threatened" status.

Many African nations have begun to realize that living elephants are of greater value than dead ones. Kenya considers a living elephant to be worth

$14,375 in tourism income for every year of its life, giving it a potential lifetime value of $900,000. The ivory from an average elephant killed for its tusks would be worth only $1,000 (the price paid before the ban on ivory took effect in October 1989).

Sources: *New Scientist,* vol. 133 (February 29, 1992), pp. 49-50, and vol. 133 (March 14, 1992), p. 11.

• What is **dolphin-safe tuna**?

Dolphin-safe tuna is tuna that is caught using methods that do not harm dolphins. One method of tuna fishing that kills large numbers of dolphins is ensnaring the fish in purse-seine nets (nets that close up to from a huge ball to be hoisted aboard ship). Dolphins, which often swim with schools of yellowfin tuna, also become entangled in the nets. Since the trapped dolphins are unable to reach the surface and breathe, they drown.

Dolphins belong to the order (category of animals) Cetacea, which also includes whales and porpoises. Humans have been hunting cetaceans, especially whales, for their valuable products since about 1000 B.C. The twentieth century, however, with its development of improved fishing methods, became the most destructive period to date for the cetacea.

In 1972, the U.S. Congress passed the Marine Mammal Protection Act. One of goals of the act was to reduce the number of dolphins killed and injured during commercial fishing operations. The number of incidental dolphin deaths and injuries in 1972 was estimated at 368,000 for U.S. fishing vessels and 55,078 for non-U.S. vessels. In 1979, the figures were reduced to 17,938 and 6,837 respectively. But in the 1980s, dolphins killed by foreign vessels rose dramatically to over 100,000 a year. Most of the slaughter occurs in the eastern Pacific Ocean from Chile to southern California.

To further reduce the numbers of dolphins killed during tuna catches, the three largest sellers of canned tuna in the United States, spearheaded by the Starkist company, decided that they would not sell tuna that has been caught by methods harmful to dolphins.

Sources: *Newsweek,* vol. 115 (April 23, 1990), p. 76; Nowak, Robert M. *Walker's Mammals of the World,* 5th ed., vol. 1, pp. 971-72; *Time,* vol. 135 (April 23, 1990), p. 63.

• How did the **dodo** become **extinct**?

The dodo, a flightless bird native to the Mascarene Islands in the Central Indian Ocean, became extinct around 1800. Pigs and monkeys, which de-

The complete skeleton of a dinosaur estimated to be 78 million years old.

stroyed dodo eggs, probably bore the greatest responsibility for the dodo's extinction. Humans contributed to the problem by slaughtering thousands of dodos for meat.

Dodos became extinct on the island of Mauritius soon after 1680 and on the island of Réunion around 1750. They remained on the island of Rodriguez until 1800.

Source: *Encyclopedia Americana*, vol. 9, pp. 232-33.

• Why did **dinosaurs** become **extinct**?

There are many theories as to why dinosaurs disappeared from the Earth about 65 million years ago. Scientists are divided between two primary schools of thought on the subject: the gradualists believe that the dinosaurs' extinction was a gradual process, and the catastrophists believe the dinosaurs were wiped out by a single catastrophic event.

The gradualists propose that the dinosaur population steadily declined at the end of the Cretaceous Period (144 to 65 million years ago) for a variety of reasons. Some claim the dinosaurs underwent biological changes which made them less competitive with other organisms, especially the mammals that were just beginning to appear. An alternate theory is that the dinosaurs suffered the effects of overpopulation. A third theory is that mammals drove dinosaurs to extinction by eating dinosaur eggs. Others believe that a variety of diseases wiped out the dinosaurs. Environmental factors also have been held responsible, such as changes in climate; continental drift (the gradual movement of land masses); volcanic eruptions; and shifts in the Earth's axis, orbit, and/or magnetic field (the portion of space near a magnetic body or current-carrying body, in which a magnetic force exists).

The catastrophists argue that a single disastrous event caused the extinction, not only of the dinosaurs, but also of a large number of other species that coexisted with them. In 1980, American physicist (a scientist specializing in the interaction between energy and matter) Luis Alvarez (1911–1988) and his geologist (a scientist specializing in the origin, history, and structure of the Earth) son, Walter Alvarez (1940–), proposed that a large comet or meteoroid (a large chunk of rock or metal from space) struck the Earth 65 million years ago. They pointed out that there is a high concentration of the element iridium in the sediments deposited at the end of the Cretaceous Period.

Iridium is rare on Earth, which makes it likely that such a large amount of the element had to come from outer space. Iridium deposits have since been discovered at more than 50 sites around the world. In 1990, tiny glass fragments, which could have been caused by the extreme heat of an impact with an extraterrestrial (beyond the Earth or its atmosphere) object, were identified in Haiti. The space object is theorized to have struck off the coast of Mexico's Yucatan Peninsula, where a 110 mile- (177 kilometer-) wide crater exists. This crater, covered by many layers of sediments, has been dated to 64.98 million years ago.

A hit by a large extraterrestrial object, perhaps as great as 6 miles (9.3 kilometers) wide, would have had a catastrophic effect upon the world's climate. Huge amounts of dust and debris would have been thrown into the atmosphere, reducing the amount of sunlight reaching the surface. Heat from the blast may also have caused large forest fires which would have added smoke and ash to the air. The lack of sunlight would have killed off

What were the smallest and largest dinosaurs?

Compsognathus, a carnivore (meat-eater) from the late Jurassic period (131 million years ago) was about the size of a chicken. It measured, at most, 35 inches (89 centimeters) from the tip of its snout to the tip of its tail. It probably weighed no more than 15 pounds (6.8 kilograms).

The largest species for which a whole skeleton has been excavated is Brachiosaurus. A specimen in the Humboldt Museum in Berlin, Germany, is 72.75 feet (22.2 meters) long and 46 feet (14 meters) tall. It weighed an estimated 34.7 tons (31,480 kilograms). Brachiosaurus was a four-footed, plant-eating dinosaur with a long neck and a long tail. It lived from about 155 to 121 million years ago.

The largest meat-eating dinosaur, the skeleton of which was discovered in 1995 in western Argentina, was Giganotosaurus. This dinosaur lived about 97 million years ago. It was about 45 to 47 feet long and weighed 7.7 to 9 tons. Giganotosaurus, running on its two hind legs, could have probably chased down and killed plant-eating dinosaurs far larger than itself. Tyrannosaurus Rex, which measured about 40 feet long, was considered the largest meat-eating dinosaur until the discovery of Giganotosaurus. (Check out the Giganotosaurus web page at http://www.giganotosaurus.com)

Sources: *The Guinness Book of Records 1996*, p. 39; Henahan, Sean. "What's News: Giganotosaurus." http://www.gene.com/ae/WN/SU/gigant597.html; Michard, Jean-Guy. *The Reign of the Dinosaurs*, p. 14; "Skull Unveiled of Largest Predator Dinosaur." http://newscenter.delphi.com/item.cfm/2115575.

plants, bringing about the starvation of herbivores (plant-eating animals) and carnivores (animals that eat other animals)—including the dinosaurs in both categories.

It is possible that the reason for the dinosaurs' extinction may have been due to a combination of gradual and catastrophic factors. The population of dinosaurs may have been gradually declining, for whatever reason, and the impact of a large object from space may have merely delivered the final blow.

The extinction of the dinosaurs has been used to argue that dinosaurs were somehow inferior to humans, or were evolutionary failures. However, dinosaurs flourished for 150 million years. By comparison, the earliest ancestors of modern-day humans appeared only about 4 million years ago.

Sources: Barnes-Svarney, Patricia. *The New York Public Library Science Desk Reference*, p. 405; Golob, Richard. *Almanac of Science and Technology: What's New and What's Known*, pp. 73-84; Michard, Jean-Guy. *The Reign of the Dinosaurs*, pp. 88-94; Norman, David. *Dinosaur!* pp. 144-59.

• Did **dinosaurs** and **humans** live at the same time?

No. Dinosaurs first appeared in the Triassic Period (about 220 million years ago) and disappeared at the end of the Cretaceous Period (about 65 million years ago). The first species of humans, *Australopithecus afarensis*, appeared about 4 million years ago. Modern humans (*Homo sapiens sapiens*) appeared only about 35,000 to 40,000 years ago.

Sources: Barnes-Svarney, Patricia. *The New York Public Library Science Desk Reference*, pp. 404-6; Norman, David. *Dinosaur!* p. 36; *The Universal Almanac 1992*, p. 512.

CONSERVATION

• Who is considered the **founder of modern conservation?**

John Muir, the founder of the modern conservation movement.

American naturalist (a scientist specializing in the study of plants and animals in their natural surroundings) John Muir (1838–1914), founder of the Sierra Club, is considered the father of the modern conservation movement. Conservation is the practice of conserving natural resources and preserving wilderness areas. Muir fought for the preservation of the Sierra Nevada Mountains as well as the creation of Yosemite National Park, both in California. He directed most of the Sierra Club's conservation efforts and was a lobbyist for the Antiquities Act, the 1906 law which preserves designated lands as national monuments.

Another pioneer of the conservation movement was George Perkins Marsh (1801–1882), a Vermont lawyer and scholar. His outstanding book

Man and Nature emphasized the mistakes of past civilizations that resulted in destruction of natural resources.

As the conservation movement swept through the United States in the last three decades of the 1800s, a number of prominent citizens joined in. Writer John Burroughs, forester (a person who cultivates, develops, and maintains forests) Gifford Pinchot, botanist (a scientist who specializes in the study of plants) Charles Sprague Sargent, and editor Robert Underwood Johnson were early advocates of conservation.

Sources: Ashworth, William. *The Encyclopedia of Environmental Studies*, p. 248; *Buzzworm: The Environmental Journal*, vol. 4, no. 2 (March-April 1992), p. 26; Harrison, C. William. *Conservation*, pp. 114-25; Hoyle, Russ. *Gale Environmental Almanac*, p. 11.

• What is a **"green product"**?

"Green products" are products that are safe for the environment, meaning they contain no chlorofluorocarbons (compounds that destroy the ozone layer), are degradable (can decompose), and are made from recycled materials. "Deep-green products" are "green" products from small suppliers who claim to be particularly sensitive to environmental issues. "Greened-up products" come from industry giants and are environmentally improved versions of established brands.

Sources: *Buzzworm: The Environmental Journal*, vol. 3, no. 6 (November-December 1991), p. 37; *Environment*, vol. 33, no. 9 (November 1991), p. 10.

• Who started **Earth Day**?

The first Earth Day, April 22, 1970, was initiated by Gaylord Nelson, who was a U.S. senator from Wisconsin and is sometimes called the "father of Earth Day." Nelson's objective was to organize a nationwide public demonstration so large that it would get the attention of politicians and force issues of environmental protection into the legislative forefront. The first Earth Day, coordinated by Harvard Law student Denis Hayes, was celebrated by more than 20 million individuals. That Earth Day is credited with spearheading the modern environmental movement.

Soon after the celebration of the first Earth Day, the following actions were taken by the U.S. government: the establishment of the Environmental Protection Agency (EPA); the creation of the President's Council on Environmental Quality; and the passage of the Clean Air Act, which established national air quality standards.

Earth Day has been celebrated every year since its beginning. In many parts of the United States, Earth Day is observed with marches, teach-ins, rallies, tree-plantings, community cleanups, and celebrations. In 1990, the twentieth anniversary of the original Earth Day (also coordinated by Denis Hayes), an estimated 200 million people in more than 140 nations marked Earth Day. Highlights included a demonstration of 350,000 in Washington, D.C., and a concert and rally of more than 1 million people in New York City.

Sources: Cunningham, William P., et al. *Environmental Encyclopedia*, p. 239; *EPA Journal*, vol. 16, no. 1 (January-February 1990), pp. 10-11, 14; *Smithsonian*, vol. 21, no. 1 (April 1990), p. 47.

• How much of the Earth is protected as **national parks** and similar sites?

Below is a table of protected areas by country for the year 1990.

Country	Percent of total land area
Venezuela	22.2
Bhutan	19.8
Chile	18.2
Botswana	17.4
Panama	16.9
Czechoslovakia	15.4
Namibia	12.7
United States	10.5
Indonesia	9.3
Australia	5.9
Canada	5.0
Mexico	4.8
Brazil	2.4
Madagascar	1.8
Former Soviet Union	1.1
WORLD	**4.9**

Source: *American Forests*, vol. 98, nos. 3 and 4 (March-April 1992), p. 42.

• What was the **United States'** first **national park**?

The U.S. government authorized Yellowstone National Park as its first national park on March 1, 1872. Yellowstone is located mostly in Wyoming, with parts of the park extending into Montana and Idaho. It is the largest national park in the United States, with 3,472 square miles. Yellowstone is home to Old Faithful, the world's most famous geyser (natural hot spring that ejects steam and hot water). There are more than 200 geysers and hot springs located in Yellowstone, which is a greater number than those existing in the rest of the world combined.

Sources: Cunningham, William P., et al. *Environmental Encyclopedia,* pp. 925-26; Kane, Joseph Nathan. *Famous First Facts,* 4th ed., p. 450

• What natural resources are saved by **recycling** one ton of paper?

Recycling 1 ton of paper saves an average of 7,000 gallons (26 liters) of water; 3.3 cubic yards (2.5 cubic meters) of landfill space; 3 barrels of oil (1 barrel equals 42 gallons); 17 trees; and 4,000 kilowatt-hours of electricity (enough energy to power the average home for 6 months).

Source: *Gale Book of Averages,* p. 428.

• What do the numbers inside the **recycling** symbol on **plastic containers** mean?

The Society of the Plastics Industry developed a voluntary coding system for plastic containers to assist recyclers in sorting plastic containers. The symbol is imprinted on the bottom of plastic containers. The numerical code appears inside a three-sided triangular arrow.

A guide to what the numbers mean is listed below. The most commonly recycled plastics are polyethylene terephthalate (PET) and high density polyethylene (HDPE).

Code	Material	Examples
1	Polyethylene terephthalate (PET)	Soft drink bottles
2	High-density polyethylene (HDPE)	Milk and water jugs

Code	Material	Examples
3	Vinyl	Shampoo bottles
4	Low-density polyethylene (LDPE)	Ketchup bottles
5	Polypropylene	Squeeze bottles
6	Polystyrene	Fast-food packaging
7	Other	

Source: Branson, Gary D. *The Complete Guide to Recycling at Home*, p. 54.

• What products are made from **recycled plastic?**

A new clothing fiber called Fortrel EcoSpun is made from recycled plastic soda bottles. The fiber is knit or woven into garments such as fleece for outerwear or long underwear. It is estimated that for every pound of Fortrel EcoSpun fiber, ten plastic bottles are kept out of landfills.

Resin	Common Uses	Products Made From Recycled Resin
HDPE	Beverage bottles, milk jugs, milk and soft drink crates, pipe, cable, film	Motor oil bottles, detergent bottles, pipes, and pails
LDPE	Film bags such as trash bag coatings and plastic bottles.	New trash bags, pallets
PET	Soft drink, detergent, and juice bottles	Carpets, fiberfill, nonfood bottles or containers
PP	Auto battery cases, screw-on caps and lids; some yogurt and margarine tubs, plastic film	Auto parts, batteries, carpets
PS	Housewares, electronics, fast food carryout packaging, plastic utensils	Insulation board, office equipment, reusable cafeteria trays
PVC	Sporting goods, luggage, pipes, auto parts. In packaging for shampoo bottles, blister packaging, and films	Drainage pipes, fencing, house siding

Sources: *Harrowsmith Country Life*, vol. 9, number 51 (May-June 1994), p. 77; *The Plastic Waste Primer*, pp. 24-25.

• What is the **Pollutant Standard Index?**

The Pollutant Standard Index (PSI) is a measure of concentrations of pollutants in the air, in parts per million. It was developed by the Environmental Protection Agency (EPA) in conjunction with the South Coast Air Quality Management District of El Monte, California. PSI measurements are used to inform the public about potential health effects due to air quality. They have been in use nationwide since 1978.

PSI Index	Health Effects	Cautionary Status
0	Good	
50	Moderate	
100	Unhealthful	
200	Very unhealthful	Alert: Elderly or ill should stay indoors and reduce physical activity.
300	Hazardous	Warning: General population should stay indoors and reduce physical activity.
400	Extremely hazardous	Emergency: All people remain indoors, windows shut, no physical exertion.
500	Toxic	Significant harm; same as above.

Source: Rovin, Jeff. *Laws of Order*, p. 246.

• What is the **Toxic Release Inventory** (TRI)?

TRI is a report containing information on the release of more than 300 individual toxic chemicals and 20 categories of chemical compounds by manufacturing facilities in the United States. Manufacturers are legally bound to report the amounts of chemicals they release directly to air, land, or water, as well as chemical wastes they transfer to off-site treatment or disposal facilities.

The U.S. Environmental Protection Agency (EPA) compiles this information into an annual inventory and makes the information available to the public in a computerized database.

In 1992, 23,630 facilities released a total of 3.2 billion pounds (1.5 billion kilograms) of toxic chemicals into the environment. More than 272 million pounds (124 million kilograms) of this total was released into surface water; 1.8 billion pounds (818 million kilograms) were emitted into the air; more than 337 million pounds (153 million kilograms) were released to land; and 725 million pounds (330 million kilograms) were injected into underground wells. The total amount of toxic chemicals released in 1992 was 6.6 percent lower than the amount released in 1991.

In the 1993 TRI, there was a total of 2.8 billion pounds of toxic substances emitted by all industry. Chemical manufacturers were responsible for 47 percent of that, or 1.3 billion pounds. Other main industries con-

> ### What causes the most forest fires in the western United States?
>
> Lightning is the single largest cause of forest fires in the western states.
>
> **Source:** *The Odds on Virtually Everything,* p. 181.

tributing to this total were: primary metals (329 million pounds); paper (216 million pounds); transportation equipment (136 million pounds); and plastics (127 million pounds).

Sources: *Chemical Marketing Reporter.* vol. 247, no. 26, June 26, 1995, p. 26; Council on Environmental Quality. *Environmental Quality,* pp. 152-53; *Toxics in the Community,* pp. xxi, 14-15.

• How many **automobile tires** are thrown away each year and what can be done with them?

Approximately 242 million tires are discarded annually in the United States. Fewer than 7 percent are recycled, 11 percent are burned for fuel, and 5 percent are exported. The remaining 78 percent are sent to landfills, stockpiled, or illegally dumped.

A major use for discarded tires is as a component in rubber-modified asphalt and concrete. Old tires can also be recycled into new products such as floor mats, blasting mats, and muffler hangers. Tires which have been ground into crumb can be used in traffic cone bases, mud flaps, moisture barriers, and other products. Whole tires can be used in artificial reefs, such as those used to control erosion.

Source: *The Biocycle Guide to Maximum Recycling,* pp. 212-15.

• When did the symbol of **Smokey Bear** begin to be used for **forest fire prevention**?

The symbol of Smokey Bear originated during World War II (1939–45). The U.S. Forest Service, concerned about maintaining a steady lumber supply for the war effort, sought to educate the public about the dangers of forest fires. With the support of the War Advertising Council, they began their campaign. On August 9, 1944, Albert Staehle, a noted illustrator of animals, created Smokey Bear. In 1947, a Los Angeles advertising agency coined the slogan "Only you can prevent forest fires."

The campaign gained a living mascot in 1950 when a firefighting crew rescued a male bear cub from a forest fire in the Capitan Mountains of New Mexico. The animal, dubbed "Smokey Bear," was sent to the National Zoo in Washington, D.C., where he remained a living symbol of forest fire protection until his death in 1976. His remains are buried at the Smokey Bear State Historical Park in Capitan, New Mexico.

Sources: *The Conservationist*, vol. 48, nos. 5 and 6 (1994), pp. 64-65; *Smithsonian*, vol. 24, no. 10, (January 1994), pp. 59-61.

METALS and OTHER MATERIALS

| METALS

• Which **metallic element** is the most abundant?

Aluminum is the most abundant metallic element on the surface of the Earth. This light metal comprises more than 8 percent of the Earth's crust. It is also the most abundant metallic element on the surface of the moon.

Aluminum does not exist in a pure form in nature. It is always found in mineral forms, in combination with oxygen, sand, iron, titanium, clay, or other substances. The principal ore of aluminum is a rock called bauxite (aluminum hydroxide). Nearly all rocks, particularly igneous rocks (rocks of volcanic origin), contain some aluminum in the form of aluminosilicate (aluminum plus silicon dioxide) minerals.

In 1854, French chemist (a scientist who specializes in the composition, structure, properties, and reactions of matter) Sainte-Claire Deville (1818–1881), in 1854, was the first to derive pure aluminum metal. With funding from French emperor Napoleon III (1808–1883), who was interested in producing aluminum for military uses, Deville invented a method of reducing aluminum chloride to get aluminum. In 1886, the American Charles Martin Hall (1863–1914) and the Frenchman Paul Louis-Toussaint

Heroult (1863–1914) independently discovered an electrolytic process (using an electric current) to produce aluminum from bauxite.

Aluminum is widely used in the manufacture of cookware and cans because it is lightweight, does not easily rust, and is an excellent conductor of heat. Aluminum is also a good conductor of electricity; for that reason it is commonly used in overhead cables. Aluminum alloys (substances made of aluminum plus at least one other metal), such as duralumin, are strong, lightweight, and hold up well under stress. Aluminum alloys are used in the manufacture of aircraft and spacecraft, as well as in other types of machinery.

Sources: *Encyclopedia of Chemical Technology*, 4th ed., vol. 2, p. 184; Giscard d'Estaing, Valerie-Anne. *The World Almanac Book of Inventions*, p. 256; *Oxford Illustrated Encyclopedia of Invention and Technology*, p. 12.

• What are the **noble metals**?

The noble metals include gold, silver, mercury, and the platinum group (including palladium, iridium, rhodium, ruthenium, and osmium). The term "noble metals" refers to those metals that are highly resistant to chemical reaction or corrosion, meaning that they will not easily dissolve in a solvent or rust. All other metals are called "base" metals and will more easily undergo chemical changes.

The term "noble metals" has its origins in ancient alchemy, the practice of attempting to transform base metals into gold. "Noble metals" is not synonymous with "precious metals," (a term used to describe expensive metals used for making coins, jewelry, and ornaments) although gold, silver, and platinum are both noble and precious metals.

Sources: Brady, George S. *Materials Handbook*, 13th ed., pp. 663-64; Thrush, Paul W. *A Dictionary of Mining, Mineral, and Related Terms*, p. 753.

• What are the **precious metals**?

Precious metals is a general term that describes expensive metals used for making coins, jewelry, and ornaments. Precious metals include gold, silver, and platinum. Precious metals are defined by two criteria: one is that they are scarce in the Earth's crust (compared to other metals); and the other is that they are noble. A noble metal is one that has a high resistance to chemical change.

> ### What is a *tiger's eye*?
>
> Tiger's eye is a semiprecious quartz gem. Running through it is a luminescent (light-producing) band, like that of a cat's eye. The band in the gem consists of veins of parallel blue asbestos fibers, which are first altered to iron oxides and then replaced by silica (a white or colorless crystalline compound). The gem has a rich color that ranges from yellow to brown.
>
> **Source:** *The New Encyclopaedia Britannica*, 15th ed., vol. 11, p. 768.

"Precious metals" is not synonymous with "noble metals." While it is true that all precious metals are noble metals, the reverse is not true.

Sources: Brady, George S. *Materials Handbook*, 13th ed., pp. 663-64; "Extraction and Processing Industries: Precious Metals." *Encyclopaedia Britannica CD 97*; Savitskii, E.M. *Handbook of Precious Metals*, pp. xv-xix.

• Where were the first successful **ironworks** in the **United States?**

Ironworks are places where iron is made or where articles made of iron are produced. The first successful ironworks in the United States was established by Thomas Dexter and Robert Bridges near the Saugus River in Lynn, Massachusetts. Dexter and Bridges hired John Winthrop Jr. to begin production. Winthrop, son of John Winthrop Sr., the first governor of the Massachusetts Bay Colony, was himself a lawyer who served as governor of Connecticut from 1659 until his death in 1676. Under the younger Winthrop's guidance, a blast furnace (a furnace in which combustion is made more intense by a forced stream of air) was made operational at the ironworks by 1645 and iron production began by 1648.

Iron ore (rock that contains iron) was first discovered in America in North Carolina in 1585. The first, unsuccessful attempt to manufacture iron was undertaken in Virginia in 1619.

Sources: Swank, James M. *History of the Manufacture of Iron in All Ages*, pp. 108-19; "Winthrop, John, The Younger." *Encyclopaedia Britannica CD 97*.

• Which countries have **uranium deposits?**

Uranium deposits are located in many parts of the world. Uranium is most plentiful in Canada and the Democratic Republic of Congo (formerly Zaire). Other significant uranium resources are found in the United States (especially Arizona, Colorado, New Mexico, North Carolina, and Utah), France, South Africa, Australia, and the former Soviet Union.

Uranium is a radioactive metallic element, meaning that its atomic nuclei undergo changes and emit radiation. Uranium is also the only natural material capable of sustaining nuclear fission—the process of splitting atoms used in the production of nuclear power. However, only one isotope, uranium-235, is suitable for fission. (Isotopes are different forms of an element, each having a unique atomic weight.) Only one molecule out of every 40 natural uranium molecules is the isotope uranium-235.

Sources: Fejer, Eva, and Cecilia Fitzsimons. *An Instant Guide to Rocks and Minerals*, p. 54; Lewis, Richard J., Sr. *Hawley's Condensed Chemical Dictionary*, 12th ed., p. 1201; *Oxford Illustrated Encyclopedia of Invention and Technology*, p. 369.

• What is **sterling silver**?

Sterling silver is a high-grade alloy (combination of two or more metals) that has a minimum silver content of 925 parts in 1,000. It is used to make fine tableware, jewelry, and electrical contacts.

Source: Brady, George S. *Materials Handbook*, 13th ed., p. 751.

• What are the chief **gold-producing countries**?

South Africa is by far the leading producer of gold. Since the breakup of the former Soviet Union in 1991, the United States has become the second largest gold-producing nation. In the United States, Nevada is the leading gold-producing state. California runs a distant second, followed by South Dakota.

Commercial usage of gold in 1993 was estimated as follows: jewelry and arts, 71 percent; industrial (mainly electronic), 22 percent; and dental, 7 percent.

World production of the top six gold-producing countries in 1993 was:

Country	Gold production
South Africa	1,365,338 pounds (619,201 kilograms)
United States	729,884 pounds (331,013 kilograms)
Australia	545,067 pounds (247,196 kilograms)
China	352,800 pounds (160,000 kilograms)
Canada	337,208 pounds (152,929 kilograms)
Russia	329,648 pounds (149,500 kilograms)

Source: *Minerals Yearbook 1993*, pp. 399-08, 414-16.

• What is **24 karat gold**?

24 karat gold is pure gold. The term "karat" refers to the percentage of gold, versus the percentage of other metals, in an alloy (an alloy is a substance made of two or more metals). Since gold is too soft to be usable in its purest form, it is usually combined with other metals.

Karatage	Percentage of fine gold
24	100
22	91.75
18	75
14	58.5
12	50.25
10	42
9	37.8
8	33.75

Source: Rovin, Jeff. *Laws of Order*, p. 32.

• Is **white gold** really gold?

White gold is a gold alloy, meaning it is a combination of gold and at least one other metal. Whereas different grades of white gold vary widely in composition, the typical alloy consists of 20 percent to 50 percent nickel, with the balance being gold. A superior class of white gold is made of 90 percent gold and 10 percent palladium. Other elements that may be included in white gold are copper and zinc. White gold alloys are mainly used by jewelers, to give gold a white color.

Sources: Brady, George S. *Materials Handbook*, 13th ed., p. 908-9; Thrush, Paul W. *A Dictionary of Mining, Mineral, and Related Terms*, p. 1235.

ROCKS, MINERALS, AND OTHER NATURAL MATERIALS

• How does a **rock** differ from a **mineral**?

Mineralogists (scientists who study minerals) use the term "mineral" for a substance that has all four of the following features:

1. It must be found in nature.

2. It must be made up of inorganic substances (substances that were never alive).

3. It must have the same chemical makeup regardless of where it is found.

4. Its atoms must be arranged in a regular pattern and form solid crystals.

"Rocks" are generally defined as an aggregates, or combinations, of two or more minerals. However, some geologists (scientists who specialize in the study of the origin, history, and structure of the Earth) extend the definition of rocks to include clay, sand, and certain types of limestone.

Sources: The American Geological Institute. *Dictionary of Geological Terms*, Rev. ed., pp. 282, 369; Barnhart, Robert K. *The American Heritage Dictionary of Science*, p. 566.

Feldspar is an example of an igneous rock.

• What are the different categories of **rocks**?

Rocks are divided into three groups: igneous, sedimentary, and metamorphic.

Igneous rocks are formed by the solidification of magma (molten rock), which exists beneath or within the Earth's crust and is ejected during volcanic eruptions. The texture and properties of the thousands of types of igneous rocks vary greatly, depending upon the composition of the magma and the conditions under which the magma solidified.

Granite, for example, which has large crystals of quartz, feldspars, and mica, is formed by the slow cooling of magma underground. Other examples of igneous rocks include pegmatite, rhyolite, obsidian, gabbro, and basalt. Igneous rocks constitute 95 percent of the Earth's crust.

Sedimentary rocks are produced by the accumulation and hardening of sediments. The sediments are either particles eroded from the surfaces of pre-existing rocks, minerals leached from rocks, or skeletons of microscopic organisms. The sediments are then carried by wind, water, or ice and de-

Granite often contains large crystals of quartz.

posited into a body of water. Over long periods of time, the sediments become compressed in layers.

The most common sedimentary rock is sandstone, which is mainly composed of quartz particles. Other examples of sedimentary rocks include brecchia, shale, limestone, chert, and coals. Sedimentary rocks are found over approximately 75 percent of land surfaces around the world.

Metamorphic rocks are rocks that originated as igneous or sedimentary rocks and were transformed by heat and pressure. Volcanic activity, as well as the formation of mountain ranges by movements of the Earth's crust, are two types of heat- and pressure-generating activities that produce metamorphic rocks.

For example, under conditions of extreme heat, limestone, a sedimentary rock, will turn to marble. Other examples of metamorphic rocks include slate, schist, gneiss, quartzite, and hornsfel.

Sources: Fejer, Eva, and Cecilia Fitzsimons. *An Instant Guide to Rocks and Minerals*, pp. 16-43; Hamilton, William R. *The Henry Holt Guide to Minerals, Rocks and Fossils*, p. 146; New York Public Library Staff. *The New York Public Library Desk Reference*, p. 385.

> ## What is a geode?
>
> A geode is a spherical, hollow, stonelike object. The inside of a geode is lined with small crystals that project inward. Geodes are frequently found in limestone beds in many parts of the world. They average 2 to 6 inches (5 to 15 centimeters) in diameter.
>
> **Sources:** American Geological Institute. *Dictionary of Geological Terms*, Rev. ed., p. 181; *The McGraw-Hill Dictionary of Scientific and Technical Terms*, 5th ed., p. 843.

• What is **petrology** and what does a **petrologist** do?

Petrology is the scientific study of rocks. A petrologist is a scientist who examines rocks to determine their origin, composition, and geologic history. By studying rocks, one can learn about past climates and geography, the past and present composition of the Earth, and conditions within the interior of the Earth.

Sources: Hamilton, William R. *The Henry Holt Guide to Minerals, Rocks, and Fossils*, p. 146; McGraw-Hill *Dictionary of Earth Science*, p. 274.

• How are **fossils** formed?

Fossils are the remains, preserved in rock, of prehistoric animals or plants. Fossils usually represent only the hard portions (and not soft tissues) of organisms, such as the bones or shells of animals and the leaves, seeds, or woody parts of plants.

Fossils are formed when a dead plant or animal becomes buried in soil or clay. As the organism decomposes, its hard body parts leave an imprint in the ground. As ground water seeps past, minerals (such as silica) from the water fill in the imprint and eventually harden into stone in a process called petrification.

Molds and casts are other common fossil types. A mold is made from an imprint, such as a dinosaur footprint, in soft mud or silt. This impression may harden, then be covered with other materials. The original footprint forms the mold and the sediments filling it in form the cast. Another class of fossils, which date to relatively recent times, are simply an organism's bones, teeth, or shells themselves.

Sources: Hamilton, William R. *The Henry Holt Guide to Minerals, Rocks, and Fossils*, p. 210; Trefil, James. *1001 Things Everyone Should Know About Science*, pp. 59-60; Zim, Herbert S., and Paul Shaffer. *Rocks and Minerals*, pp. 130-32.

A 35-million-year-old fly fossilized in amber.

• How is **petrified wood** formed?

Petrified wood is the remains, preserved in rock, of prehistoric trees. It is formed over thousands of years, as mineral-rich water seeps through the wood of a tree. The minerals in the water, such as calcium carbonate ($CaCO_3$) and silica salts, either replace or enclose the tree's organic (living) matter and eventually harden into stone, in a process called petrification. Botanists (scientists who specialize in the study of plants) find these types of fossils to be very important since they allow for the study of the internal structure of extinct plants.

There are some instances in which the petrification of a tree is so complete that even the cellular structure of the tree is preserved. The best examples of this can be found in the Petrified Forest National Park in Arizona.

Source: Tidwell, William D. *Common Fossil Plants of Western North America*, p. 29.

• How old are **fossils**?

The oldest known fossils are of blue-green algae, which are single-celled organisms that do not have a nucleus. The algae fossils were found in 3.2-billion-year-old cherts, shales, and sandstone from Transvaal, South Africa. The oldest known fossils of multicellular organisms date back about 700 million years ago.

The largest number of fossils are from the Cambrian period (570 to 505 million years ago), when living organisms began to develop bones and shells. An organism's soft tissues will likely decompose before leaving an imprint in soil or clay. Organisms with hard body parts were more likely to leave an imprint in the ground and become fossilized.

Sources: Fenton, Carroll L. *The Fossil Book*, pp. 91, 93; Trefil, James. *1001 Things Everyone Should Know About Science*, pp. 59-61.

• Are there any **diamond mines** in the **United States?**

The only significant diamond deposit in North America is at Murfreesboro, Arkansas. It is on government-owned land and has never been systematically developed. For a small fee, tourists can dig there and try to find diamonds. The largest crystal found there weighed 40.23 carats (one carat equals about 200 milligrams) and was named the "Uncle Sam" diamond.

Diamonds crystallize directly from melted rock that is rich in magnesium and saturated with carbon dioxide gas (saturated means that it contains the maximum possible amount). Diamonds form when the melted rock, originating deep in the Earth's mantle (the layer of Earth beneath the crust), is subjected to high pressures and temperatures exceeding 2559° Fahrenheit (1400° Celsius).

Diamonds are minerals composed entirely of the element carbon, with an isometric (having three equal axes at right angles to each other) crystalline structure. Gem diamonds, the type used in jewelry, are the hardest natural substance and are also used in glass-cutting tools.

Sources: Arem, Joel E. *Color Encyclopedia of Gemstones*, 2nd ed., p. 81; Parker, Sybil P. *McGraw-Hill Concise Encyclopedia of Science and Technology*, 2nd ed., p. 572.

• How can a genuine **diamond** be identified?

There are several tests that can be performed to determine whether or not a diamond is real, without the aid of tools. To the trained eye, a genuine diamond can be told by its shine, by the straightness and flatness of its surfaces, and by the way it reflects light.

A simple test to determine authenticity is to expose the stones to warm and cold surroundings. After each exposure touch the stones to your lips. True diamonds become warm if the surroundings are warm and cool if the surroundings are cool. This test is especially effective if the results are compared to the results obtained using a diamond known to be genuine.

Another test is to attempt to pick up the stone with a moistened fingertip. If this can be done, then the stone is likely to be a diamond. Most other stones cannot be picked up in this way.

A third test is the water test, in which one places a drop of water on a table. A genuine diamond has the ability to almost "magnetize" water, keeping the water from spreading.

Finally, an instrument called a diamond probe can detect even the most sophisticated fakes. Gemologists (people who study gemstones) always use this as part of their inspection.

Source: Hudgeons, Marc. *The Official Investors Guide: Buying, Selling, Gold, Silver, and Diamonds*, pp. 166-67.

• Which **diamond** is the **world's largest?**

The Cullinan Diamond, weighing 3,106 carats, is the world's largest (one carat equals about 200 milligrams). It was discovered on January 25, 1905, at the Premier Diamond Mine, in Transvaal, South Africa. Named for Sir Thomas M. Cullinan, chairman of the Premier Diamond Company, it was cut into 9 major stones and 96 smaller stones called "brilliants." The total weight of the cut stones was 1,063 carats—only 35 percent of the original weight.

The largest of the major stones, which remains the largest cut diamond in the world, is called Cullinan I. Also known as the "Greater Star of Africa" or the "First Star of Africa," it is a pear-shaped diamond weighing 530.2 carats. It is 2.12 inches (5.4 centimeters) long, 1.75 inches (4.4 centimeters) wide, and 1 inch (2.5 centimeters) thick at its deepest point. It was presented to Britain's King Edward VII in 1907 and was set in the British monarch's scepter.

Cullinan II, also known as the "Second Star of Africa," is an oblong diamond which weighs 317.4 carats. It was set in the British Imperial State Crown.

Sources: Argenzio, Victor. *Diamonds Eternal*, pp. 40-43; Field, Leslie. *The Queen's Jewels*, pp. 72-75; *How In the World?: A Fascinating Journey Through the World of Human Ingenuity*, pp. 144-45.

> ## Which **woods** are used for **telephone poles**?
>
> The principal woods used for telephone poles are southern pine, Douglas fir, western red cedar, and lodgepole pine. Other woods used include: ponderosa pine, red pine, jack pine, western larch, northern white cedar, and other cedars.
>
> **Source:** U.S. Forest Products Laboratory. *Encyclopedia of Wood*, p. 294.

• How much **wood** is used to make a ton of **paper**?

It takes two cords of wood to make one ton of a typical paper (one cord equals 128 cubic feet). The paper-making process also requires 55,000 gallons (208,000 liters) of water, 102 pounds (46 kilograms) of sulfur, 350 pounds (159 kilograms) of lime, 289 pounds (131 kilograms) of clay, 1.2 tons of coal, 112 kilowatt hours of power, 20 pounds (9 kilograms) of dye and pigments, and 108 pounds (49 kilograms) of starch. It uses smaller amounts of other ingredients.

In the United States, the wood used for the manufacture of paper is mainly from small-diameter, softwood trees, such as spruce.

Source: Haygreen, John G. *Forest Products and Wood Science*, 2nd ed., pp. 410-12.

• Does any type of **wood** sink in water?

Ironwood is a name applied to many species of hardwood trees, the wood of which is so dense and heavy that it sinks in water. North American ironwoods include the American hornbeam, the mesquite, the desert ironwood, and leadwood (*Krugiodendron ferreum*).

Water has a specific gravity, or relative density, of 1. To sink in water, a substance must have a specific gravity greater than 1. Leadwood has a specific gravity between 1.34 and 1.42, making it the densest wood in the United States.

The world's most dense wood is black ironwood (*Olea laurifolia*), also called South African ironwood. Found in the West Indies, it has a specific gravity of 1.49 and weighs up to 93 pounds (42.18 kilograms) per foot. The lightest wood is *Aeschynomene hispida*, found in Cuba, with a specific gravity of 0.044 and a weight of 2.5 pounds (1.13 kilograms) per foot. Balsa

323

wood (*Ochroma pyramidale*) varies between 2.5 and 24 pounds (1 and 10 kilograms) per foot.

Sources: *Encyclopedia Americana*, vol. 15, p. 467; *The Guinness Book of Records 1992*, p. 140.

• Why are **essential oils** called "essential"?

Essential oils are called "essential" because they easily dissolve in alcohol to form essences. (Essences are extracts that have the fundamental properties of a substance in concentrated form.) Essential oils are used in flavorings, perfumes, disinfectants, medicines, and other products. One of the main ingredients of these oils is a substance belonging to the terpene group (terpene is a type of hydrocarbon). Essential oils are naturally occurring, volatile (readily convert to a gas), scented oils found in the leaves, pods, and other parts of plants.

Examples of essential oils include bergamot, eucalyptus, ginger, pine, spearmint, and wintergreen oils. These oils are extracted by distillation (the process in which the components of a substance are separated, by boiling and subsequent condensation) or enfleurage (a process in which odorless fats or oils absorb the fragrance) and mechanical pressing. These oils can now be created in a laboratory, as well.

Source: *Oxford Illustrated Encyclopedia of Invention and Technology*, p. 123.

• What is **diatomite**?

Diatomite, also called diatomaceous earth, is a white or cream-colored, crumbly, porous rock. It is made of the fossil remains of diatoms, which are single-celled water plants with silica (a white or colorless crystalline compound) cell walls. Diatom fossils build up on the ocean bottoms to form diatomite. In some places, where the oceans have receded over time, diatomaceous earth exists as dry land.

Diatomite is chemically unreactive and has a rough texture and other unusual physical properties that make it suitable for many scientific and industrial purposes. Among the uses of diatomite are: filtering agent; building material; heat, cold, and sound insulator; catalyst carrier; filler absorbent; abrasive; and ingredient in medicines. By soaking diatomite in liquid explosive nitroglycerin, one can produce dynamite.

Sources: Barnhart, Robert K. *The American Heritage Dictionary of Science*, p. 161; Parker, Sybil P. *McGraw-Hill Concise Encyclopedia of Science and Technology*, 2nd ed., p. 574.

MANUFACTURED MATERIALS

• When was **plastic** first invented?

English inventor Alexander Parkes (1813–1890) created the earliest form of plastic in 1855. He mixed pyroxylin, a partially nitrated form of cellulose (cellulose is the major component of plant cell walls), with alcohol and camphor. This produced a hard but flexible transparent material, which he called "Parkesine." Parkes teamed up with a manufacturer to produce Parkesine; however, they were unable to market it. The material was so strange and new that no one knew how to use it.

In 1868, an American inventor, John Wesley Hyatt (1837–1920), acquired the patent to Parkesine and set out to produce artificial ivory for billiard balls. Hyatt modified Parkes's process—he first soaked cotton in nitric acid and then added camphor. This yielded a hard, flexible material called celluloid. Celluloid was soon used to make of a variety of household items, such as buttons, letter openers, boxes, hatpins, combs, fountain pens, and knife handles. The material was also produced in the form of celluloid strips, which were coated with a light-sensitive "film." Celluloid strips proved ideal for shooting and showing movie pictures.

In 1904, a Belgian scientist, Leo Hendrik Baekeland (1863–1944), brought plastic a step closer to the modern-day material. Baekeland produced a synthetic shellac from formaldehyde and phenol. He then subjected this material to high heat and pressure, creating a hard plastic called "bakelite." Bakelite and other, more versatile plastics eventually replaced

325

How is **bulletproof glass** made?

Bulletproof glass is composed of two sheets of plate glass with a sheet of transparent resin (adhesive) in between, molded together under heat and pressure. When subjected to a severe blow, it will crack without shattering. Today's bulletproof glass contains multiple glass and plastic layers molded together.

Sources: Brady, George S. *Materials Handbook*, 13th ed., p. 564-65; Diamond, Freda. *The Story of Glass*, pp. 128-30.

celluloid. By the 1940s, the market for celluloid had shrunk to the point that it was no longer of commercial importance.

Sources: *The American Heritage Dictionary of Science and Technology*, vol. 3, no. 1 (Summer 1987), pp. 18-23; De Bono, Edward. *Eureka!* p. 89; Travers, Bridget, ed. *World of Invention*, pp. 132-33; 487-88.

• Who invented **thermopane glass?**

Thermopane insulated window glass was invented by C. D. Haven in the United States in 1930. It consists of two sheets of glass that are bonded together in such a manner that they trap air in the space between them. Often this space is filled with an inert (unreactive) gas which increases the insulating quality of the window.

Glass traps warmth in a building because it allows the short wavelengths of light to pass through it, but prohibits nearly all of the long waves of reflected radiation (heat) from passing back through it.

Sources: Drake, George R. *Weatherizing Your Home*, pp. 153-54; DuVall, Nell. *Domestic Technology*, p. 254.

• Who developed **fiberglass?**

Fiberglass is a material composed of very fine threads of glass and sometimes other materials, loosely grouped together in bundles. Fiberglass has many impressive qualities, among them strength, flexibility, heat trapping, and fire-resistance. Fiberglass is used in vehicle construction, woven into cloths to make them fire resistant, and as insulation.

The earliest form of fiberglass, which consisted of coarse glass fibers, was used by the ancient Egyptians. They incorporated the fibers into pottery, as a decorative trim.

The first modern process for making fiberglass was developed by Parisian craftsman Dubus-Bonnel. He would spin and weave strands of hot glass on a loom. Dubus-Bonnel was granted a patent for his product in 1836. (A patent is a grant made by a government that allows the creator of invention the sole right to make, use, and sell that invention for a set period of time.) Then in 1893, the Libbey Glass Company exhibited lampshades at the World's Columbian Exposition in Chicago that were made of coarse glass thread woven together with silk.

Between 1931 and 1939 in the United States, the Owens Illinois Glass Company and the Corning Glass Works developed the first practical methods of making fiberglass commercially. The greatest technical challenge they faced was creating long glass strands as thin as $\frac{1}{5000}$ of an inch. Once they crossed that hurdle, the industry began to produce glass fiber for thermal insulation and air filters, among other uses.

During World War II (1939–45), glass fibers were combined with plastics to create a new material called glass-fiber-reinforced plastics (GFRP). Glass fibers did for plastics what steel did for concrete—they gave plastics strength and flexibility. GFRP is now used extensively in boat and ship construction, sporting goods, automobile bodies, and circuit boards in electronics.

Sources: Diamond, Freda. *The Story of Glass*, pp. 197-224; Giscard d'Estaing, Valerie-Anne. *The World Almanac Book of Inventions*, p. 274; *Oxford Illustrated Encyclopedia of Invention and Technology*, p. 129; Travers, Bridget, ed. *World of Invention*, p 247.

• What is **buckminsterfullerene**?

Buckminsterfullerene is a recently discovered carbon chemical comprised of large molecules shaped like soccer balls, each containing 60 carbon atoms. Also called "buckyballs," the molecules of buckminsterfullerine are hollow, spherical objects with 32 faces—12 of them pentagons (having 5 sides) and the rest hexagons (having 6 sides). This shape is technically called a "truncated icosahedron." This substance was named buckminsterfullerene because of its molecules' structural resemblance to the geodesic domes designed by American architect R. Buckminster Fuller (1895–1983). (Geodesic domes are lightweight domes that incorporate the geometric properties of the tetrahedron and the sphere.)

Before chemist (a scientist specializing in the composition, structure, properties, and reactions of matter) Richard Smalley identified buckminsterfullerene in 1985, it was believed that the only substances comprised to-

American architect Buckminster Fuller developed the geodesic dome.

tally of carbon were graphite and diamonds. However, it was suspected that other pure-carbon molecules did exist. For instance, large molecules containing only carbon atoms have been known to exist around certain types of carbon-rich stars. And similar molecules are also thought to be present in soot formed during the incomplete combustion (burning) of organic (living) materials.

Buckminsterfullerene is formed by using a laser to vaporize material from a graphite surface. Buckminsterfullerene is unique in many ways. For instance, it easily gives up and accepts electrons. For this reason, it can be used as an electrical insulator, conductor, semiconductor, and superconductor in various compounds. Buckminsterfullerene is also known to have unusual chemical and magnetic characteristics. Its potential uses in medicine and as a component in building materials are currently being studied.

Sources: Barnes-Svarney, Patricia. *The New York Public Library Science Desk Reference*, pp. 251, 384; Golob, Richard. *Almanac of Science and Technology: What's New and What's Known*, pp. 209-10; *Technology Review*, vol. 97 (January 1994), pp. 54-62.

• Why is **sulfuric acid** important?

Sulfuric acid is essential for the production of many commonly used manufactured items. Sometimes called "oil of vitriol," sulfuric acid (H_2SO_4) is prepared industrially by the reaction of water with sulfur trioxide. Sulfur trioxide is made by combining sulfur dioxide and oxygen.

The first widespread use of sulfuric acid was in the manufacture of soda in the eighteenth century. Its greatest use today is in the production of fertilizers. It is also used in the refining of petroleum, as well as in the produc-

> ## What material is used to make a **tuning fork**?
>
> Tuning forks are made of steel. A tuning fork is an instrument that, when struck, emits a constant musical pitch.
>
> **Source:** *McGraw-Hill Encyclopedia of Science and Technology,* 7th ed., vol. 18, pp. 608-9.

tion of automobile batteries, explosives, pigments, iron and other metals, and paper pulp.

Sources: McNeil, Ian. *An Encyclopedia of the History of Technology,* pp. 221-23; *Van Nostrand Reinhold Encyclopedia of Chemistry,* 4th ed., pp. 909-10; *World Book Encyclopedia,* vol. 18, p. 968.

• How is **dry ice** made?

Dry ice is composed of carbon dioxide, which at room temperature is a gas. The carbon dioxide used to make dry ice is liquefied and then stored and shipped in highly pressurized tanks.

To make dry ice, the liquid carbon dioxide is withdrawn from the tank and allowed to evaporate at a normal pressure in a porous bag (a porous material is one through which air and water molecules can pass). This rapid evaporation consumes so much heat from the surrounding air that part of the liquid carbon dioxide freezes to a temperature of -109° Fahrenheit (-78° Celsius). The frozen liquid is then compressed by machines into blocks of "dry ice" which will sublimate (return to the gaseous state) when set out at room temperature.

Dry ice was first made commercially in 1925 by the Prest-Air Devices Company of Long Island City, New York, through the efforts of Thomas Benton Slate. It was used by Schrafft's of New York in July 1925 to prevent ice cream from melting. The first large sale of dry ice was made later in that year to Breyer Ice Cream Company of New York.

Sources: Kane, Joseph N. *Famous First Facts,* 4th ed., p. 316; Sutton, Caroline, and Duncan M. Anderson. *How Do They Do That?* p. 154.

• How is **sandpaper** made?

Sandpaper consists of a flexible paper backing, with a film of adhesive (glue) that holds and supports a coating of abrasive grains. Sandpaper belongs to a class of materials called "coated abrasives." The first record of a coated abrasive is in thirteenth-century China, when crushed seashells were bound with natural gums to backing material. The first known article on coated abrasives was published in 1808. It described how heat-processed, ground pumice (a type of abrasive) was mixed with varnish and spread on paper with a brush.

Most abrasive papers are now made with aluminum oxide or silicon carbide, although they are still called "sandpaper." Quartz grains are also used for wood polishing. The paper used is heavy, tough, and flexible. The grains are bonded with a strong glue made from a variety of resins.

Sources: Brady, George S. *Materials Handbook,* 13th ed., p. 698; *Coated Abrasives: Modern Tool of Industry,* pp. 7-8; *World Book Encyclopedia,* vol. 21, p. 401.

• What is **solder**?

Solder is an alloy, which is a combination of two or more metals. It is heated to its melting point and used to join together other metals. The most common solder is called half-and-half, or "plumber's" solder, and is composed of equal parts of lead and tin. Other metals used in solder are aluminum, cadmium, zinc, nickel, gold, silver, palladium, bismuth, copper, and antimony.

Soldering is an ancient joining method. It is mentioned in the Bible (Isaiah 41:7) and there is evidence of its use in Mesopotamia some 5,000 years ago. (Mesoptamia was an ancient republic located in present-day Iraq.) Solder was later used in Egypt, Greece, and Rome. Solder is frequently used today in the construction of electronic circuitry.

Sources: Brady, George S. *Materials Handbook,* 13th ed., pp. 768-70; Manko, Howard H. *Solders and Soldering,* 2nd ed., p. xv.

• What is **creosote**?

Creosote is a yellowish, poisonous, oily liquid obtained from the distillation of coal tar. (Distillation is the process in which the components of a substance are separated by boiling and subsequent condensation.) Coal tar is a by-product of the process of "dry" distillation, or carbonization, of coal into the solid fuel product coke.

Crude creosote oil, also called dead oil or pitch oil, is used as a wood preservative. Railroad ties, poles, fence posts, marine pilings, and lumber for

---

What is slag?

Slag is a nonmetallic by-product of smelting. Smelting is the process by which a metal is separated from its ore (a mineral compound that is mined for one of the elements it contains, usually a metal element) in a blast furnace (a furnace in which combustion is made more intense by a forced stream of air). Slag is formed in the smelting of iron, copper, lead, and other metals.

Slag consists primarily of silica (a white or colorless crystalline compound) and lime. It is used as an ingredient in cements, concrete, and roofing materials. It is also placed under roads and railways to lend stability.

Source: Brady, George S. *Materials Handbook,* 13th ed., pp. 756-57.

---

outdoor use are all soaked in creosote. This treatment can greatly extend the life of wood that is exposed to the weather.

Sources: Brady, George S. *Materials Handbook,* 13th ed., p. 256-57; *Van Nostrand Reinhold Encyclopedia of Chemistry,* 4th ed., pp. 264-65.

• Why is **titanium dioxide** the most widely used white pigment?

Titanium dioxide is the principal white pigment used throughout the world not only because it is the whitest known pigment, but it is unrivaled in opacity (the opposite of transparency), stain resistance, and durability. It is also nontoxic. The industries that consume the bulk (60 to 70 percent) of titanium dioxide are paint, printing inks, plastics, and ceramics.

Sources: *Encyclopedia of Chemical Technology,* 4th ed., vol. 23, p. 143; Morgans, W. M. *Outlines of Paint Technology,* p. 52; *The Timetable of Technology,* p. 28.

WEATHER and CLIMATE

| ATMOSPHERIC BASICS

• What is **barometric pressure** and what does it mean?

Barometric pressure, also called air pressure or atmospheric pressure, is the pressure exerted by the weight of air over a given area of Earth's surface. This value is a function of how many molecules of air there are in a specific area, how fast those molecules are moving, and how often they collide. (Molecules are particles made by the chemical combination of two or more atoms.) Barometric pressure is measured by an instrument called a barometer.

At sea level (the level of the ocean's surface used as a standard in determining land elevation and sea depths), where gravity is strongest and attracts the greatest number of molecules, air pressure is greatest. Because gravity weakens as you go up, air pressure is lower at higher altitudes. So while the average air pressure at sea level is 14.7 pounds per square inch, at 1,000 feet (304 meters) above sea level the pressure drops to 14.1 pounds per square inch. And if you travel four miles above the ground—the point at which half of the atmosphere's mass (measure of the total amount of matter in an object) is above and half is below you—the air pressure is about 7.3 pounds per square inch.

The barometric pressure at any given location is constantly changing. Those changes produce the winds, bring in clouds, or clear the way for

An aneroid barometer is used to measure the barometric pressure.

sunny skies. Air pressure readings are important in weather forecasting. For instance, rising barometric pressure often coincides with clearing skies and fair weather; falling pressure indicates that wet or stormy weather may be on the way. Areas of very low pressure are associated with severe storms, such as hurricanes.

Sources: Engelbert, Phillis. *The Complete Weather Resource*, vol. 1, pp. 14-18, vol. 3, pp. 393-4; Lee, Sally. *Predicting Violent Storms*, pp. 16-17; Tufty, Barbara. *1001 Questions Answered About Hurricanes, Tornados, and Other Natural Air Disasters*, p. 316; Williams, Jack. *The Weather Book*, p. 30.

• What are the **highest and lowest** recorded **temperatures** on Earth?

The highest temperature in the world was 136° Fahrenheit (58° Celsius), recorded at El Azizia, Libya, on the edge of the Sahara Desert, on September 13, 1922. The highest temperature ever recorded in the United States was 134° Fahrenheit (56.7° Celsius) in Death Valley, California, on July 10, 1913. The unofficial high temperature, which does not meet the international weather standards, was 140° Fahrenheit (60° Celsius). This was recorded at Delta, Mexico, in August 1953. Another unofficial high of 136.4° Fahrenheit (58° Celsius) was recorded at San Luis, Mexico, on August 11, 1933.

The lowest temperature on record is -128.6° Fahrenheit (-89.6° Celsius), measured at Vostok Station in Antarctica on July 21, 1983. The record cold temperature for an inhabited area was -90.4° Fahrenheit (-68° Celsius) at Oymyakon, Siberia (population 4,000), on February 6, 1933. This temperature is the same as the readings at Verkhoyansk, Siberia, on January 3, 1885, and February 5 and 7, 1892. The lowest temperature reading in the United States was -79.8° Fahrenheit (-62.1° Celsius) on January 23, 1971, in Prospect Creek, Alaska. For the contiguous 48 states (the con-

> ### Why are the **horse latitudes** called by that name?
>
> The horse latitudes are two high-pressure belts characterized by low winds, at about 30 degrees north and south of the equator. Dreaded by early sailors, these areas have undependable winds with long periods of calm. In the Northern Hemisphere, particularly near Bermuda, sailing ships carrying horses from Spain to the New World (the Americas) were often stalled. When water supplies ran low, these animals were the first to go without water. Dying from thirst or tossed overboard, the animals were sacrificed to conserve water for the men. Explorers and sailors reported that the seas were "strewn with bodies of horses." This is one explanation of how these areas came to be called the horse latitudes.
>
> The term might also be rooted in complaints by sailors who were paid in advance and received no overtime when the ships slowly proceeded through the windless regions. During this time, they were said to be "working off a dead horse."
>
> **Sources:** *Encyclopedic Dictionary of Science*, p. 121; Rovin, Jeff. *Laws of Order*, p. 87; Tufty, Barbara. *1001 Questions Answered About Hurricanes, Tornadoes, and Other Natural Air Disasters*, pp. 189-90.

tinental United States, which excludes Alaska and Hawaii), the coldest temperature was -69.7° Fahrenheit (-56.5° Celsius) at Rogers Pass, Montana, on January 20, 1954.

Sources: Ahrens, C. Donald. *Meteorology Today: An Introduction to Weather, Climate, and the Environment*, 5th ed., p. 505; *The Guinness Book of Records 1995*, pp. 63-64.

• What is the **Coriolis effect?**

The Coriolis effect is the apparent curvature of global winds, ocean currents, and anything else that moves freely across the Earth's surface, due to the rotation of the Earth on its axis. It was discovered by, and is named for, nineteenth century French engineer Gaspard C. Coriolis (1792–1843). Coriolis used mathematical formulas to explain that the path of any object set in motion above a rotating surface will curve in relation to objects on that surface.

If not for the spinning of the Earth, global winds would blow in straight north-south lines. In reality, global winds blow diagonally—for instance, from the northwest to the southeast. The Coriolis effect influences the direction of winds around the world as follows: In the Northern Hemisphere (the half of the Earth north of the equator), it curves them to the right; in the Southern Hemisphere (the area south of the equator) it curves them to the left.

The Coriolis effect is strongest at the north and south poles. It does not exist at all at the equator, where opposing forces (the turn to the right and the turn to the left) cancel each other out.

Sources: Bair, Frank E. *The Weather Almanac*, 6th ed., pp. 192-93; Engelbert, Phillis. *The Complete Weather Resource*, vol. 1, pp. 20-22; Great Britain Meteorological Office. *Meteorological Glossary*, p. 287; Williams, Jack. *The Weather Book*, p. 21

• What are **jet streams** and when were they discovered?

Jet streams are the world's fastest upper-level winds. They are narrow bands of wind that zip through the top of the troposphere in a west-to-east direction, usually at speeds between 80 and 190 miles per hour (129 and 306 kilometers per hour). (The troposphere is the lowest level of the Earth's atmosphere, extending to a height of about 30,000 feet [9 kilometers] above the surface.) Jet streams are usually a few miles deep, up to 100 miles (160 kilometers) wide, and well over 1,000 miles (1,600 kilometers) long. Jet stream winds have been clocked at a maximum of over 345 miles (552 kilometers) per hour.

Jet streams were discovered by World War II (1939–45) bomber pilots flying over Japan and the Mediterranean Sea. Jet planes, which are capable of flying at the top of the troposphere, take advantage of the jet stream's great speeds.

Jet streams occur where there are largest differences in air temperature, and hence pressure, at high altitudes. In both Northern and Southern Hemispheres, jet streams exist at around 60 degrees latitude (distance north and south of the equator measured in degrees). At that latitude relatively warm "westerly" winds meet cold air coming from the poles. There is also a subtropical jet stream in each hemisphere at around 30 degrees latitude. That is where westerlies from 60 degrees latitude meet the warm trade winds (winds that blow throughout the tropics, circulating air between the equator and 30 degrees latitude, north and south), which are coming from the equator.

Sources: Considine, Glenn D. *Van Nostrand's Scientific Encyclopedia*, 8th ed., vol. 2, p.1796; *Encyclopedia of Aviation*, p. 107; Engelbert, Phillis. *The Complete Weather Resource*, vol. 1, pp. 30-31, 90, 97.

• What is the **dew point** and how does **dew** form?

The dew point is the temperature at which the air becomes saturated, meaning it reaches 100 percent relative humidity. (Relative humidity is the amount of moisture in the air, expressed as a percentage of how much moisture the air can hold at a given temperature.) If the temperature falls below the dew point, water vapor within the air begins to condense (changes from a gas to a liquid). The dew point is so-named because it's the temperature below which dew forms on a cold surface.

The concept of dew point rests on the premise that cold air can hold less water vapor than can warm air. Consider air that at 77° Fahrenheit (25° Celsius) has a relative humidity of 56 percent. If that temperature is lowered to 59° Fahrenheit (15° Celsius) and the amount of moisture held constant, the air will have 100 percent relative humidity. Therefore, the dew point of that air is 59° Fahrenheit.

If a thin layer of air contacts a surface and is chilled to its dew point, dew will form on the surface. Fog and clouds develop when large volumes of air are cooled to their dew point.

Magnification of dew on a blade of grass.

Sources: Engelbert, Phillis. *The Complete Weather Resource*, vol. 1, pp. 49-50; Ludlum, David M. *The Audubon Society Field Guide to North American Weather*, p. 610; *World Book Encyclopedia*, vol. 5, p. 176.

• When does **frost** form?

Frost is a crystalline deposit of small, thin ice crystals. This deposit forms on objects when the air directly above those objects reaches the frost point. The frost point is the temperature at which a given volume of air becomes saturated and thus can no longer hold water in the vapor state—provided that the air temperature is at or below freezing.

In the formation of frost, a layer of water initially freezes onto the surface. The layer of frost grows as water vapor from the air directly solidifies into ice without going through the liquid phase; this process is called deposition.

Usually frost forms on clear, calm nights, especially during early autumn when the air above the Earth is quite moist. A light frost generally damages only the most tender plants and vines, whereas a heavy frost (a heavy deposit of crystallized water) may kill even hearty (nonwoody) plants.

Sources: Engelbert, Phillis. *The Complete Weather Resource*, vol. 1, pp. 51-52; Tufty, Barbara. *1001 Questions Answered About Hurricanes, Tornadoes, and Other Natural Air Disasters*, pp. 276-78.

• What is the **heat index**?

The heat index, also called the humiture index or temperature-humidity index, is a way to measure how hot and muggy it feels. This index gives an indication of how stressful outdoor activity will be for the average person.

The heat index is most useful during the hottest part of the day. The lower the heat index, the more comfortable the air is. Any value over 89 is considered to be muggy and uncomfortably hot. Heat exhaustion and sunstroke are of greatest concern when the heat index reaches 105. The chart below provides the heat index for some temperatures and relative humidities (the amount of moisture in the air at a given temperature).

Air Temperature (°F)

Relative Humidity	70	75	80	85	90	95	100	105	110	115	120
	Feels like (°F)										
0%	64	69	73	78	83	87	91	95	99	103	107
10%	65	70	75	80	85	90	95	100	105	111	116
20%	66	72	77	82	87	93	99	105	112	120	130
30%	67	73	78	84	90	96	104	113	123	135	148
40%	68	74	79	86	93	101	110	123	137	151	
50%	69	75	81	88	96	107	120	135	150		
60%	70	76	82	90	100	114	132	149			
70%	70	77	85	93	106	124	144				
80%	71	78	86	97	113	136					
90%	71	79	88	102	122						
100%	72	80	91	108							

• **Sources:** Engelbert, Phillis. *The Complete Weather Resource*, vol. 3, pp. 424-25; *World Almanac 1996*, p.186

What is meant by the **windchill** factor?

In cold weather, the windchill factor (also called the windchill equivalent temperature or windchill index) is included in weather reports. The windchill factor is a measure of how cold the air feels, due to the interaction of wind and temperature. Wind intensifies the effects of low temperature by removing heat from the body more rapidly than usual.

The windchill factor is the temperature at which the body would lose an equivalent amount of heat, if there were no wind. For instance, if it were 10° Fahrenheit (-12° Celsius) and winds were blowing between 29 and 32 miles per hour (46 and 51 kilometers per hour), the windchill factor would be -35° Fahrenheit (-37° Celsius).

The accompanying chart is used to determine windchill. Find the wind speed in the column on the left and the temperature at the row on top. The square where this column and row intersect gives the windchill factor.

Sources: Ahrens, C. Donald. *Meteorology Today: An Introduction to Weather, Climate, and the Environment*, 5th ed., pp. 77-79; Vergara, William. *Science in Everyday Life*, pp. 168-69.

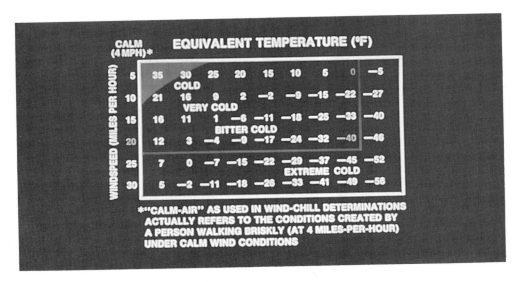

CALM (4 MPH)*	EQUIVALENT TEMPERATURE (°F)								
5	35	30	25	20	15	10	5	0	—5
		COLD							
10	21	16	9	2	—2	—9	—15	—22	—27
		VERY COLD							
15	16	11	1	—6	—11	—18	—25	—33	—40
		BITTER COLD							
20	12	3	—4	—9	—17	—24	—32	—40	—46
25	7	0	—7	—15	—22	—29	—37	—45	—52
					EXTREME COLD				
30	5	—2	—11	—18	—26	—33	—41	—49	—56

WINDSPEED (MILES PER HOUR)

*"CALM-AIR" AS USED IN WIND-CHILL DETERMINATIONS ACTUALLY REFERS TO THE CONDITIONS CREATED BY A PERSON WALKING BRISKLY (AT 4 MILES-PER-HOUR) UNDER CALM WIND CONDITIONS

Wind chill table.

• When and by whom were **clouds** first **classified**?

The French naturalist (a scientist specializing in the study of plants and animals in their natural surroundings) Jean Baptiste Pierre Antoine de Monet Lamarck (1744–1829) proposed the first system for classifying clouds in 1802. However, his work did not receive wide recognition. One year later, Englishman Luke Howard (1772–1864) developed a cloud classification system that has been generally accepted and is still used, in a modified form, today.

Clouds are distinguished by their general appearance and by their height above the ground. Howard assigned the following names to the four categories of clouds, based on appearance: cumuliform ("piled") for puffy, heaped-up clouds; cirriform ("hair-like") for thin, wispy, feathery swirls of clouds; stratiform ("layered") for continuous, flat sheets or layers of clouds; and nimbus ("cloud") for dark, rain- and snow-producing clouds.

Howard assigned combinations of these names to specific cloud types. Nimbostratus, for instance, is a rain-producing, layered cloud, and stratocumulus is a continuous sheet of bumpy clouds.

Sources: Ahrens, C. Donald. *Meteorology Today: An Introduction to Weather, Climate, and the Environment*, 5th ed., p. 163; Engelbert, Phillis. *The Complete Weather Resource*, vol. 1, p. 75; Williams, Jack. *The Weather Book*, pp. 160-61.

- ## What are the **four major cloud categories,** based on height in the sky?

The first scientific method of classifying clouds was developed in 1803 by English naturalist (a scientist specializing in the study of plants and animals in their natural surroundings) and pharmacist Luke Howard (1772–1864). In an article titled "On the Modifications of Clouds," Howard designated Latin names to four cloud categories, based on appearance: cumuliform ("piled") for puffy, heaped-up clouds; cirriform ("hair-like") for thin, wispy, feathery swirls of clouds; stratiform ("layered") for continuous, flat sheets or layers of clouds; and nimbus ("cloud") for dark rain clouds. Meteorologists again took up the topic of cloud classification in 1874, at the first meeting of the International Meteorological Congress. There a classification system was devised that used Howard's cloud names as a starting point. The new system included four categories of clouds based on their height in the sky. Those categories were subdivided into ten groupings of clouds based on appearance.

1. **High Clouds**—composed almost entirely of ice crystals, the bases of these clouds start at 16,500 feet (5,005 meters) and reach 45,000 feet (13,650 meters).

Cirrus (from Latin "lock of hair")—are thin featherlike crystal clouds in patches or narrow bands. The large ice crystals that often trail downward in well-defined wisps are called "mares' tails."

Cirrostratus—is a thin, white cloud layer that resembles a veil or sheet. This layer can be striated or fibrous. Because of the ice content, these clouds are associated with the halos that surround the sun or moon.

Cirrocumulus—are thin clouds that appear as small white flakes or cotton patches and may contain supercooled water.

2. **Middle Clouds**—composed of ice and water. The height of the cloud bases range from 6,500 to 23,000 feet (1,972 to 6,977 meters).

Altostratus—appears as a bluish or grayish veil or layer of clouds that can gradually merge into altocumulus clouds. The sun may be dimly visible through it, but flat, thick sheets of this cloud type can obscure the sun.

Altocumulus—is a white or gray layer or patches of solid clouds with rounded shapes.

3. **Low Clouds**—composed almost entirely of water that may at times be supercooled (liquid below the freezing point); at subfreezing tem-

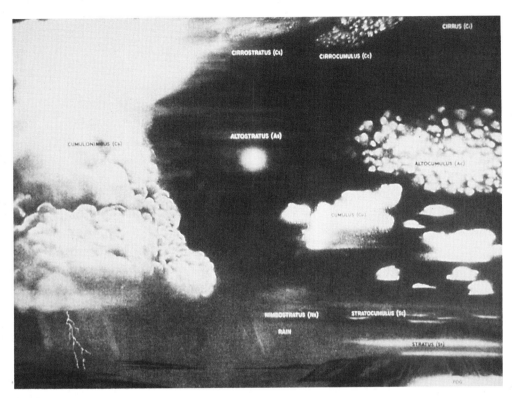

Types of clouds.

peratures, snow and ice crystals may be present as well. The bases of these clouds start near the Earth's surface and climb to 6,500 feet (1,972 meters) in the middle latitudes.

Stratus—are gray uniform sheetlike clouds with a relatively low base or they can be patchy, shapeless, low gray clouds. Thin enough for the sun to shine through, these clouds bring drizzle and snow.

Stratocumulus—are globular rounded masses that form at the top of the cloud layer.

Nimbostratus—are seen as a gray or dark relatively shapeless massive cloud layer containing rain, snow, and ice pellets.

4. **Clouds with Vertical Development**—contain supercooled water and grow to great heights. The cloud bases range from 1,000 feet (303 meters) to 10,000 feet (3,033 meters).

Cumulus—are detached, fair weather clouds with relatively flat bases and dome-shaped tops. These usually do not have extensive vertical development and do not produce precipitation.

Cumulonimbus—are unstable large vertical clouds with dense boiling tops that bring showers, hail, thunder, and lightning.

Sources: Ahrens, C. Donald. *Meteorology Today: An Introduction to Weather, Climate, and the Environment*, 5th ed., p. 164; Bair, Frank E. *The Weather Almanac*, 6th ed., pp. 198-200; Engelbert, Phillis. *The Complete Weather Resource*, vol.1, pp. 78-91.

• What is the **Beaufort Scale?**

The Beaufort scale is a handy device for estimating wind speed. It was devised in 1805 by a British Admiral, Sir Francis Beaufort (1774–1857). Beaufort's intention was to create a standard method of assessing wind speed, based on sailors' descriptions of the wind's effect on the water. In 1926 the scale was modified so it could also be used on land.

The Beaufort Scale designates numbers from 0 to 17 to indicate wind speeds, as shown in the table below.

Beaufort Wind Scale

Wind speed (mph)	Beaufort Number	Wind Effect on Land	Official Description
Less than 1	0	Calm; smoke rises vertically.	CALM
1–3	1	Wind direction is seen in direction of smoke, but is not revealed by weather vane.	LIGHT AIR
4–7	2	Wind can be felt on face; leaves rustle; wind vane moves.	LIGHT BREEZE
8–12	3	Leaves and small twigs in motion; wind extends light flag.	GENTLE
13–18	4	Wind raises dust and loose papers; small branches move.	MODERATE
19–24	5	Small trees with leaves begin to sway; crested wavelets appear on inland waters.	FRESH
25–31	6	Large branches move; telegraph wires whistle; umbrellas become difficult to control.	STRONG
32–38	7	Whole trees sway and walking into the wind becomes difficult.	NEAR GALE
39–46	8	Twigs break off trees; cars veer on roads.	GALE

Wind speed (mph)	Beaufort Number	Wind Effect on Land	Official Description
47–54	9	Slight structural damage occurs (roof slates may blow away, etc.).	STRONG GALE
55–63	10	Trees are uprooted; considerable structural damage is caused.	STORM
64–72	11	Widespread damage is caused.	VIOLENT STORM
73 or more	12	Widespread damage is caused.	HURRICANE

Source: Williams, Jack. *The Weather Book*, p. 43.

• Is **Chicago** the **windiest city**?

In 1990, Chicago ranked twenty-first in the list of 68 windy cities, with an average wind speed of 10.3 miles (16.6 kilometers) per hour. Cheyenne, Wyoming, with an average wind speed of 12.9 miles (20.8 kilometers) per hour, ranks number one. It is closely followed by Great Falls, Montana, which has an average wind speed of 12.8 miles (20.6 kilometers) per hour.

The highest surface wind speed ever recorded was on Mount Washington, New Hampshire, at an elevation of 6,288 feet (1.9 kilometers). On April 12, 1934, its wind was 231 miles (371.7 kilometers) per hour and its average wind speed was 35 miles (56.3 kilometers) per hour.

Sources: Krantz, Les. *The Best and Worst of Everything*, pp. 102-3; Williams, Jack. *The Weather Book*, p. 43.

• What is a **chinook**?

A chinook is a warm, dry wind that blows down the eastern side of the Rocky Mountains from New Mexico to Canada. Chinooks occur in winter or early spring and bring a noticeable rise in temperature to the plains just east of the Rocky Mountains.

The chinook is classified as a katabatic wind. A katabatic wind is a strong, downhill wind that forms as cold, dense, surface air travels down a mountainside and sinks into the valley. The air is dried and heated as it streams down the slope. Sometimes the falling air becomes warmer than the air it displaces below.

"Chinook" is an Arapaho Indian word meaning "snow eater." This wind is so-named because it brings a dramatic warming to cold regions, melting the snow in its path. Chinooks can raise the temperature of an area by more

> ### *How much water is there in an inch of snow?*
>
> On average, 10 inches (25 centimeters) of snow is equal to 1 inch (2.5 centimeters) of water. Heavy, wet snow may contain as much as 16 percent meltwater by volume. A dry, powdery snow may be as little as 1/13 meltwater by volume.
>
> **Sources:** Ahrens, C. Donald. *Meteorology Today: An Introduction to Weather, Climate, and the Environment*, 5th ed., p. 212; *Mineral Information Service*, vol. 23 (September 1970), p. 189.

than 36° Fahrenheit (20° Celsius) in just one hour and by as much as 60° Fahrenheit (15° Celsius) in one day.

Another type of warm katabatic wind is the Santa Ana, which brings warm, dry conditions—conditions ripe for forest fires—to southern California.

Sources: Bair, Frank E. *The Weather Almanac*, 6th ed., p. 280-81; Eagleman, J. R. *Severe and Unusual Weather*, pp. 50-52; Engelbert, Phillis. *The Complete Weather Resource*, vol. 1, pp. 128-30; Ludlum, David M. *The Audubon Society Field Guide to North American Weather*, p. 630.

PRECIPITATION AND THUNDERSTORMS

• How does **snow** form?

Snowflakes, the basic unit of snow, originate as tiny ice crystals within "cold clouds." Cold clouds are clouds that exist within air that is at, or below, the freezing point. As an ice crystal is blown back and forth between the top and bottom of the cloud, it grows in two ways: by coalescence and by deposition. In coalescence, the ice crystal collides, and sticks to the cold water droplets it encounters in the cloud. In deposition, water vapor molecules (particles made by the combination of two or more atoms) within the cloud freeze directly onto the ice crystal.

As the ice crystal grows, it bonds with other ice crystals and takes on the six-sided shape of a snowflake. When the snowflake becomes heavy enough, it falls to the ground.

Sources: Ahrens, C. Donald. *Meteorology Today: An Introduction to Weather, Climate, and the Environment*, 5th ed., pp. 201-3; Engelbert, Phillis. *The Complete Weather Resource*, vol. 2, pp. 189-95; Spar, Jerome. *The Way of the Weather*, p. 103.

Is it ever too cold to **snow**?

No. The air always holds some moisture, regardless of its temperature. Moisture falls from clouds in very cold air in the form of tiny snow crystals.

Frigid air, particularly polar air that sweeps into a region in the wake of a cold front, produces scant snow. In contrast, heavy snowfalls occur when relatively mild air is brought to a region by a warm front. (A front is the boundary between warm and cold air masses.)

The fact that snow piles up year after year in Arctic regions illustrates that it is never too cold to snow.

Sources: Forrester, Frank. *1001 Questions Answered About the Weather*, p. 286; Sanders, Ti. *Weather*, p. 165.

A snowflake.

• Can two **snowflakes** be alike?

No two snowflakes are identical, molecule for molecule. (Molecules are particles made by the combination of two or more atoms.) A snowflake is made up of more than 180 billion water molecules that come together under a variety of conditions. Furthermore, molecules are constantly freezing to and evaporating from snowflakes, meaning that snowflakes, at the molecular level, are constantly changing.

However, it does appear that two snowflakes can be identical in size. This was proven in 1989 by Nancy Knight, a cloud physicist (a scientist specializing in the interaction between matter and energy) with the National Center for Atmospheric Research. Knight collected snow samples from an airplane over Wasau, Wisconsin, and found two snowflakes that were both 250 microns long and 170 microns wide. (A micron is one-millionth of a meter.)

Sources: Engelbert, Phillis. *The Complete Weather Resource*, vol. 2, p. 197; Williams, Jack. *The Weather Book*, pp. 98-100.

> ## Where is the **rainiest place** on Earth?
>
> The wettest place in the world is Tutunendo, Colombia, with an average rainfall of 463.4 inches (1177 centimeters) per year. The place that has the most rainy days per year is Mount Wai-'ale'ale on the island of Kauai, Hawaii. It has up to 350 rainy days annually.
>
> In contrast, the longest rainless period in the world was 14 years, from October 1903 to January 1918, at Arica, Chile. In the United States the longest dry spell was 767 days at Bagdad, California—from October 3, 1912, to November 8, 1914.
>
> **Sources:** *The Guinness Book of Records 1996*, p 64; Williams, Jack, *The Weather Book*, p. 89.

• What is the difference between **freezing rain** and **sleet**?

Freezing rain is rain that falls from a cloud as a liquid but turns to ice on contact with a freezing object. It forms a smooth ice coating called glaze. Usually freezing rain only falls for a short time, because as the air temperature changes even slightly, freezing rain either turns to rain or to snow.

Sleet is frozen or partially frozen raindrops, in the form of ice pellets. Sleet forms as rain passes through a layer of freezing air above the ground. The rain freezes to form hard, clear, tiny ice pellets. These pellets hit the ground so fast that they bounce off with a sharp click.

In the United States, the term "sleet" refers to ice pellets. In Australia and Great Britain, however, "sleet" is defined as a mixture of rain and wet snow. Wet snow is made of partially melted snowflakes (the ice crystals on the edges of the snowflakes have melted, making the snow sticky and wet).

Sources: Ahrens, C. Donald. *Meteorology Today: An Introduction to Weather, Climate, and the Environment*, 5th ed., pp. 205-7; Tufty, Barbara. *1001 Questions Answered About Hurricanes, Tornadoes, and Other Natural Air Disasters*, p. 275.

• When and where do **thunderstorms** occur in the **United States**?

In the United States, thunderstorms usually occur in the late spring and summer, especially from May through August. The formation of thunderstorms requires warm, moist air, such as the tropical air masses that come from the Gulf of Mexico and move across the United States. Storms usually develop at the time of day when the surface air is warmest (2 to 4 p.m.).

Compared to other parts of the United States, thunderstorms are relatively rare in Alaska, New England, North Dakota, Montana, and other

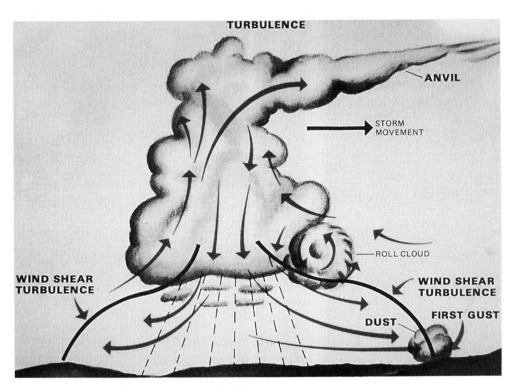

A diagram showing the cross-section of a thunderstorm.

northern states where the air is generally cold. These storms are also rare along the Pacific Coast, since the summertime air there is relatively dry.

Florida's Gulf Coast experiences the greatest number of thunderstorms of any U.S. location. Thunderstorms occur there on 130 days per year, on average. Throughout the rest of Florida, plus the Gulf Coasts of Alabama and Mississippi, thunderstorms occur between 80 and 100 days. The rest of the southeastern United States has thunderstorms approximately 60 to 80 days.

The rest of the country has the following annual average number of thunderstorm days: the central portion of the Rockies, 50 to 70; the Corn Belt (Iowa, Indiana, and Illinois) and Great Plains states (states just east of the Rockies), 50; the portion of the Midwest that lies east of Iowa, as well as the mid-Atlantic states and New England, 20 to 40.

Sources: Engelbert, Phillis. *The Complete Weather Resource*, vol. 2, pp. 216-17; *The Guinness Book of Records 1994*, p. 46; Schaefer, Vincent J., and John A. Day. *A Field Guide to the Atmosphere*, p. 25; Tufty, Barbara. *1001 Questions Answered About Hurricanes, Tornadoes, and Other Natural Air Disasters*, pp. 115-17.

Lightning over Tamworth, New South Wales, Australia.

• How hot is **lightning**?

The temperature of the air around a bolt of lightning is about 54,000° Fahrenheit (30,000° Celsius), which is six times hotter than the surface of the sun.

Remarkably, many people have been struck by lightning and survived. American park ranger Roy Sullivan, for example, was hit by lightning seven times between 1942 and 1977. As long as the lightning does not pass through the heart or spinal column, the victim of a lightning strike will most likely survive.

Sources: *How in the World?: A Fascinating Journey Through the World of Human Ingenuity*, p. 298; Magill, Frank N. *Magill's Survey of Science: Earth Science Series*, vol. 3, p. 1374.

• How is the distance between **lightning** and an observer calculated?

Count the number of seconds between seeing a flash of lightning and hearing thunder. Divide that number by 5 to determine how many miles away the lightning is. For instance, if 5 seconds has elapsed between seeing lightning and hearing thunder, the storm is one mile away.

Source: *World Book Encyclopedia*, vol. 19, p. 272.

> ## What *color* is *lightning?*
>
> Lightning takes on a range of colors, depending on conditions in the clouds and in the air.
>
> *Blue lightning* within a cloud indicates the presence of hail.
>
> *Red lightning* within a cloud indicates the presence of rain.
>
> *Yellow or orange lightning* occurs when there is a large concentration of dust in the air.
>
> *White lightning* is a sign of low humidity (amount of moisture in the air). White is the color of lightning that most often ignites forest fires.
>
> **Sources:** Burroughs, William J., et. al. *The Nature Company Guides: Weather*, p. 240; Field, Frank. *Doctor Frank Field's Weather Book*, p. 201.

• What is **ball lightning?**

Ball lightning is a rare and mysterious form of lightning. Numerous people throughout history claim to have seen it; however, it has never been photographed. Ball lightning is reported to look like a luminous white or colored sphere, from .4 to 40 inches (1 to 100 centimeters) in diameter. It is reported to last from a few seconds to several minutes, either hanging in the air or floating horizontally at a speed of about 10 feet per second. It either disappears silently or with a bang. Spheres have been reported to vanish harmlessly, or to pass into or out of rooms leaving a sign of their passage, such as a hole in a window pane.

There are various theories as to the cause of ball lightning. One recent theory claims that ball lightning is an "electromagnetic knot" created by the linked lines of magnetic force that form in the wake of an ordinary lightning bolt. Some scientists, however, suggest that ball lightning is merely an optical illusion experienced by people who have just witnessed ordinary lightning bolts.

Other types of lightning include the common streak lightning (a single or multiple zigzagging line from cloud to ground); forked lightning (lightning forming two branches simultaneously); sheet lightning (a shapeless flash that illuminates clouds); ribbon lightning (streak lightning blown sideways by the wind to make it appear like several parallel strokes); bead or chain lightning (a stroke that is blown by the wind and broken into evenly

---

How many **volts** are in **lightning**?

A stroke of lightning discharges up to several hundred million volts of electricity and produces a current up to several hundred thousand amperes. (Volts and amperes are measures of electricity.) In an average lightning stroke there are 30,000 amperes. By way of comparison, 240 volts and a current of 1 ampere flow through a 100-watt light bulb.

Sources: Robinson, Andrew. *Earthshock*, p. 148; Tufty, Barbara. *1001 Questions Answered About Hurricanes, Tornadoes, and Other Natural Air Disasters*, p. 126.

---

spaced segments or beads); and heat lightning (silent lightning from a storm which is too far away for the thunder to be heard).

Sources: Bair, Frank E. *The Weather Almanac*, 6th ed., p. 107; Browne, Malcolm W. "Scientists Still Baffled by the Ancient Mystery of Ball Lightning." *Ann Arbor News.* September 12, 1996, pp. D1+; Engelbert, Phillis. *The Complete Weather Resource*, vol. 2, p. 235; Great Britain Meteorological Office. *Meteorological Glossary*, p. 37.

• How large can **hailstones** become?

While most hailstones are the size of peas (about 0.25 in [0.63 cm] in diameter), they sometimes grow larger than softballs. Large hailstones have been responsible for destroying crops, breaking windows, and denting cars, and have caused the deaths of many people and animals.

The largest hailstones ever reported, weighing up to 7.5 pounds (3.4 grams), fell in the state of Hyderabad, India, in 1939. However, scientists believe that these huge hailstones may have been several stones that partially melted and stuck together. On April 14, 1986, hailstones weighing 2.5 pounds (1 kilogram) each were reported to have fallen in the Gopalgang district of Bangladesh.

The largest hailstone ever recorded in the United States fell in Coffeyville, Kansas, on September 3, 1970. It measured 5.57 inches (14.1 centimeters) in diameter and 17.2 inches (44 centimeters) in circumference, and weighed 1.67 pounds (0.75 kilogram).

Hailstones are balls of ice that fall from tall clouds, usually during thunderstorms. They are round, have either a smooth or jagged surface, and are totally or partially transparent. Hailstones usually are made of concentric, or onionlike, layers of ice alternating with partially melted and refrozen

Hailstones.

snow structured around a tiny central core. They are formed in thunderclouds when freezing water and ice cling to small particles in the air, such as dust. The winds in the cloud blow the particles through zones of different temperatures, causing them to accumulate additional layers of ice and melting snow and grow larger.

Sources: Battan, Louis J. *Weather in Your Life*, pp. 56-57; Engelbert, Phillis. *The Complete Weather Resource*, vol. 2, pp. 206-9; Tufty, Barbara. *1001 Questions Answered About Hurricanes, Tornados, and Other Natural Air Disasters*, pp. 151-53.

TORNADOES AND HURRICANES

• Which month is the most dangerous for **tornadoes** in the **United States?**

A tornado is a violent, destructive, whirling wind that is accompanied by a funnel-shaped cloud that progresses in a narrow path over land. Tornadoes occur every month of the year in the United States. They occur with the greatest frequency in the spring and early summer months, April through June, and with the lowest frequency in December and January. According to one study, May is the most dangerous month for tornadoes in the United States, with an average of 329.

Across the United States, tornadoes peak in frequency at various times. For instance, in the lower Great Plains states (Kansas, Oklahoma, and Texas) and from Iowa east to Ohio, tornadoes occur with the greatest frequency in April through June. In Nebraska and South Dakota, as well as in Pennsylvania, tornado season peaks in May through August. In North Dakota, Michigan, and the New England states, the greatest number of tornadoes occurs in June through August. In the Gulf Coast states, such as

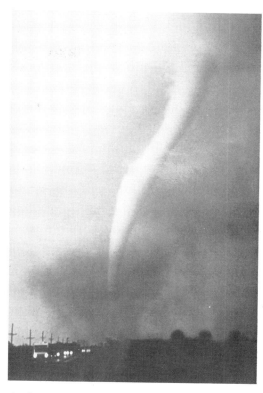

A photograph of a tornado that hit Union City, Oklahoma, on May 24, 1973.

Louisiana, Mississippi, and Alabama, tornadoes peak in March through May, with a secondary peak in November.

Sources: Bair, Frank E. *The Weather Almanac*, 6th ed., p. 83; *The Public Health Consequences of Disasters 1989*, p. 52; U.S. Department of Commerce. *Tornadoes . . . Nature's Most Violent Storms*.

• What is the **Fujita and Pearson Tornado Scale?**

The Fujita and Pearson Tornado Scale, otherwise known as the Fujita Scale of Tornado Intensity or simply the "Fujita Scale," categorizes tornadoes by their wind speed and the severity of damage they created. It also takes into account a tornado's path length and width. The Fujita scale places tornadoes into groups ranging from F0 (very weak) to F6 (inconceivable).

The Fujita Scale was created in the late 1960s by T. Theodore Fujita, a meteorology professor at the University of Chicago, and Allen Pearson, former director of the National Severe Storm Forecast Center.

F0—Light damage: damage to trees, billboards, and chimneys.

F1—Moderate damage: mobile homes pushed off their foundations and cars pushed off roads.

F2—Considerable damage: roofs torn off, mobile homes demolished, and large trees uprooted.

F3—Severe damage: even well-constructed homes torn apart, trees uprooted, and cars lifted off the ground.

F4—Devastating damage: houses leveled, cars thrown, and objects become flying missiles.

F5—Incredible damage: structures lifted off foundations and carried away; cars become missiles. Less than 2 percent of tornadoes are in this category.

F6—Maximum tornado winds are expected to exceed 318 miles per hour (511 kilometers per hour).

Fujita and Pearson Tornado Scale

Scale	Speed miles per hour	Path length in miles	Path width
0	<72	<1.0	<17 yards
1	73–112	1.0–3.1	18–55 yards
2	113–157	3.2–9.9	56–175 yards
3	158–206	10.0–31.0	176–556 yards
4	207–260	32.0–99.0	0.34–0.9 miles
5	261–318	100–315	1.0–3.1 miles
6	319–380	316–999	3.2–9.9 miles

Sources: Ahrens, C. Donald. *Meteorology Today: An Introduction to Weather, Climate, and the Environment*, 5th ed., pp. 417-18; Bair, Frank E. *The Weather Almanac*, 6th ed., p. 90; *The Public Health Consequences of Air Disasters 1989*, p. 40; Tufty, Barbara. *1001 Questions Answered About Hurricanes, Tornadoes, and Other Natural Air Disasters*, pp. 356-57.

• How are **hurricanes** classified?

Hurricanes are tropical cyclones with winds of 74 miles per hour or greater. They usually occur in the western Atlantic Ocean. The Saffir-Simpson Hurricane Damage-Potential scale is a tool for measuring the disaster potential of a hurricane's winds and its accompanying storm surge (the wall of water that rushes onshore as the eye of a hurricane passes overhead). The purpose of the scale is to help disaster agencies gauge the potential danger posed by these storms and to determine whether or not to evacuate coastal residents.

The scale, on which each hurricane is assigned a number 1 through 5, was developed in 1971. The creators of the scale are Herbert Saffir, the engineer who designed Miami's hurricane-proof building code, and Robert Simpson, former director of the National Hurricane Center.

Saffir-Simpson Hurricane Intensity Scale

| Scale number (category) | Central pressure | | Wind speed | | Storm surge | | Damage |
	mb	in.	mi/hr	km/hr	ft	m	
1	≥980	≥28.94	74–95	119–154	4–5	1–2	Minimal
2	965–979	28.50–28.91	96–110	155–178	6–8	2–3	Moderate
3	945–9643	27.91–28.47	111–130	179–210	9–12	3–4	Extensive
4	920–944	27.17–27.88	131–155	211–250	13–18	4–6	Extreme
5	<920	<27.17	>155	>250	>18	>6	Catastrophic

Damage categories:

Minimal—No real damage to building structures. Some tree, shrubbery, and mobile home damage. Coastal road flooding and minor pier damage.

Moderate—Some roof, window, and door damage. Considerable damage to vegetation, mobile homes, and piers. Coastal and low-lying escape routes flood two to four hours before center of storm arrives. Small craft can break moorings (equipment such as anchors) in unprotected areas.

Extensive—Some structural damage to small or residential buildings. Mobile homes destroyed. Flooding near coast destroys structures and flooding of homes 5 feet (1.5 meters) above sea level (level of the ocean's surface) as far inland as 6 miles (9.5 kilometers).

Extreme—Extensive roof, window, and door damage. Major damage to lower floors of structures near the shore, and some roof failure on small residences. Complete beach erosion. Flooding of terrain 10 feet (3 meters) above sea level as far as 6 miles (9.5 kilometers) inland requiring massive residential evacuation.

Catastrophic—Complete roof failure to many buildings; some complete building failure with small utility buildings blown away. Major damage to

A computer enhanced image of Hurricane Diana just off the coast of South and North Carolina, at its strongest on September 11, 1984. Winds within it were 130 mph (209 kph).

lower floors of all structures 19 feet (5.75 meters) above sea level located within 500 yds (547 meters) of the shoreline. Massive evacuation of residential areas on low ground 5 to 10 miles (8 to 16 kilometers) from shoreline may be required.

Sources: Bair, Frank E. *The Weather Almanac*, 6th ed., p. 42; *The Public Health Consequences of Disasters 1989*, p. 34; Williams, Jack. *The Weather Book*, p. 137.

• Which **U.S. hurricanes** have caused the most deaths?

The ten deadliest United States hurricanes are listed below.

Hurricane	Year	Deaths
1. Texas (Galveston)	1900	6,000
2. Florida (Lake Okeechobee)	1928	1,836
3. Florida (Keys/S. Texas)	1919	600–900+
4. New England	1938	600
5. Florida (Keys)	1935	408
6. Audrey (Louisiana/Texas)	1957	390
7. Northeast U.S.	1944	390
8. Louisiana (Grand Isle)	1909	350
9. Louisiana (New Orleans)	1915	275
10. Texas (Galveston)	1915	275

Source: *The Public Health Consequences of Disasters 1989*, p. 35.

• What were the deadliest and costliest **natural disasters** in **United States** history?

The deadliest natural disaster occurred when a hurricane struck Galveston, Texas, on September 8, 1900, killing over 6,000 people. Winds gusted to more than 100 miles (160 kilometers) per hour and a 20-foot storm surge (wall of water) crashed onto shore, entirely submerging the island. The hurricane dumped ten inches (25 centimeters) of rain on the island, as well. Almost every structure in town was leveled.

The costliest national disaster to date was Hurricane Andrew, which hit Florida on August 31, 1992, and Louisiana on September 1, 1992. Early warning kept the death toll to 58, but property damage came to over $30 billion. Over 200,000 homes and business were damaged or destroyed and 160,000 people were left homeless.

Sources: De Blij, Harm J. *Nature on the Rampage*, pp. 122; National Climatic Data Center. Billion Dollar U.S. Weather Disasters, 1980-1996. [Online] Available http://www.ncdc.noaa.gov/, November 19, 1996; *Newsweek*, vol. 120 (September 7, 1992), p. 23; Williams, Jack. *The Weather Book*, pp. 4-5.

• How do **hurricanes** get their **names**?

Since 1950, meteorologists (scientists who study weather and climate) have been assigning names to all hurricanes and tropical storms that form in the western North Atlantic Ocean, the Caribbean Sea, and the Gulf of Mexico. (A tropical storm is weaker than a hurricane and has maximum sustained winds of 39 to 73 miles per hour [63 to 117 kilometers per hour].) They have been naming eastern Pacific storms since 1959.

Names are assigned in advance for six-year cycles. The names are suggested by countries that lie in the path of hurricanes. The names must be approved by the Region 4 Hurricane Committee of the World Meteorological Organization, which is made up of representatives of countries affected by hurricanes. Once a tropical storm develops, staff members at the National Hurricane Center near Miami, Florida, automatically assign it the next name on the list.

After the six-year cycle has ended, hurricane names may be used again. The names of hurricanes that cause widespread damage, however, such as Gilbert, Gloria, Hugo, and Andrew, are taken off the list for at least ten years.

1996	1997	1998	1999	2000
Arthur	Ana	Alex	Arlene	Alberto
Bertha	Bill	Bonnie	Bret	Beryl
Cesar	Claudette	Charley	Cindy	Chris
Diana	Danny	Danielle	Dennis	Debbie
Edouard	Erika	Earl	Emily	Ernesto
Fran	Fabian	Frances	Floyd	Florence
Gustav	Grace	Georges	Gert	Gordon
Hortense	Henri	Hermine	Harvey	Helene
Isidore	Isabel	Ivan	Irene	Isaac
Josephine	Juan	Jeanne	Jose	Joyce
Klaus	Kate	Karl	Katrina	Keith
Lili	Larry	Lisa	Lenny	Leslie
Marco	Mindy	Mitch	Maria	Michael
Nana	Nicholas	Nicole	Nate	Nadine
Omar	Odette	Otto	Ophelia	Oscar
Paloma	Peter	Paula	Philippe	Patty
Rene	Rose	Richard	Rita	Rafael
Sally	Sam	Shary	Stan	Sandy
Teddy	Teresa	Tomas	Tammy	Tony
Vicky	Victor	Virginie	Vince	Valerie
Wilfred	Wanda	Walter	Wilma	William

Sources: Bair, Frank E. *The Weather Almanac*, pp. 44-45; Engelbert, Phillis. *The Complete Weather Resource*, vol. 2, pp. 289-90; *Weatherwise*, vol. 36 (August 1983), p. 179; Williams, Jack. *The Weather Book*, p. 145.

OPTICAL EFFECTS

• What is the order of colors in a **rainbow**?

A rainbow is composed of the entire spectrum of colors of visible light, from the longest wavelength, red, to the shortest wavelength, violet. The order of colors in a rainbow is easiest to remember by the following mnemonic (a formula that helps one remember something): ROY G. BIV. R=red, O=orange, Y=yellow, G=green, B=blue, I=indigo, and V=violet. Red is at the top edge of the rainbow and violet is at the bottom edge, with the other colors in between.

Rainbows are created both by reflection and refraction (bending) of sunlight in raindrops. As sunlight enters a raindrop, it bends and it is separated into its constituent colors (the colors that comprise white light [ROY G. BIV]. Some of the light—that which travels at a "critical" angle—is reflected off the back of the raindrop. (A "critical" angle is the angle at which sunlight must strike the back of the raindrop, in order to be reflected back to the front of the drop.) Each color strikes the back of the raindrop at a slightly different angle, thus each color emerges from the front of the raindrop at a slightly different angle.

Only one color exits from each raindrop at the exact angle necessary to reach the observer's eye. An observer sees only one color at a time reflecting from each raindrop. For this reason, it takes millions of raindrops to create a rainbow.

Sources: Ahrens, C. Donald. *Meteorology Today: An Introduction to Weather, Climate, and the Environment,* 5th ed., pp. 100-103; Engelbert, Phillis. *The Complete Weather Resource,* vol. 2, pp. 331, 333; Schaefer, Vincent J., and John A. Day. *A Field Guide to the Atmosphere,* p. 163; *World Book Encyclopedia,* vol. 16, p. 128.

• What is a **halo**?

A halo is a thin ring of light that sometimes appears around the sun or the moon. Halos are formed by the refraction (bending) of light as it passes through small, hexagonal (six-sided), pencil-shaped ice crystals high in the sky.

The two most common types of halo are the 22 degrees halo and the 46 degrees halo. The number of degrees in a halo refers to the angle by which light is refracted through the ice crystals. For instance, if light is bent at an

359

A solar halo seen above the Isle of Skye in Scotland.

angle of 22 degrees, it will form a circle of light with a radius (the length of a line segment from the center of a circle to its boundary) of 22 degrees. The 22-degree halo is smaller than the 46-degree halo and more tightly encircles the sun.

A 22-degree halo is formed by ice crystals that are randomly arranged. The light enters one of the six sides and exits through another of the six sides. The ice crystals that produce a 46-degrees halo are all arranged the same way, so that sunlight strikes one of a crystal's six sides and exits through one of its two ends.

Haloes may form at the leading edge of an advancing storm system. For that reason, they are often looked upon as a sign of rain. However, a halo is not an entirely reliable forecasting tool; the storm front may change direction or gently pass through without producing rain.

Sources: Ahrens, C. Donald. *Meteorology Today: An Introduction to Weather, Climate, and the Environment*, 5th ed., pp. 98-99; Engelbert, Phillis. *The Complete Weather Resource*, vol. 2, pp. 328-29.

• What are **sundogs** and **moon dogs**?

Sundogs, also called "mock suns" or "parahelia" (Greek for "beside the sun"), appear as one or two patches of light on either or both sides of the sun. Sundogs give the illusion that there are two or three suns in the sky. Sundogs may be white or colored, and often appear along the path of a 22 degrees halo (a thin ring of light around the sun).

These patches of light are occasionally seen around a very bright, full moon. In that case, they are called moon dogs.

Sundogs are produced by the refraction (bending) of sunlight through relatively large ice crystals. Sundogs and moon dogs form only in cold regions.

Sources: Ahrens, C. Donald. *Meteorology Today: An Introduction to Weather, Climate, and the Environment*, 5th ed., pp. 99-100; Engelbert, Phillis. *The Complete Weather Resource*, vol. 2, pp. 329-31.

Sunset and sun dogs over the frozen sea at Cape Churchill.

• When does the **green flash** phenomenon occur?

On rare occasions, the final portion of a setting sun appears bright green. This "green flash," as it is known, is due to both refraction (bending) and scattering (reflection in every direction) of sunlight in the atmosphere.

The different color components of sunlight, each having a different wavelength, are refracted to different degrees as sunlight passes through the Earth's atmosphere. Red light, which has the longest wavelength, is bent the least, and violet light, which has the shortest wavelength, is bent the most. In between these two extremes are (from longest to shortest wavelength): orange, yellow, green, blue, and indigo.

As the sun sets over the horizon, yellow, orange, and red (the colors bent the least) are the first wavelengths of light to disappear. However, they are usually the only colors of a setting sun that we see. This is because the colors that are bent the most (blue, indigo, and violet) are scattered by air molecules. Green is the shortest wavelength of sunlight not scattered in this way.

So why aren't green sunsets a regular occurrence? Air pollution. Dust and other particles that are usually present in the air scatter green light.

361

Your best chance to see the green flash is on a boat at sea, where the air is relatively clean and there is a distant, well-defined horizon.

Sources: *Weatherwise.* December 1996-January 1997, pp. 31-34. Forrester, Frank H. *1001 Questions Answered About the Weather,* p. 169.

• What is **Saint Elmo's fire?**

Saint Elmo's fire is a flash of light, most likely produced by an electrical discharge. It forms around tall, grounded metal objects, such as ship's masts, antennae, and chimney tops.

Because Saint Elmo's fire often occurs during thunderstorms, it has been suggested that the source of the electrical buildup is lightning. Another theory is that Saint Elmo's fire is initiated by weak static electricity, created when an electrified cloud touches a tall metal object. Molecules (particles made by the combination of two or more atoms) of gas in the air around the object then become ionized (take on an electrical charge) and glow.

This phenomenon was first described by sailors, who witnessed the display of spearlike or tufted flames on the tops of their ships' masts. It was named for Saint Elmo (originally called Saint Ermo), the patron saint of sailors.

Sources: Forrester, Frank. *1001 Questions Answered About the Weather,* pp. 182-83; Schaefer, Vincent J., and John A. Day. *A Field Guide to the Atmosphere,* p. 196.

• How does an **airplane** produce a **glory?**

A glory is a set of colored rings that appears on the top surface of a cloud, directly beneath the observer. Although it's possible to view a glory by climbing a mountain until you're above the clouds, it's much easier to look at one from an airplane window. Because they are most often seen from airplanes, glories are generally thought of as the rings of color that surround the shadow of an airplane.

A glory is not produced by an airplane, but by a complex process involving the interaction of sunlight and cloud droplets. First, sunlight is refracted (bent) as it enters a droplet. The refracted light then reflects off the back of the droplet. Next, the light skims the opposite surface of the droplet. As it follows the edge of the droplet, it bends slightly. The light then exits the droplet on a path that's parallel to its entry path.

As the sunlight bends around the droplet, it becomes separated into its constituent colors (the colors that comprise the white light [ROY G. BIV]). Red light, which has the longest wavelength, bends the least, and violet light, which has the shortest wavelength, bends the most. For this reason, the innermost ring of the glory appears purple and the outermost ring appears red, with the rest of the color spectrum lying in between.

Sources: Ahrens, C. Donald. *Meteorology Today: An Introduction to Weather, Climate, and the Environment*, 5th ed., pp. 105-7; Engelbert, Phillis. *The Complete Weather Resource*, vol. 2, pp. 336-37; Williams, Jack. *The Weather Book*, pp. 153-54.

FORECASTING AND CLIMATE

• When did the first **television** and **radio weather forecasts** take place?

The first televised weather forecast in the United States was on October 14, 1941. It appeared on WNBT (later WNBC) in New York City. The weather was presented by a cartoon character named "Wooly Lamb." Each day the lamb would sing a little song, after which a written forecast for the next day's weather would appear on the screen.

The first radio broadcast of a weather forecast was presented on January 3, 1921, by the University of Wisconsin's station 9XM in Madison, Wisconsin.

Sources: Fields, Alan. *Partly Sunny: The Weather Junkie's Guide to Outsmarting the Weather*, p. 9; Robertson, Patrick. *The Book of Firsts*, p. 200.

• How accurate are **forecasts**?

For most parts of the world, weather forecasts for 12 to 24 hours in advance are correct about 87 percent of the time; for 24 hours in advance they're correct about 80 percent of the time; and for 3 to 5 days in advance they're correct about 65 percent of the time (up from 55 percent in the mid-1980s).

Source: Christian, Spencer, and Tom Biracree. *Spencer Christian's Weather Book*, pp. 123-24.

• What is **nowcasting**?

Nowcasting is a form of very short-range weather forecasting, covering only a very specific geographic area. A nowcast is loosely defined as a forecast for the coming 12-hour period, based on very detailed observational data. A more restrictive definition of a nowcast is a detailed description of current weather conditions, from which one can extrapolate (project) the weather conditions for the following two hours.

Source: *McGraw-Hill Encyclopedia of Science and Technology*, 7th ed., vol. 12, p. 116.

• What is a **radiosonde**?

A radiosonde is an electronic instrument package that hangs beneath a hydrogen- or helium-filled weather balloon. The instruments in a radiosonde are used to measure temperature, air pressure, and relative humidity as they float upward to a maximum height of 19 miles (30.6 kilometers). (Relative humidity is the amount of moisture in the air, expressed as a percentage of how much moisture are can hold at a given temperature.) Attached to radiosondes are radio transmitters, which continuously send upper-air readings back to weather stations on the ground.

Some radiosondes, called rawinsondes, emit a signal so their location can be tracked by radar on the ground. The path of a rawinsonde gives an indication of how wind speed and wind direction change with height.

Radiosondes in the United States contain parachutes, so they can gently drift back to the ground. Each radiosonde comes with a prepaid mail bag and instructions, and a request that the finder return it to the National

Weather Service (NWS). About 20 percent of all radiosondes are returned to the NWS and reused.

Sources: Burroughs, William J., et. al. *The Nature Company Guides: Weather*, pp. 74, 100; Christian, Spencer, and Tom Biracree. *Spencer Christian's Weather Book*, pp. 115-16; Engelbert, Phillis. *The Complete Weather Resource*, vol. 3, p. 409.

• Is the **world** actually getting **warmer**?

By most indications, we are in a warming trend. According to the National Aeronautics and Space Administration (NASA), 1995 was the hottest year on record. The average temperature around the world was approximately 59.8° Fahrenheit , which is .8° higher than the average temperature for the years 1950 to 1980. And since the 1880s, the world's eight warmest years have all taken place since 1979.

On the other hand, annual average temperatures in the continental United States have varied from decade to decade, with no significant upward or downward trend throughout the century. The United States began the century with cool temperatures, the 1920s through 1950s were warm, the 1960s and 1970s were cool, and the 1980s were warm.

Sources: *Ann Arbor News.* July 14, 1996, pp. A1+; *Chemical and Engineering News*, vol. 70 (April 27, 1992), pp. 7-8; Famighetti, Robert, ed. *The World Almanac and Book of Facts 1992*, p. 206; Leggett, Jeremy. *Global Warming*, p. 18; Williams, Jack. *The Weather Book*, p. 186.

SPACE

| EARTH AND SUN

• How hot is the **sun**?

The surface, or photosphere, of the sun is about 10,000° Fahrenheit (5,500° Celsius). Cool, dark areas of magnetic disturbance that erupt on the photosphere, called sunspots, are only about 6,700° Fahrenheit (4,000° Celsius).

The layer of the sun's atmosphere that lies just beyond the photosphere, called the chromosphere, is only about 1,900 miles (3,000 kilometers) thick. Where it meets the photosphere, the chromosphere is about 7,800° Fahrenheit (4,300° Celsius). The temperature rises throughout the chromosphere. Where the chromosphere merges with the sun's outermost atmospheric layer, the corona, it is about 180,000° Fahrenheit (100,000° Celsius). Temperatures rise to 3,600,000° Fahrenheit (2,000,000° Celsius) in the part of the corona that's farthest from the sun.

The sun is hottest at its center—about 27,000,000° Fahrenheit (15,000,000° Celsius)!

Sources: Abell, George O. *Realm of the Universe*, 5th ed., pp. 225-28; Asimov, Isaac. *Isaac Asimov's Guide to Earth and Space*, pp. 159-61; Moore, Patrick. *Atlas of the Solar System*, p. 19.

• When will the **sun** die?

The sun is about 4.5 billion years old and it is estimated to still possess a 5-billion year supply of hydrogen (hydrogen is the fuel that drives nuclear fusion on the sun). Therefore, it is predicted that our sun will die in approximately 5 billion years.

Once the sun has converted all its hydrogen into helium, the sun will change from its current form, a yellow dwarf, into a red giant. As a red giant, its diameter will extend well beyond the orbit of Venus, and even possibly beyond the orbit of Earth. When the sun enters the red giant phase, in which it will spend the final 10 percent of its lifetime, the Earth will be burned to a cinder.

Sources: Pasachoff, Jay M. *Contemporary Astronomy*, pp. 205-6; *The Universal Almanac 1992*, pp. 482-83.

• When do **solar eclipses** happen?

A solar eclipse occurs when the moon passes between the Earth and the sun, and all three bodies exist in a straight line. There are three types of solar eclipse: total, annular, and partial. In a total eclipse the sun is completely blocked from view; in an annular eclipse a ring of sunlight is visible around the silhouette of the moon; and in a partial eclipse only part of sun is blocked from view.

During a solar eclipse, the shadow of the moon sweeps across the Earth. There are two parts to the moon's shadow: the central, dark part called the umbra, and the lighter region that surrounds the umbra, the penumbra. In a total eclipse, the umbra covers a portion of the Earth. The portion of the Earth's surface across which the umbra travels, called the "track of totality," is just 100 to 200 miles (160 to 320 kilometers) wide.

During totality, which averages 2.5 minutes but may last up to 7.5 minutes, the sky is dark and stars and planets are easily seen. The corona, the sun's outer atmosphere, is also visible. Just before totality, the only parts of the sun that are visible are a few points of light called Baily's beads, shining through valleys on the moon's surface. Sometimes a last bright flash of sunlight, called the diamond ring effect, occurs just before totality.

If the moon is at a point along its orbit where it's relatively far from Earth, it may not appear large enough in the sky to completely cover the sun. It is this condition that produces an annular eclipse. Although the sky

> ### When will the next *total solar eclipse* be visible in the **United States**?
>
> The next total solar eclipse will occur on August 21, 2017, across a 70-mile- (113-km-) wide path stretching from Salem, Oregon, to Charleston, South Carolina.
>
> **Sources:** Brewer, Bryan. *Eclipse*, 2nd ed., p. 89; *Weatherwise*, vol. 47, no. 2 (April-May 1994), p. 28.

may darken, it will not be dark enough to see the stars. Nor will the sun's corona be visible during an annular eclipse.

During a partial eclipse the moon covers only part of the sun. Since only the penumbra of the moon's shadow strikes the Earth, the sky does not darken noticeably. A partial eclipse can be seen on either side of the track of totality of an annular or total eclipse.

Sources: Abell, George O. *Realm of the Universe*, 5th ed., pp. 75-84; Menzel, Donald H., and Jay M. Pasachoff. *A Field Guide to Stars and Planets*, 2nd ed., pp. 404-10; Moore, Patrick. *International Encyclopedia of Astronomy*, p. 382.

• What is the safest way to view a **solar eclipse**?

Punch a pinhole in an index card and hold it 2 to 3 feet in front of another index card. The projected image of the eclipse can be viewed safely on the bottom index card. Adjust the distance between the two cards to bring the image into focus. There are also special glasses with aluminized Mylar lenses that may be purchased.

Damage to the eye's retina can occur if the eclipse is viewed directly or with inappropriate equipment like photographic filters, exposed film, smoked glass, camera lenses, telescopes, or binoculars.

Sources: *Pittsburgh Post-Gazette*, May 9, 1994, sec. A, p. 6; *Sky and Telescope*, vol. 87 (May 1994), pp. 73-74.

• What is the **distance from Earth** to the **sun**?

The sun is, on average, 92,955,630 miles (149,597,870 kilometers) from Earth. That distance has been designated an astronomical unit (AU) and is used as a standard for measuring distances to other bodies in the solar system. If a bridge to the sun existed, it would take 177 years, driving at a constant 60 miles per hour (97 kilometers per hour), to get there.

Sources: *The Facts On File Dictionary of Astronomy*, 1994, pp. 34, 325; Rovin, Jeff. *Laws of Order*, p. 213; *The Universal Almanac 1992*, p. 531.

• Is it true that during the Northern Hemisphere winter, the **Earth is closer to the sun** than it is during the Northern Hemisphere summer?

Yes. Seasons exist because the Earth's axis, the line around which the planet rotates, is tilted at an angle of 23.5 degrees with respect to the Earth's plane of revolution around the sun. (A plane is an imaginary surface running through all points along an orbit.) When Earth is closest to the sun, about January 3, the Northern Hemisphere is tilted away from the sun. Thus, it is winter in the Northern Hemisphere and summer in the Southern Hemisphere.

When the Earth is farthest from the sun, around July 4, the situation is reversed and the Northern Hemisphere tilts toward the sun. At this time it is summer in the Northern Hemisphere and winter in the Southern Hemisphere.

Sources: Magill, Frank N. *Magill's Survey of Science* (Earth Science Series), vol. 1, p. 401; *McGraw-Hill Encyclopedia of Science and Technology*, 7th ed., vol. 5, p. 524.

• What is the **circumference of the Earth**?

The Earth is an oblate ellipsoid, meaning it is a sphere that is slightly flattened at the poles and bulging at the equator. The distance around the Earth at the equator is 24,902 miles (40,075 kilometers). The distance around the Earth through the poles is 24,860 miles (40,008 kilometers).

Sources: *The New Encyclopaedia Britannica*, 15th ed., vol. 4, p. 320; *Science and Technology Illustrated*, vol. 9., p. 1049.

• What is **solar wind**?

Solar wind is the outflow of charged particles from the sun's outer atmosphere (corona). The charged particles, or ions, are created under the conditions of extreme heat that exist in the corona—up to 3.6 million degrees Fahrenheit (2 million degrees Celsius). Atoms within the gases of the corona heat up, collide, and lose electrons. Solar wind is a state of matter called plasma, which is different from a solid, liquid, or gas.

The solar wind flows away from the sun at a speed of 310 miles (500 kilometers) per second. As solar wind approaches Earth and other planets, it gets caught up in the planetary magnetosphere. The magnetosphere is the region surrounding a planet, occupied by the lines of force of its magnetic field. The magnetosphere protects a planet from the effects of solar wind.

In 1959, the Soviet spacecraft *Luna 2* confirmed the existence of solar wind and made the first measurements of its properties.

Sources: Engelbert, Phillis. *Astronomy and Space: From the Big Bang to the Big Crunch*, vol. 3, pp. 572-73; *The Facts on File Dictionary of Astronomy*, 3rd ed., p. 352; *World Book Encyclopedia*, vol. 18, pp. 581-82.

• What are **auroras** and how often do they appear?

Auroras are displays of colored light in the night sky, which typically occur in polar regions. There are two types of aurora: the Aurora borealis (Northern Lights) and the Aurora australis (Southern Lights).

Auroras are produced when charged particles from the sun, called solar wind, enter the Earth's atmosphere. This stream of particles becomes trapped for a time in the outermost parts of the Earth's magnetic field, eventually spiraling down toward the north and south magnetic poles. In the process they ionize (create an electric charge within) the oxygen and nitrogen gas in the atmosphere, causing the atmosphere to glow.

There is no fixed frequency with which auroras occur. Auroras are dependent upon solar wind, which in turn is dependent upon sunspot activity. Sunspots are dark areas of magnetic disturbance on the surface of the sun. It has been shown that during times of greatest sunspot activity, the sun ejects the greatest concentration of charged particles. And it is during this time of greatest solar activity that auroras are most likely to appear.

Sources: Engelbert, Phillis. *Astronomy and Space: From the Big Bang to the Big Crunch*, vol. 1, pp. 44-45; Hopkins, Jeanne. *Glossary of Astronomy and Astrophysics*, p. 10; *World Book Encyclopedia*, vol. 1, pp. 891-92.

Aurora borealis.

| PLANETS AND MOONS

• How old is the **solar system**?

Current estimates put the age of the solar system at 4.5 billion years. There have been several theories advanced, over time, as to the origin of the solar system. The most widely accepted theory today is called the "modified nebular hypothesis." It claims that the solar system was formed from an immense cloud of gas and dust (a nebula). Gravity and rotational forces caused the cloud to flatten into a disc.

Much of the cloud's mass drifted into the center and became the sun. The left over parts of the cloud formed small bodies called planetesimals. These planetesimals collided with each other, gradually forming larger and larger bodies, some of which became the planets. This process is thought to have taken about 25 million years.

Sources: Moore, Patrick. *Atlas of the Solar System*, pp. 10-11; Van Andel, Tjeerd H. *New Views On an Old Planet*, p. 28.

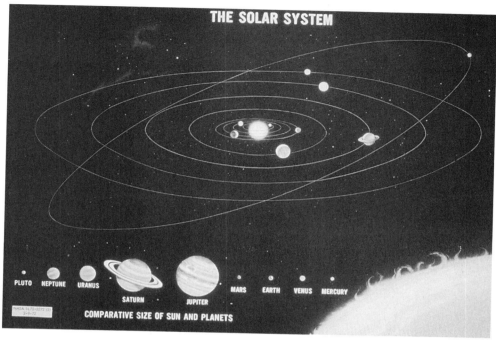

An illustration showing the orbits of the planets in the solar system (top) and their comparative sizes (bottom).

• How far are the **planets** from the **sun?**

The planets revolve around the sun in elliptical (oval-shaped) orbits. The sun does not sit at the center of the ellipse, rather it is situated near one of the elongated ends. Thus, a planet is closer to the sun at some points along its orbit and farther from the sun at other points along its orbit.

The table below lists each planet's average distance from the sun. It begins with Mercury, the planet closest to the sun, and continues with planets successively farther from the sun.

Planet	Average distance	
	Miles	Kilometers
Mercury	35,983,000	57,909,100
Venus	67,237,700	108,208,600
Earth	92,955,900	149,598,000
Mars	141,634,800	227,939,200
Jupiter	483,612,200	778,298,400
Saturn	888,184,000	1,427,010,000

| Planet | Average distance | |
	Miles	Kilometers
Uranus	1,782,000,000	2,869,600,000
Neptune	2,794,000,000	4,496,700,000
Pluto	3,666,000,000	5,913,490,000

Sources: Beatty, J. Kelly, Brian O'Leary, and Andrew Chaikin. *The New Solar System*, p. 219; *The Guinness Book of Answers*, 8th ed., p. 14.

• What are the diameters of the **planets?**

The nine planets differ tremendously in diameter. The four gaseous planets—Jupiter, Saturn, Uranus, and Neptune—are by far the largest of the nine planets. And, with the exception of Pluto, these four gas giants are the farthest from the sun. In the following list, diameters are measured at each planet's equator.

| Planet | Diameter | |
	Miles	Kilometers
Mercury	3,031	4,878
Venus	7,520	12,104
Earth	7,926	12,756
Mars	4,221	6,794
Jupiter	88,846	142,984
Saturn	74,898	120,536
Uranus	31,763	51,118
Neptune	31,329	50,530
Pluto	1,423	2,290

Sources: *The Guinness Book of Answers*, 8th ed., p. 15; Moore, Patrick. *Atlas of the Solar System*, p. 442.

• What are the colors of the **planets?**

As you can see in the following list, there is a virtual rainbow of colors in the sky represented by the planets.

Planet	Color
Mercury	Orange
Venus	Yellow
Earth	Blue, brown, green

Saturn and its rings.

Planet	Color
Mars	Red
Jupiter	Yellow, red, brown, white
Saturn	Yellow
Uranus	Green
Neptune	Blue
Pluto	Yellow

Sources: Curtis, Anthony R. *Space Almanac*, p. 580; Moore, Patrick. *International Encyclopedia of Astronomy*, p. 120

• Which **planets** have **rings**?

Jupiter, Saturn, Uranus, and Neptune all have rings. Jupiter's rings were discovered by the interplanetary space probe *Voyager 1* in March 1979. The rings extend 80,240 miles (129,130 kilometers) from the center of the planet. They are about 4,300 miles (7,000 kilometers) wide and less than 20 miles (30 kilometers) thick. A faint inner ring is believed to extend to the edge of Jupiter's atmosphere.

Saturn has the largest, most spectacular set of rings in the solar system. Saturn's rings were first recognized by Dutch astronomer Christiaan Huygens (1629–1695) in 1659 and were examined in detail by the *Voyager 1* and *Voyager 2* missions in 1980 and 1981. Saturn's rings are about 41,168 miles (66,400 kilometers) wide and 169,800 miles (273,200 kilometers) in diameter, but less than 10 miles (16 kilometers) thick. There are six different rings, the largest of which appears to be divided into thousands of ringlets. The rings appear to be composed mainly of frozen water—in the form of snowflakes, snowballs, hailstones, and icebergs—ranging in size from 3 inches to more than 10 yards in diameter.

In 1977, when Uranus occulted (passed in front of) a star, scientists observed that the light from the star flickered or winked several times before the planet totally blocked the star from view. The same flickering occurred as Uranus continued on its path and the star came back into view. The reason for this flickering was determined to be the presence of rings around Uranus. Nine rings were initially identified and *Voyager 2* discovered two more in 1986, bringing the total to eleven. The rings are thin, narrow, and very dark.

Voyager 2 also discovered a series of at least five very faint rings around Neptune in 1989. The rings are made up of particles, some of which are greater than one mile in diameter and are considered "moonlets." Where these particles clump together, they create relatively bright areas called "arcs."

Sources: Abell, George O. *Realm of the Universe*, 5th ed., p. 193; Famighetti, Robert, ed. *The World Almanac and Book of Facts 1996*, pp. 279-81; *The Guinness Book of Answers*, 8th ed., pp. 19-22; Hamilton, Calvin J. Voyager Uranus Science Summary: December 21, 1988, [Online] Available http://bang.lanl.gov/solarsys/vgrur.htm; *The Planetary Report*, vol. 12, no. 2 (March-April 1992) pp. 4-9; Rudd, Richard. Voyager Project Home Page. [Online] Available http://vraptor.jpl.nasa.gov/voyager/voyager.html July 2, 1996.

• How many **moons** does each **planet** have?

All planets except Mercury and Venus have at least one moon. Saturn has the greatest number of moons—18. In 1995, the Hubble Space Telescope detected what appeared to be four additional moons of Saturn; however, that discovery has yet to be confirmed.

Planet	Number of Moons	Names of Moons
Mercury	0	
Venus	0	
Earth	1	The Moon (sometimes called Luna)
Mars	2	Phobos, Deimos

Planet	Number of Moons	Names of Moons
Jupiter	16*	Metis, Adrastea, Amalthea, Thebe, Io, Europa, Ganymede, Callisto, Leda, Himalia, Lysithia, Elara, Ananke, Carme, Pasiphae, Sinope
Saturn	18*	Atlas, 1981S13 (unnamed as yet), Prometheus, Pandora, Epimetheus, Janus, Mimas, Enceladus, Ththys, Telesto, Calypso, Dione, Helene, Rhea, Titan, Hyperion, Iapetus, Phoebe
Uranus	15	Cordelia, Ophelia, Bianca, Cressida, Desdemona, Juliet, Portia, Rosalind, Belinda, Puck, Miranda, Ariel, Umbriel, Titania, Oberon
Neptune	8	Naiad, Thalassa, Despina, Galatea, Larissa, Proteus, Triton, Nereid
Pluto	1	Charon

*Several other satellites have been reported but not confirmed.

Sources: Famighetti, Robert, ed. *World Almanac and Book of Facts 1996*, pp. 279-80; *The Universal Almanac 1992*, pp. 17-22.

• How long do the **planets** take to go around the **sun**?

There is a tremendous variation among the planets in the time it takes to complete a single revolution around the sun. For planets that are closer to the sun than Earth is, a year is shorter than an Earth year; for planets that are farther from the sun than Earth is, a year is longer than an Earth year.

Planet	Period of revolution	
	Earth days	Earth years
Mercury	88	0.24
Venus	224.7	0.62
Earth	365.26	1.00
Mars	687	1.88
Jupiter	4,332.6	11.86
Saturn	10,759.2	29.46
Uranus	30,685.4	84.01
Neptune	60,189	164.8
Pluto	90,777.6	248.53

Sources: *The Guinness Book of Answers*, 8th ed., p. 13; Pasachoff, Jay M. *Contemporary Astronomy*, p. A6.

• Is a day the same on all **planets**?

No. A day, the period of time it takes for a planet to make one complete turn on its axis, varies from planet to planet. A day on Venus, Mercury, and

Pluto is several times longer than a day on Earth. A Martian day is closest in length to our own. The rest of the planets have shorter days than we do.

Planet	Earth Days	Length of Day Hours	Minutes
Mercury	58	15	30
Venus	243		32
Earth		23	56
Mars		24	37
Jupiter		9	50
Saturn		10	39
Uranus		17	14
Neptune		16	03
Pluto	6	09	18

Source: *The Guinness Book of Answers*, 8th ed., p. 15.

• How can an observer distinguish **planets** from **stars**?

In general, planets emit a constant light or shine, whereas stars appear to twinkle. The twinkling effect of stars is due to the refraction, or bending, of starlight as it passes through the Earth's atmosphere. And because stars are so far away and appear only as points of light, the twinkling is very noticeable.

Light from planets is also refracted by the Earth's atmosphere. However, because the planets are closer to Earth than the stars, the planets appear as disks. Their disklike shapes mask the twinkling effect. The exception to this rule occurs when planets are observed near the horizon. Near the horizon, the light from planets must travel through the greatest depth of Earth's atmosphere, which causes the planets to appear to twinkle.

Source: *The Encyclopedia Americana*, p. 594.

• Is it true that **Pluto** is not always the outermost **planet** in the solar system?

Yes. Pluto travels on a tilted orbit that crosses the plane shared by all other planetary orbits. (A plane is an imaginary surface that runs through all the points of an orbit.) Although Pluto's orbit is usually outside that of its closest neighbor, Neptune, at times it crosses over Neptune's orbit. For example, Pluto moved inside Neptune's orbit on January 23, 1979, making Neptune the farthest planet from the sun. Pluto will remain inside Neptune's orbit until March 15, 1999.

Pluto was discovered in 1930 by American astronomer (a scientist specializing in the study of matter in outer space) Clyde Tombaugh (1906–). It is by far the smallest planet in the solar system, with a diameter of 1,457 miles (2,344 kilometers). Pluto is thought to be composed of rock and water ice. There are bright areas on the planet's surface, which are probably nitrogen ice, solid methane, and carbon monoxide. Pluto has a thin atmosphere, which is most likely made of nitrogen, carbon monoxide, and methane.

Pluto has a single moon, Charon, discovered by American astronomer James Christy in 1978. Charon (pronounced "Karen") has a diameter of 741 miles (1,192 kilometers). This makes Charon, at half the size of Pluto, a very large moon relative to its planet. Because of Charon's large size, some astronomers consider Pluto and Charon to be a double planet system.

Sources: *The Ann Arbor News*, March 8, 1996, p. A6; Arnett, Bill. Pluto. [Online] Available http://seds.lpl.arizona.edu/billa/tnp/pluto.html, March 14, 1996; *The Guinness Book of Answers*, 8th ed., p. 22; Miller, Ron, and William K. Hartmann. *The Grand Tour: A Traveler's Guide to the Solar System*, pp. 126-27; Moore, Patrick. *Atlas of the Solar System*, pp. 396-97.

• What is **Planet X**?

There are presently nine known planets in the solar system. It is possible that a tenth planet, referred to as "Planet X," exists and is waiting to be discovered.

Soon after German astronomer (a scientist specializing in the study of matter in outer space) William Herschel discovered Uranus in 1781, scientists noticed that Uranus was changing direction from its predicted orbit. This led them to hypothesize that there was another planet out there, the gravitational field of which was tugging at Uranus. The next planet, Neptune, was discovered in 1841 independently by English astronomer John Couch Adams and French astronomer Urbain Leverrier. The existence of Neptune, however, was not able to totally explain Uranus's orbital disturbances. Neptune showed movement away from its predicted orbit, as well. The search for Planet X continued.

The next planet to be discovered, by American astronomer Clyde Tombaugh (1906–) in 1930, was Pluto. Pluto was at first believed to be

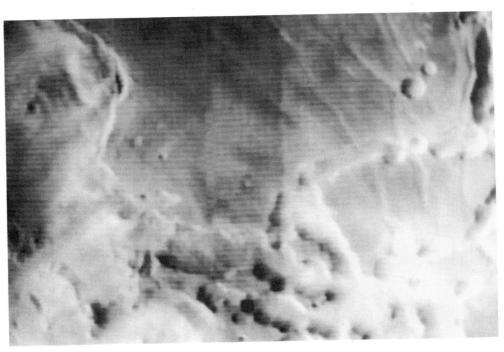

A photograph of the surface of Mars taken by one of the _Viking_ Landers.

Planet X. It was soon realized, however, that Pluto is much too small to influence the orbits of objects the size of Uranus or Neptune.

This leads to the question: Is there a Planet X still out there? While there have been no sightings of this tenth planet, the search continues. There is a possibility that the deep space probes _Pioneer 10_ and _11_ and _Voyager 1_ and _2_, now heading out of the solar system, will be able to locate this elusive object.

Sources: Engelbert, Phillis. _Astronomy and Space: From the Big Bang to the Big Crunch_, vol. 2, pp. 444-45; Golob, Richard. _Almanac of Science and Technology: What's New and What's Known_, p. 82; Moore, Patrick. _Atlas of the Solar System_, p. 397

• Is there life on **Mars?**

Three experiments conducted on the composition of the Martian soil and atmosphere carried out by the Viking Lander in July 1976 offered no evidence of life on Mars. However, new findings have raised the possibility that there may have once been life on the red planet.

In early August 1996, a team of nine researchers led by the National Aeronautics and Space Administration (NASA) detected possible evidence of ancient Martian life. This evidence is contained in a Martian meteorite that landed on Earth 13,000 years ago.

In 1984, American scientists in Antarctica discovered the four-and-a-half-billion-year-old, squash-sized chunk of rock (named ALH 84001). They originally identified it as a fragment of an asteroid (a rocky chunk of material in orbit around the sun). Ten years later scientists took another look at the rock and found that its chemical composition matched that of the surface of Mars.

Researchers discovered tiny, sausage-shaped markings on ALH 84001 that resemble the fossilized bacteria found in rocks on Earth. They believe these particles, which are only the size of a billionth of a pinhead, may be remains of primitive Martian life.

It remains to be determined whether these findings are, in fact, evidence of ancient life on Mars. In an attempt to answer that question, NASA has begun a renewed program of exploration of Mars. Over the next decade NASA will launch a series of spacecraft to orbit Mars and land on its surface. The Mars Pathfinder, which landed on Mars on July 4, 1997, and Mars Global Surveyor, which was launched on November 7, 1996, and will reach Mars on September 11, 1997, missions will be followed by the launchings of two spacecraft every two years until 2005. These missions will focus on studying the conditions for the emergence of life on Mars, particularly the history of climate and water. Starting in 2005, missions will collect rocks from three regions on Mars. It is expected that the first samples will be returned to Earth during the same year. These robotic explorations will pave the way for a human expedition sometime around 2020.

Sources: Beatty, J. Kelly. Life from Ancient Mars? *Sky and Telescopes Weekly News Bulletin: Special Edition.* [Online] Available http://www.skypub.com/news/marslife.html, August 8, 1996; Engelbert, Phillis. *Astronomy and Space: From the Big Bang to the Big Crunch*, vol. 2, pp. 356-57; NASA Mars Pathfinder Homepage [Online] Available http://mpfwww.jpl.nasa/gov/defautl.html, August 17, 1997.

• How far is the **moon** from the Earth?

Since the moon's orbit is elliptical (oval-shaped), its distance varies from about 221,463 miles (356,334 kilometers) at perigee (closest approach to Earth) to 251,968 miles (405,503 kilometers) at apogee (farthest point).

A photograph of the Earth rising over the moon taken by the *Apollo* 8 spacecraft.

The average distance from the moon to the Earth is 238,857 miles (384,392 kilometers).

Sources: *McGraw-Hill Encyclopedia of Science and Technology,* 7th ed., vol. 5, p. 470; *The Universal Almanac 1992,* p. 16.

• What are the **phases of the moon?**

A phase of the moon is defined by the shape of the illuminated portion of the moon, as it appears to observers on Earth. The moon's appearance changes throughout the month, as it travels on its orbit around the Earth. The relative positions of the sun, Earth, and moon determine which portion of the moon's sunlit surface can be seen.

When the moon is between the Earth and the sun, its daylight side is turned away from the Earth, so the moon can't be seen at all. This is called the "new moon." As the moon continues its revolution around the Earth, a slice of its surface becomes visible. This is called the "waxing crescent" phase. About a week after the new moon, half the moon is visible. This is the "first quarter" phase.

> ### *Why does the **moon** always keep the same face toward the Earth?*
>
> Only one side of the moon is seen because it takes the exact same length of time for the moon to rotate once about its axis, as it does to complete one revolution around the Earth. The result of this combination of motions (called "captured rotation") is that the moon always keeps the same side toward Earth.
>
> **Sources:** Moore, Patrick. *Atlas of the Solar System*, p. 147; Pickering, James S. *1001 Questions Answered About Astronomy*, p. 23.

During the following week, more than half the surface of the moon can be seen; this is called the "waxing gibbous" phase. Finally, about two weeks after the new moon, the moon and sun are on opposite sides of the Earth. The side of the moon facing the sun is also facing the Earth, and the moon's entire illuminated side is seen as a "full moon."

For the rest of the month, the moon goes through the reverse process, appearing as a progressively smaller portion of a circle. During the third week the moon is in the "waning gibbous" phase; at the end of that week it appears as a half-circle and is called a "third quarter" moon. It then enters the "waning crescent" phase. Less and less of the moon is visible each day until a new moon occurs again.

Sources: Abell, George O. *Realm of the Universe*, 5th ed., pp. 72-73; Menzel, Donald H., and Jay M. Pasachoff. *A Field Guide to Stars and Planets*, pp. 318-22.

• Is the **moon** really blue during a **blue moon**?

A blue moon is the second full moon in a single month. The term does not refer to the color of the moon.

A blue moon occurs, on average, every 2.72 years. Since 29.53 days pass between full moons, there can never a blue moon in February because this month only contains 28 days. On rare occasions, a blue moon can be seen twice in one year, but only in certain parts of the world. The next pair of blue moons will occur in 1999, during the months of January and March.

Sometimes the moon does appear bluish; however, this effect is caused by the way moonlight is scattered as it enters the Earth's atmosphere. A

383

A photograph of a full moon taken by the *Apollo 17* spacecraft.

bluish moon was observed was on September 26, 1950, due to Canadian forest fires which had released dust and soot high into the atmosphere.

Sources: *Country Journal*, vol. 15 (May 1988), p. 14; Moore, Patrick. *International Encyclopedia of Astronomy*, p. 83.

• Why do **lunar eclipses** happen?

A lunar eclipse occurs only during a full moon when the moon and sun are on opposite sides of the Earth and all three bodies exist in a straight line. In this configuration the Earth blocks the sun's rays, thus casting a shadow on the moon. The Earth, moon, and sun only rarely line up in this manner because the plane of the Earth's orbit around the sun is different from the plane of the moon's orbit around the Earth. (A plane is an imaginary surface that runs through all the points of an orbit.) Only once every six months or so do these planes intersect, creating the conditions required for an eclipse.

In a total lunar eclipse the Earth's shadow completely covers the moon and the moon seems to disappear from the sky. A total lunar eclipse may last up to 1 hour and 40 minutes.

If only part of the moon is covered by the Earth's shadow, a partial eclipse occurs. It is difficult to detect this type of eclipse from Earth. However, if you were standing on the moon it would appear that the Earth was blocking part of the sun.

Sources: Abell, George O. *Realm of the Universe*, 5th ed., p. 84; *World Book Encyclopedia*, vol. 6, p. 49.

METEORS, ASTEROIDS, AND COMETS

• How does a **meteorite** differ from a **meteor**?

A meteorite is a natural object that comes from space, survives the passage through the Earth's atmosphere, and hits the Earth's surface. It is a chunk of rock and/or metal that has broken off a larger space object, such as an asteroid (rocky chunks of matter in orbit around the sun) or comet (a luminous celestial body that has a tail and follows an orbit around the sun). The primary metals in meteorites are iron and nickel. Meteorites range in size from pebbles to three-ton chunks.

Meteorites are often mistakenly called meteors. Meteors, also known as "shooting stars," are small particles that burn up as they enter the Earth's atmosphere. Meteors originate as dust or tiny rocks ejected by a comet's tail. A meteor looks like streak of light across the sky, never reaching the ground.

"Meteoroid" is the term that collectively describes all forms of meteoric material, including meteors and meteorites.

Sources: Engelbert, Phillis. *Astronomy and Space: From the Big Bang to the Big Crunch*, vol. 2, pp. 374-75; Moore, Patrick. *Atlas of the Solar System*, pp. 406-7; *The Planetary Report*, vol. 2, no. 6 (November-December 1991), pp. 8-11.

• When do **meteor showers** occur?

Meteors, also called "shooting stars" (the streaks we see cross the sky on clear summer nights), are small particles of dust left behind by a comet's tail (a comet is a celestial body that has a tail and follows an orbit around the

385

sun). Although some meteors streak through the sky every day and night, meteor activity greatly intensifies ten times during the year. These periods are known as "meteor showers" and occur when the Earth passes through the orbit of a comet or the debris left behind by a comet.

Meteor showers are named for the area of sky, or constellation, where the meteors originate. Listed below are ten meteor showers and when they can be seen.

Name of Shower	Dates
Quadrantids	January 1–6
Lyrids	April 19–24
Eta Aquarids	May 1–8
Perseids	July 25–August 18
Orionids	October 16–26
Taurids	October 20–November 20
Leonids	November 13–17
Phoenicids	December 4–5
Geminids	December 7–15
Ursids	December 17–24

Source: Rovin, Jeff. *Laws of Order*, p. 217.

• What are the **largest meteorites** that have been found in the world?

A meteorite is a chunk of rock and/or metal that has broken off a larger space object, such as an asteroid (rocky chunks of matter in orbit around the sun) or comet (celestial bodies that have tails and follow an orbit around the sun), and strikes the Earth's surface. The famous Willamette (Oregon) iron, displayed at the American Museum of Natural History in New York, is the largest specimen found in the United States. It is 10 feet (3.05 meters) long and 5 feet (1.52 meters) high. This and other weighty meteorites are listed below.

Name	Location	Weight	
		Tons	Tonnes
Hoba West	Namibia	66.1	60
Ahnighito (The Tent)	Greenland	33.5	30.4
Bacuberito	Mexico	29.8	27

Name	Location	Weight	
		Tons	Tonnes
Mbosi	Tanzania	28.7	26
Agpalik	Greenland	22.2	20.1
Armanty	Outer Mongolia	22	20
Willamette	Oregon, USA	15.4	14
Chupaderos	Mexico	15.4	14
Campo del Cielo	Argentina	14.3	13
Mundrabilla	Western Australia	13.2	12
Morito	Mexico	12.1	11

Source: Moore, Patrick. *Atlas of the Solar System*, p. 406.

• Where are **asteroids** found?

Asteroids, also called "minor planets," are rocky chunks of matter in orbit around the sun. They are smaller than any of the nine major planets and they are not moons of any major planet. Some asteroids are as small as 0.62 miles (1 kilometer) in diameter. The term asteroid means "starlike" because asteroids appear as points of light when seen through a telescope.

Most asteroids are located in belts that lie between the orbits of Mars and Jupiter, at a distance of 2.1 to 3.3 AUs from the sun. (An AU is an astronomical unit, the distance between the Earth and sun, about 92 million miles.) Other asteroids, called Trojan asteroids, exist in two clusters, one on either side of Jupiter. And the Apollo asteroids cross Earth's orbit, sometimes even coming closer than the moon. There is yet another group of asteroids that crosses the orbits of several planets.

Ceres, the first asteroid to be discovered, is also the largest known asteroid with a diameter of 582 miles (936 kilometers). Ceres was discovered on January 1, 1801, by an Italian monk, Giuseppe Piazzi. A second asteroid, Pallas, was discovered in 1802 by German scientist Heinrich Olbers. Since then, more than 18,000 asteroids have been identified and astronomers have determined orbits for about 5,000 of them.

Originally, astronomers thought the asteroids were remnants of a planet that had been destroyed. However, it turns out that asteroids are so small that even if all known asteroids were combined, they would form an object much smaller than our moon. Astronomers now believe that asteroids are ancient chunks of matter that originated with the formation of our solar system, but never came together to form a planet.

Sources: Menzel, Donald H., and Jay M. Pasachoff. *A Field Guide to Stars and Planets*, 2nd ed., pp. 243-45; *The Planetary Report*, vol. 11, no. 6 (November-December 1991), pp. 8-11; *Scientific American*, vol. 265, no. 4 (October 1991), pp. 88-94.

• What was the **Tunguska Event**?

On June 30, 1908, a violent explosion occurred in the atmosphere over the Podkamennaya Tunguska River in a remote part of central Siberia. The blast's consequences were similar to a hydrogen bomb explosion. It sent up a mushroom cloud, leveled thousands of square miles of forest, and wiped out a herd of reindeer. The shock of the explosion shattered windows 600 miles (960 kilometers) away. A number of theories have been proposed to account for this event.

Some people thought that a large meteorite or a piece of antimatter had fallen to earth. (Antimatter is a substance that is the opposite of matter; it is believed that when matter and antimatter come into contact, they destroy each other.) However, a meteorite, composed of rock and metal, would have created a crater and none was found at the impact site. Nor were high radiation levels, which would have resulted from the collision of antimatter and matter, detected in the area.

Two other theories include: a small-black hole striking the Earth or the crash of an extraterrestrial spaceship. (A black hole is the remains of a massive star, which has become transformed into a single point of infinite mass and gravity.) However, a small-black hole would have passed straight through the Earth, and there is no record of a corresponding explosion on the other side of the world. As for the spaceship, no wreckage of such a craft was ever found.

The most likely cause of the explosion was the entry into the atmosphere of an asteroid or a piece of a comet. Either of these would have produced a large fireball and blast wave. If the asteroid had exploded in midair, it would not have carved a crater in the ground. And since a comet is composed primarily of ice, the fragment would have melted during its passage through the Earth's atmosphere, also leaving no impact crater. Since the Tunguska Event coincided with the Earth's passage through the orbit of Comet Encke, the explosion may have been caused by a piece of that comet.

Sources: Angelo, Joseph A. *The Extraterrestrial Encyclopedia*, Rev. and updated ed., p. 220; Calder, Nigel. *The Comet Is Coming*, pp. 124-26; Engelbert, Phillis. *Astronomy and Space: From the Big Bang to the Big Crunch*, vol. 1, p. 38.

This 1927 photograph of the site of the Tunguska event shows how devastating the damage was.

• Where do **comets** originate?

The most commonly accepted theory about where comets (celestial bodies that have tails and follow an orbit around the sun) originate was developed by Dutch astronomer (a scientist specializing in the study of matter in outer space) Jan Oort in 1950. According to Oort, trillions of inactive comets lie on the outskirts of the solar system, between 50,000 and 150,000 AUs from the sun. (An AU is an astronomical unit, the distance between the Earth and sun, about 92 million miles.) They remain there in a large cloud of gas and dust, called an Oort cloud, until a passing star or gas cloud jolts a comet into orbit around the sun.

In 1951, another Dutch astronomer, Gerard Kuiper, suggested that a second cometary reservoir exists just beyond the orbit of Pluto, around 1,000 times closer to the sun than the Oort cloud. His proposed Kuiper belt is located somewhere between 35 and 1,000 AUs from the sun. It is believed to contain an estimated 10 million to 1 billion comets.

Comets, sometimes called "dirty snowballs," are made of clumps of rocky material, dust, frozen methane, ammonia, and water. When a comet moves closer to the sun, the dust and ice of the core (nucleus) heats up, producing a tail of material which trails along behind it. The tail is swept back by the solar wind (outflow of charged particles from the sun) and always points away from the sun.

Most comets have highly elliptical (oval-shaped) orbits that carry them around the sun and then fling them out to the outer reaches of the solar system, never to return. Occasionally however, a comet is drawn into a smaller orbit as it passes by a planet and is influenced by that planet's gravitational field.

A comet that remains within the solar system and passes close to the sun at regular intervals is called a "short-period comet." The most famous short-period comet is Halley's comet which reaches perihelion (the point in its orbit nearest to the sun) about every 76 years.

Sources: Abell, George O. *Realm of the Universe*, 5th ed., pp. 210-15; Horgan, John. "Beyond Neptune: Hubble Telescope Spots a Vast Ring of Ice Protoplanets." *Scientific American*, October 1995, pp. 24+; Miller, Ron, and William K. Hartmann. *The Grand Tour: A Traveler's Guide to the Solar System*, pp. 173-79; Sagan, Carl, and Ann Druyan. *Comet*, p. 5; Weissman, Paul R. "Comets at the Solar System's Edge." *Sky and Telescope*, January 1993, pp. 26-29.

• What is **Comet Hale-Bopp**?

Comet Hale-Bopp was discovered on July 23, 1995, by amateur astronomers (scientists specializing in the study of matter in outer space) Alan Hale and Thomas Bopp. This comet astounded astronomers around the world, as it was the brightest comet to pass by Earth in about 400 years. Comet Hale-Bopp was visible to the naked eye for more than 8 months. It was visible in the early morning sky in the fall and winter of 1996, and in the early evening sky in the early spring of 1997.

At 25 miles (40 kilometers) across, Comet Hale-Bopp is a relatively large comet. In contrast, Comet Hyakutake, the comet that passed by Earth in the spring of 1996, was only about 1 mile across. However, since Hale-Bopp never came closer than 120 million miles to Earth and Hyakutake came within 10 million miles of Earth, the two comets appeared equally bright in the night sky.

Sources: *Astronomy*, vol. 24 (February 1996), pp. 68-73; Grantham, Russell. "Now showing at a Sky Near You: The Comet." *The Ann Arbor News*, March 8, 1997, pp. A1+.

• When will **Halley's comet** return?

Halley's comet comes close to Earth about every 76 years. It was most recently seen in 1985 and 1986 and is predicted to appear again in 2061. Every appearance of what is now known as Comet Halley has been recorded by astronomers (scientists specializing in the study of matter in outer space) since the year 239 B.C.

The comet is named for famed English astronomer Edmund Halley (1656–1742). In 1682, Halley observed a bright comet and noted that it was moving along an orbit similar to comets that had been noted in 1531 and 1607. He concluded that the three comets were actually one, and that the comet completed an orbit around the sun once every 76 years.

In 1705, Halley published *A Synopsis of the Astronomy of Comets* in which he predicted that this comet would return in 1758. On Christmas night, 1758, a German farmer and amateur astronomer named Johann Palitzsch spotted the comet in the precise area of the sky that Halley had foretold.

Prior to Halley's study of comets, no one knew where comets came from or what paths they followed. Comets were often thought to be evil omens or signs of impending disaster. Halley proved that they are natural objects subject to the laws of gravity.

Sources: Moore, Patrick. *International Encyclopedia of Astronomy*, p. 177; Sagan, Carl, and Ann Druyan. *Comet*, p. 364.

STARS, GALAXIES, AND THE UNIVERSE

• Which **star** is closest to Earth?

The sun, at a distance of about 92 million miles, is the closest star to Earth. After the sun, the closest stars are the members of the triple star system known as Alpha Centauri (Alpha Centauri A, Alpha Centauri B, and Alpha Centauri C, sometimes called Proxima Centauri). They are 4.3 light-years away. (A light-year is the distance light travels in one year, about 5.9 trillion miles.)

Sources: Flaste, Richard, ed. *The New York Times Book of Science Literacy: What Everyone Needs to Know From Newton to Knuckleball*, p. 19; Moore, Patrick. *International Encyclopedia of Astronomy*, p. 22.

• How are **stars born** and how do they **die?**

A star is formed from the condensation of a hot cloud of gas and dust in space. When the cloud gets hot and dense enough, fusion—the combination of hydrogen atoms into helium atoms—begins to occur, producing starlight. Depending on the size of the cloud, a single star, a binary star (a system of two stars that orbit around a common center of gravity), or a cluster of stars may be formed.

The main phase of a star's life lasts as long as a star has plenty of hydrogen fuel. A star enters the final 10 percent of its life once its hydrogen supply runs low. What happens next is determined by the size of the star.

An average-sized star, like our sun, will spend its final phase as a red giant. In the red giant phase, the star takes on a reddish color and its diameter expands by ten to one thousand times its original size. The star's surface temperature drops to between 3,140° Fahrenheit and 6,741° Fahrenheit (1,727° Celsius and 3,727° Celsius).

The star's atmosphere eventually dislodges. This leaves the Earth-sized glowing core, called a white dwarf, to cool for eternity.

The second possibility, which applies to a star at least 1.4 times as massive as the sun, is that once it runs out of fuel it will undergo a supernova explosion, shedding much of its mass. In most cases the star will then end up as an extremely dense, compact, neutron-filled body called a neutron star. The fate of the most massive stars is the subject of the next question.

Sources: Abell, George O. *Realm of the Universe*, 5th ed., pp. 373-77; Engelbert, Phillis. *Astronomy and Space: From the Big Bang to the Big Crunch*, vol. 3, pp. 621-22.

• What is a **black hole?**

A black hole is a single point in space where pressure and density are infinite. It is the remains of a massive star (a star at least two or three times the mass of our sun) that has burned out its nuclear fuel and collapsed under tremendous gravitational force. Any object—even light—that gets too close to a black hole gets pulled in, stretched to infinity, and remains forever trapped. While black holes are impossible to see, they may account for 90 percent of the content of the universe.

The concept of black holes was introduced by English geologist (a scientist specializing in the origin, history, and structure of the Earth) John Michell and French astronomer (a scientist specializing in the study of outer space) Pierre-Simon Laplace in the late eighteenth century. Scientists first called black holes "gravitationally collapsed objects." Russian scientists later re-named them "collapsars." It wasn't until 1969 that American physicist (a scientist specializing in the interaction between matter and energy) John Wheeler came up with the name "black holes." Black holes have been popularized by the research of mathematics professor Stephen Hawking of Cambridge University in England.

A black hole can be detected only if it exists near another star. In that arrangement, the black hole draws matter from the other star into itself and, in the process, emits tremendous quantities of X-rays.

A black hole may exist in our galaxy, beside a star called Cygnus X-1. Cygnus X-1, which gives off intense X-rays, is believed to be a member of a binary star system—an arrangement in which two stars exist close together and orbit each other around a common point of gravity. It is possible that the star paired with Cygnus X-1 is actually a black hole and is pulling material away from Cygnus X-1.

Sources: *Astronomy*, November 1991, pp. 51-55; *Encyclopedic Dictionary of Science*, p. 46; *The Facts on File Dictionary of Astronomy*, 3rd ed., pp. 50-52; Hathaway, Nancy. *The Friendly Guide to the Universe*, pp. 253-58; Moore, Patrick. *The International Encyclopedia of Astronomy*, pp. 64, 81.

• What does the **color of a star** indicate?

The color of a star is an indication of its brightness, temperature, and age. Stars are classified into groups called "spectral types." From oldest to youngest and hottest to coolest, the types of stars are:

Type	Color	Temperature Fahrenheit	Celsius
O	Blue	45,000-75,000	25,000-40,000
B	Blue	20,800-45,000	11,000-20,000
A	Blue-white	13,500-20,000	7,500-11,000
F	White	10,800-13,500	6,000-7,500
G	Yellow	9,000-10,800	5,000-6,000
K	Orange	6,300-9,000	3,500-5,000
M	Red	5,400-6,300	3,000-3,500

Each spectral type is further subdivided on a scale of 0 to 9. The sun, for instance, is a type G2 star.

Sources: *The Guinness Book of Answers*, 8th ed., p. 11; Rovin, Jeff. *Laws of Order*, p. 214.

• What is the **Big Dipper**?

The Big Dipper, called "the Plough" in Great Britain, is a group of seven stars which are part of the constellation Ursa Major. (A constellation is one of 88 groups of stars in the sky, named for mythological beings.) The stars of the Big Dipper appear to form a spoon with a long handle.

The Big Dipper is almost always visible in the night sky in the Northern Hemisphere (the half of the globe north of the equator). It serves as a convenient reference point for locating other stars. For example, if you draw an arc between the three stars forming the Big Dipper's handle, and extend that arc from the last star in the handle, you'll come to Arcturus, one of the closest, brightest stars in the sky. It is part of the constellation Bootes.

Source: Booth, Nicholas. *The Concise Illustrated Book of Planets and Stars*, p. 30.

• How many **constellations** are there and how were they named?

There are 88 constellations—groups of stars in the sky—which are named for mythological beings. Although some constellations may resemble the animals or people they are named for, others were merely named in honor of those figures. The constellations are spread throughout the whole celestial sphere, the imaginary sphere in space that surrounds the Earth.

Constellations are visible on any clear night. The particular constellations you can see depends on your location, the time of year, and the time of night. As the Earth makes its daily rotation about its axis and its yearly revolution around the sun, the celestial sphere appears to shift. As a result, different constellations come into view.

Until 1930, the constellations had no fixed boundaries. In that year the International Astronomical Union defined limits for the constellations that are still accepted today. These boundaries are imaginary lines, running north to south and east to west across the entire celestial sphere. Every point in the sky exists within one of the sections that is named for the constellation it contains.

The naming of constellations began in ancient times. Alexandrian (Egyptian) astronomer (a scientist specializing in the study of matter in outer space) Ptolemy, in A.D. 1400, indexed the original 48 constellations. All of these except one are still considered constellations. Several new constellations were defined in later centuries, mostly in previously unexplored parts of the sky in the Southern Hemisphere (the portion of the Earth south of the equator).

Many of the constellations were originally given Greek names. These names were later replaced by their Latin translations, names by which they are still known today. Some of these include Aquila (the Eagle); Cancer (the Crab); Cygnus (the Swan); and Leo (the Lion).

Individual stars in a constellation are usually assigned Greek letters in the order of brightness: the brightest star is alpha, the second brightest is beta, and so on. The possessive (or genitive) form of the constellation name is used in individual stars. Alpha Orionis, for example, is the brightest star in the constellation Orion.

Constellation	Genitive	Abbreviation	Meaning
Andromeda	Andromedae	And	Chained Maiden
Antlia	Antliae	Ant	Air Pump
Apus	Apodis	Aps	Bird of Paradise
Aquarius	Aquarii	Aqr	Water Bearer
Aquila	Aquilae	Aql	Eagle
Ara	Arae	Ara	Altar
Aries	Arietis	Ari	Ram
Auriga	Aurigae	Aur	Charioteer
Boötes	Boötis	Boo	Herdsman
Caelum	Caeli	Cae	Chisel
Camelopardalis	Camelopardalis	Cam	Giraffe
Cancer	Cancri	Cnc	Crab
Canes Venatici	Canum Venaticorum	CVn	Hunting Dogs
Canis Major	Canis Majoris	CMa	Big Dog

Constellation	Genitive	Abbreviation	Meaning
Canis Minor	Canis Minoris	CMi	Little Dog
Capricornus	Capricorni	Cap	Goat
Carina	Carinae	Car	Ship's Keel
Cassiopeia	Cassiopeiae	Cas	Queen of Ethiopia
Centaurus	Centauri	Cen	Centaur
Cepheus	Cephei	Cep	King of Ethiopia
Cetus	Ceti	Cet	Whale
Chamaeleon	Chamaeleonis	Cha	Chameleon
Circinus	Circini	Cir	Compass
Columba	Columbae	Col	Dove
Coma Berenices	Comae Berenices	Com	Berenice's Hair
Corona Australis	Coronae Australis	CrA	Southern Crown
Corona Borealis	Coronae Borealis	CrB	Northern Crown
Corvus	Corvi	Crv	Crow
Crater	Crateris	Crt	Cup
Crux	Crucis	Cru	Southern Cross
Cygnus	Cygni	Cyg	Swan
Delphinus	Delphini	Del	Dolphin
Dorado	Doradus	Dor	Goldfish
Draco	Draconis	Dra	Dragon
Equuleus	Equulei	Equ	Little Horse
Eridanus	Eridani	Eri	River Eridanus
Fornax	Fornacis	For	Furnace
Gemini	Geminorum	Gem	Twins
Grus	Gruis	Gru	Crane
Hercules	Herculis	Her	Hercules
Horologium	Horologii	Hor	Clock
Hydra	Hydrae	Hya	Hydra, Greek monster
Hydrus	Hydri	Hyi	Sea Serpent
Indus	Indi	Ind	Indian
Lacerta	Lacertae	Lac	Lizard
Leo	Leonis	Leo	Lion
Leo Minor	Leonis Minoris	LMi	Little Lion
Lepus	Leporis	Lep	Hare
Libra	Librae	Lib	Scales
Lupus	Lupi	Lup	Wolf
Lynx	Lyncis	Lyn	Lynx
Lyra	Lyrae	Lyr	Lyre or Harp

Constellation	Genitive	Abbreviation	Meaning
Mensa	Mensae	Men	Table Mountain
Microscopium	Microscopii	Mic	Microscope
Monoceros	Monocerotis	Mon	Unicorn
Musca	Muscae	Mus	Fly
Norma	Normae	Nor	Carpenter's Square
Octans	Octanis	Oct	Octant
Ophiuchus	Ophiuchi	Oph	Serpent Bearer
Orion	Orionis	Ori	Orion, the Hunter
Pavo	Pavonis	Pav	Peacock
Pegasus	Pegasi	Peg	Winged Horse
Perseus	Persei	Per	Perseus, a Greek hero
Phoenix	Phoenicis	Phe	Phoenix
Pictor	Pictoris	Pic	Painter
Pisces	Piscium	Psc	Fish
Piscis Austrinus	Piscis Austrini	PsA	Southern Fish
Puppis	Puppis	Pup	Ship's Stern
Pyxis	Pyxidis	Pyx	Ship's Compass
Reticulum	Reticuli	Ret	Net
Sagitta	Sagittae	Sge	Arrow
Sagittarius	Sagittarii	Sgr	Archer
Scorpius	Scorpii	Sco	Scorpion
Sculptor	Sculptoris	Scl	Sculptor
Scutum	Scuti	Sct	Shield
Serpens	Serpentis	Ser	Serpent
Sextans	Sextantis	Sex	Sextant
Taurus	Tauri	Tau	Bull
Telescopium	Telescopii	Tel	Telescope
Triangulum	Trianguli	Tri	Triangle
Triangulum Australe	Triangli Australis	TrA	Southern Australe Triangle
Tucana	Tucanae	Tuc	Toucan
Ursa Major	Ursae Majoris	UMa	Big Bear
Ursa Minor	Ursae Minoris	UMi	Little Bear
Vela	Velorum	Vel	Ship's Sail
Virgo	Virginis	Vir	Virgin
Volans	Volantis	Vol	Flying Fish
Vulpecula	Vulpeculae	Vul	Little Fox

Sources: Engelbert, Phillis. *Astronomy and Space: From the Big Bang to the Big Crunch*, vol. 1, pp. 108-11; Famighetti, Robert, ed. *The World Almanac and Book of Facts 1996*, pp. 287-88; *The Universal Almanac 1992*, pp. 484-85.

An artist's impression of our galaxy, the Milky Way, seen edge-on.

• What is the **Milky Way**?

The Milky Way is a hazy band of light that can be seen arcing across the night sky. This light comes from the stars that make up the Milky Way galaxy, the galaxy to which the sun, the Earth, and our entire solar system belong. The Milky Way contains at least 100 billion stars, possibly one or more black holes, planets, glowing nebulae (clouds), dust, and empty space.

Astronomers (scientists specializing in the study of matter in outer space) estimate that the Milky Way galaxy is about 80,000 to 100,000 light-years in diameter and 2,000 light-years thick (a light-year is the distance light travels in one year, about 5.9 trillion miles). The Milky Way is classified as a "spiral galaxy"—it is shaped like a phonograph record with a central bulge, or nucleus, and spiral arms curving out from the center.

Sources: *The Facts On File Dictionary of Astronomy*, 3rd ed., p. 283; Hathaway, Nancy. *The Friendly Guide to the Universe*, p. 303.

> ## Which *galaxy* is closest to us?
>
> The Andromeda Galaxy is the galaxy closest to our own Milky Way galaxy. The Andromeda is estimated to be 2.2 million light-years away from Earth. (A light-year is the distance light travels in one year, about 5.9 trillion miles.) Bigger than the Milky Way, Andromeda is a spiral-shaped galaxy. It is the only galaxy other than the Milky Way that is visible in the night sky without a telescope.
>
> **Source:** Curtis, Anthony. *Space Almanac*, 1990, p. 768.

• How **old** is the **universe?**

The universe is all matter and energy including the Earth, the galaxies, and the contents of space, regarded as a whole. Recent data collected by the Hubble Space Telescope suggest that the universe may be only 8 billion years old. This contradicts the previous belief the universe is somewhere between 15 billion and 20 billion years old.

The 8-billion-year figure was derived using Hubble's constant, which is the rate of expansion of the universe. Hubble's constant is calculated by dividing the speed at which a galaxy is moving away from Earth by its distance from Earth. The age of the universe can be calculated by working backward from the present—that is, divide the galaxy's distance from Earth by that galaxy's recessional speed. In this way, you can determine a time when all matter existed at a single point.

The velocity (speed of motion) with which galaxies are moving, their distances from Earth, and the rate of universal expansion are all mere approximations. Therefore, many scientists believe that the age of the universe cannot be calculated with any certainty.

Sources: Brennan, Richard P. *Dictionary of Scientific Literacy*, pp. 310-11; *Science*, vol. 266, December 23, 1994, p. 1928; Van Andel, Tjeerd H. *New Views on an Old Planet*, p. 28.

• What was the "Big Bang"?

The Big Bang theory is the explanation most commonly accepted by astronomers (scientists specializing in the study of matter in outer space) for the origin of the universe. It proposes that the universe began 15 to 20 billion years ago as a single point that underwent a tremendous explosion, called the Big Bang. Particles were spewed forth and became the building blocks of matter. In time, this matter came together in huge clumps to form the galaxies. Smaller clumps within the galaxies formed stars. Parts of at least one clump of matter became the planets of our solar system.

The first piece of hard evidence in support of the Big Bang theory was provided in 1929 by American astronomer Edwin Hubble (1889–1953). Hubble demonstrated that the universe is expanding. Soon thereafter, Belgian astronomer Georges-Henri Lemaître (known as the "Father of the Big Bang") determined that if the universe is expanding, then by going back in time one would find that everything began at a single point.

The Big Bang theory received a boost in 1948, when Russian-born American physicist (a scientist specializing in the interaction between matter and energy) George Gamow deduced that if a bang had occurred, it would have left traces of background radiation. By the present era, Gamow argued, that radiation would have cooled to just a few degrees above absolute zero (the lowest possible temperature at which matter can exist, equal to -273° Celsius or -459° Fahrenheit). Gamow's theory was confirmed in the mid-1960s by radio engineers Arno A. Penzias (1933–) and Robert W. Wilson (1936–) of Bell Telephone Laboratories. Penzias and Wilson detected faint radiation, coming from all parts of the sky, matching that which Gamow had described.

Sources: Abell, George O. *Realm of the Universe*, 5th ed., pp. 447-59; *McGraw-Hill Encyclopedia of Science and Technology*, 7th ed., vol. 2, pp. 550-52; *World Book Encyclopedia*, vol. 4, p. 1078.

• What is a **pulsar**?

A pulsar is a rapidly spinning, blinking neutron star. It gives off sharp regular pulses of radio waves at a rate of up to one thousand times per second. "Pulsar" is the abbreviated form of "pulsating radio source." When the first pulsar was discovered, it was almost mistaken for communication attempts by an alien civilization.

A neutron star is the extremely dense, compact, neutron-filled remains of a massive star—a star with at least 1.4 times the mass of the sun. When such a star reaches the end of its lifetime, it undergoes a supernova explosion. It then folds in on itself, becoming so compact that it measures only about 12 miles (20 kilometers) across. In the process, the protons and electrons in the star become converted into neutrons.

Neutron stars spin extremely fast. For example, a neutron star in the Crab nebula (a huge cloud of gas and dust in the constellation Taurus) rotates about 30 times per second. This spinning generates a magnetic field and the star spews radio waves out of its magnetic poles. If the magnetic axis is tilted in a certain way, the spinning star's on-and-off signal is visible from Earth.

Pulsar signals were first detected in 1967 by Jocelyn Bell (1943–) and Antony Hewish (1924–) of Cambridge University. The link between pulsars and neutron stars was made by astronomers Thomas Gold (1920–) of Cornell University and his associate, Franco Pacini.

Hundreds of pulsars have now been identified. Many of these are in locations where a supernova is known to have occurred. Scientists believe that more than 100,000 pulsars may exist in our galaxy.

Sources: *Astronomy*, November 1991, pp. 51-55; Engelbert, Phillis. *Astronomy and Space: From the Big Bang to the Big Crunch*, vol. 2, pp. 460-61; Menzel, Donald H., and Jay M. Pasachoff. *A Field Guide to Stars and Planets*, 2nd ed., pp. 112-14.

• What are **quasars**?

The name quasar is short for *quasi*-stellar radio source. Quasars are extremely bright, starlike objects that emit various types of radiation, including radio waves. Quasars are the oldest known objects in the universe.

Quasars appear to be faint, close stars, but in reality they are extremely distant. They are moving away from Earth at tremendous speeds, some at up to 90 percent of the speed of light. (The speed of light is 186,282.397 miles

A photograph of Quasar 3C273, the first quasar found.

per second.) Because a quasar is so far away, it takes several billion years for its light to reach Earth. And these mysterious objects are so bright that they shine with more light than 100 galaxies combined.

Quasars were first identified in 1963 by astronomer (a scientist specializing in the study of matter in outer space) Maarten Schmidt (1929–) at the Palomar Observatory in California. Schmidt noted that a star-like object he was studying had a tremendous redshift. A redshift is the shift of an object's visible light spectrum toward the red-wavelength-end. It indicates that the object is moving away from the observer.

The exact nature of quasars is still unknown, but many believe quasars to be the cores of distant galaxies or objects formed by collisions between two galaxies.

Sources: Engelbert, Phillis. *Astronomy and Space: From the Big Bang to the Big Crunch*, vol. 3, pp. 487-89; Hartmann, William, and Ron Miller. *Cycles of Fire*, pp. 154-57; Trefil, James. *1001 Things Everyone Should Know About Science*, p. 259.

SPACE TRAVELERS AND SPACECRAFT

• Who was the **first man in space**?

Yuri Gagarin (1934–1968), a cosmonaut from the former Soviet Union, became the first man in space on April 12, 1961. Gagarin made a full orbit of the Earth in the spacecraft *Vostok I*. Gagarin's flight lasted only 1 hour and 48 minutes. As the first man in space, he became an international hero.

The first American in space was Alan B. Shepard Jr. (1923–). On May 5, 1961, Shepard flew aboard *Freedom 7*. This flight only reached an altitude of 116.5 miles (187.45 kilometers), which is below the altitude necessary to orbit the Earth.

On May 25, 1961, U.S. president John F. Kennedy (1917–1963) announced that the United States would land a man on the moon before the end of the decade. The United States took its first step toward that goal when it launched the first American into orbit on February 20, 1962. Astronaut John H. Glenn Jr. (1921–), completed three orbits in *Friendship 7* and traveled about 81,000 miles (130,329 kilometers).

Source: *The Cambridge Encyclopedia of Space*, pp. 50-55.

• Which **astronauts** have walked on the **moon**?

Twelve astronauts, all from the United States, have walked on the moon. Each Apollo flight had a crew of three. One crew member remained in orbit in the command service module (CSM) while the other two actually landed on the moon.

Apollo 11, July 16-24, 1969
> Neil A. Armstrong
> Edwin E. Aldrin, Jr.
> Michael Collins (CSM pilot, did not walk on the moon)

Apollo 12, November 14-24, 1969
> Charles P. Conrad
> Alan L. Bean
> Richard F. Gordon, Jr. (CSM pilot, did not walk on the moon)

Apollo 14, January 31-February 9, 1971
> Alan B. Shepard, Jr.
> Edgar D. Mitchell
> Stuart A. Roosa (CSM pilot, did not walk on the moon)

Apollo 15, July 26-August 7, 1971
> David R. Scott
> James B. Irwin
> Alfred M. Worden (CSM pilot, did not walk on the moon)

Apollo 16, April 16-27, 1972
> John W. Young
> Charles M. Duke, Jr.
> Thomas K. Mattingly, II (CSM pilot, did not walk on the moon)

Apollo 17, December 7-19, 1972
> Eugene A. Cernan
> Harrison H. Schmitt
> Ronald E. Evans (CSM pilot, did not walk on the moon)

Sources: Curtis, Anthony R. *Space Almanac*, pp. 30, 43, 66; Magill, Frank N. *Magill's Survey of Science* (Space Exploration Series), vol. 1, pp. 28-32.

• Who were the **first man and woman** to **walk in space**?

A spacewalk, also called an extravehicular activity, is an activity performed in space by an astronaut attached by a tether to the outside of a spacecraft. On March 18, 1965, cosmonaut Alexei Leonov (1934–) of the former Soviet Union became the first person to walk in space. He spent ten minutes outside his *Voskhod 2* spacecraft. The first woman to walk in space was Soviet cosmonaut Svetlana Savitskaya (1947–). During her second flight aboard the *Soyuz T-12*, on July 17, 1984, she performed 3.5 hours of extravehicular activity.

The first American to walk in space was Edward White II (1930–1967), from the spacecraft *Gemini 4*, on June 3, 1965. Kathryn D. Sullivan (1951–) became the first American woman to walk in space on October 11, 1984. Sullivan spent 3.5 hours outside the *Challenger* orbiter during the space shuttle mission 41G.

American astronaut Bruce McCandless II (1937–) performed the first untethered space walk from the space shuttle *Challenger* on February 7, 1984. He wore a manual maneuvering unit (MMU) backpack.

Sources: *The Guinness Book of Records 1994*, p. 92; Hawthorne, Douglas B. *Men and Women of Space*, 1992, pp. 415-19, 620-23, 709-11, 795-97; Spangenburg, Ray, and Diane Moser. *Space People From A-Z*, pp. 65, 71-72.

Russian cosmonaut Valentina Tereshkova was the first woman in space.

• Who was the **first woman** in **space**?

Valentina V. Tereshkova (1937–), a cosmonaut from the former Soviet Union, became the first woman in space on June 16, 1963. She orbited Earth 48 times over the course of three days, aboard the *Vostok 6*. Although Tereshkova had little cosmonaut training, she was an accomplished parachutist and was especially fit for the rigors of space travel. On her return from space, Tereshkova received a hero's welcome and embarked on a world speaking tour. Tereshkova is presently chair of the Russian Association of International Cooperation.

The U.S. space program did not put a woman in space until 20 years after the Soviet Union. On June 18, 1983, Sally K. Ride (1951–) made American history as she flew aboard the space shuttle *Challenger* mission STS-7. In 1987, Ride became an administrator for the National Aeronautics and Space Administration (NASA). In that capacity she issued the "Ride Report" which recommended future missions and direction for NASA. She retired from NASA in August 1986 and is presently the director of the California Space Institute at the University of California-San Diego.

Sources: Hawthorne, Douglas B. *Men and Women of Space*, 1992, pp. 718-21; McMurray, Emily J., and Donna Olendorf, eds. *Notable Twentieth-Century Scientists*, vol. 4, pp. 1992-93; Spangenburg, Ray, and Diane Moser. *Space People From A-Z*, pp. 61, 72.

• Who was the **first African American in space?**

Guion S. Bluford Jr. (1942–), became the first African American to fly in space during the space shuttle *Challenger* mission STS-8 of August 30 to September 5, 1983. Bluford, who holds a Ph.D. in aerospace engineering, made a second shuttle flight aboard *Challenger* on mission STS-61-A/ Spacelab D1 of October 30 to November 6, 1985.

Mae C. Jemison became the first African American woman in space on September 12, 1992. She flew aboard the space shuttle *Endeavour* mission Spacelab-J.

Source: Hawthorne, Douglas B. *Men and Women of Space*, 1992, pp. 75-78, 357-59.

• When was the **first animal** sent into **orbit?**

On November 3, 1957, a small female dog named Laika was the first animal (and first living creature) sent into orbit. Laika traveled aboard the Soviet *Sputnik 2*. This event followed the successful Soviet launch on October 4, 1957, of *Sputnik 1*, the first human-made satellite ever placed in orbit.

Laika sat in a pressurized compartment within a capsule that weighed 1,103 pounds (500 kilograms). She died after a few days in orbit. On April 14, 1958, *Sputnik 2* reentered the Earth's atmosphere. According to some sources, the dog was actually a Russian breed called a samoyed laika, and was named "Kudyavka" or "Limonchik."

Sources: *The Cambridge Encyclopedia of Space*, p. 48; Curtis, Anthony R. *Space Almanac*, p. 425; Wood, Gerald L. *The Guinness Book of Pet Records*, p. 39.

• What are some of the accomplishments of **female astronauts?**

First American woman in space: Sally K. Ride—June 18, 1983, aboard *Challenger* STS-7.

First American woman to walk in space: Kathryn D. Sullivan—October 11, 1984, aboard *Challenger* STS 41G.

First woman to make five spaceflights and set American endurance record for time spent in space on a single mission: Shannon W. Lucid—June 17, 1985; October 18, 1989; August 2, 1991; October 18, 1993; and March 23, 1996. On her final flight she spent 188 days aboard the Russian space station *Mir*.

First African American woman in space: Mae C. Jemison—September 12, 1992, aboard *Endeavour*.

First American woman space shuttle pilot: Eileen M. Collins—February 3, 1995, aboard *Discovery*.

Sources: *Aviation Week and Space Technology*, vol. 142 (February 20, 1995), p. 60; Famighetti, Robert, ed. *World Almanac and Book of Facts 1996*, p. 317; Hawthorne, Douglas B. *Men and Women of Space*, 1992, pp. 442, 590, 709; Lyndon B. Johnson Space Center. Biographical Data: Shannon W. Lucid. [Online] Available http://www.jsc.nasa.gov/Bios/htmlbios/lucid.html, June 23, 1997.

• Who was the "father" of the **Soviet space program?**

Sergei P. Korolëv (1907–1966), sometimes spelled "Korolyov," is considered the father of the Soviet space program. Largely due to the efforts of Korolëv, the former Soviet Union became the first nation to put a satellite into orbit around the Earth, send a person into space, and land an unpiloted spacecraft on the moon.

Trained as an aeronautical engineer, in 1931 Korolëv became director of the rocket research group in Moscow, Russia. During World War II (1939–45), Korolëv was forced by the Soviet secret police to design aircraft and weapons for use in the war. In August 1957 he developed the first Soviet intercontinental ballistic missile (ICBM). The Soviets used a modified ICBM-rocket to launch the world's first satellite, *Sputnik 1*, on October 4, 1957.

Korolëv was next involved in designing the spacecraft *Luna 3*, which in 1959 gave humans their first view of the far side of the moon. Two years later Korolëv designed *Vostok 1*, the spacecraft in which Yuri Gagarin (1934–1968) became the first person in space. In 1966, another spacecraft designed by Korolëv, *Luna 9*, landed on the moon and sent back television footage of the lunar surface.

Sources: *The Cambridge Encyclopedia of Space*, p. 34; McMurray, Emily J., and Donna Olendorf, eds. *Notable Twentieth-Century Scientists*, vol. 2, pp.1127-29.

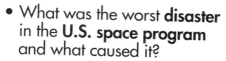

- ## What was the worst **disaster** in the **U.S. space program** and what caused it?

The worst disaster in the U.S. space program was the explosion of the space shuttle *Challenger*, on January 28, 1986. The explosion occurred 73 seconds after lift-off. All seven people on board were killed and the spacecraft was completely destroyed. Those killed included astronauts Gregory Jarvis, Ronald McNair, Ellison Onizuka, Judith Resnick, Francis Scobee, Michael Smith, and schoolteacher Christa Mc-Auliffe.

The investigation of the *Challenger* tragedy was performed by the Rogers Commission, established and named for its chairman, former Secretary of State William Rogers. The Rogers Commission studied the accident for several months and

The space shuttle *Challenger* exploding in midair.

concluded that it had been caused by a leak in one of the two solid rocket boosters that ignite the main fuel tank. The leak had occurred because of a faulty rubberized seal called an "O-ring."

Although the commission did not place blame for the tragedy on particular individuals, they indicated that the launch should not have been made that day. The weather was unusually cold at Cape Canaveral and temperatures had dipped below freezing during the night. Test data had suggested that the O-rings around the solid rocket booster joints lose much of their effectiveness in very cold weather.

Sources: Engelbert, Phillis. *Astronomy and Space: From the Big Bang to the Big Crunch*, vol. 1, pp. 90-92; Gurney, Gene. *Space Shuttle Log*, p. 269; Magill, Frank N. *Magill's Survey of Science* (Space Exploration Series), vol. 4, p. 1813; Neal, Valerie, et. al. *Spaceflight: A Smithsonian Guide*, p. 127; Smith, Marcia. *Space Activities of the United States and Other Launching Countries/Organizations: 1957-1991*, p. CRS-35.

• How many **fatalities** have occurred during **space-related missions?**

The 14 astronauts and cosmonauts listed below died in space-related accidents.

Date	Astronaut/Cosmonaut	Mission
January 27, 1967	Roger Chaffee (U.S.)	*Apollo 1*
January 27, 1967	Edward White II (U.S.)	*Apollo 1*
January 27, 1967	Virgil "Gus" Grissom (U.S.)	*Apollo 1*
April 24, 1967	Vladimir Komarov (U.S.S.R.)	*Soyuz 1*
June 29, 1971	Viktor Patsayev (U.S.S.R.)	*Soyuz 11*
June 29, 1971	Vladislav Volkov (U.S.S.R.)	*Soyuz 11*
June 29, 1971	Georgi Dobrovolsky (U.S.S.R.)	*Soyuz 11*
January 28, 1986	Gregory Jarvis (U.S.)	STS 51L
January 28, 1986	Christa McAuliffe (U.S.)	STS 51L
January 28, 1986	Ronald McNair (U.S.)	STS 51L
January 28, 1986	Ellison Onizuka (U.S.)	STS 51L
January 28, 1986	Judith Resnik (U.S.)	STS 51L
January 28, 1986	Francis Scobee (U.S.)	STS 51L
January 28, 1986	Michael Smith (U.S.)	STS 51L

Chaffee, Grissom, and White died in a cabin fire during a ground test of *Apollo 1*. Komarov was killed in *Soyuz 1* when the capsule's parachute failed. Dobrovolsky, Patsayev, and Volkov were killed during the *Soyuz 2*'s reentry into the Earth's atmosphere, when a valve accidentally opened and the air in the capsule escaped. Jarvis, McAuliffe, McNair, Onizuka, Resnik, Scobee, and Smith died when the space shuttle *Challenger* exploded 73 seconds after lift-off.

In addition, 19 astronauts and cosmonauts have died of nonspace-related causes. Fourteen of these died in air crashes, four died of natural causes, and one died in an auto crash.

Sources: *Astronauts and Cosmonauts Biographical and Statistical Data: Report to the Committee on Science, Space, and Technology, U.S. House of Representatives 1989*, p. 447; Bali, Mrinal. *Space Exploration*, p. 143.

• When was the first **United States satellite** launched?

On January 31, 1958, *Explorer 1* became the first U.S. satellite launched into orbit. It came four months after the launch of the world's first satellite, the former Soviet Union's *Sputnik 1*. While the Soviet satellite weighed

184 pounds (83.5 kilograms), the U.S. satellite weighed only 31 pounds (14.06 kilograms) and was nicknamed "the grapefruit."

Explorer 1 carried instrumentation that led to the discovery of the Van Allen belts (or zones), which are two rings of highly charged particles encircling the Earth. The belts are named for James Van Allen (1914–), the professor of physics who designed *Explorer's* instruments. (A physicist is a scientist specializing in the interaction between matter and energy.)

Sources: Braun, Wernher von, and Frederick I. Ordway III. *Space Travel: A History,* pp. 170-73; Curtis, Anthony R. *Space Almanac,* p. 13.

• What did **NASA** mean by *Voyager 2* taking a **"grand tour"** of the planets?

Voyager 2, launched in 1977, visited four planets—Jupiter, Saturn, Uranus, and Neptune—before exiting the solar system. The spacecraft was able to undertake this "grand tour" because of the particular way the outer planets were lined up in the late 1970s. The planets formed a continuous curve, so that a spacecraft could rely on a technique called "gravity assist" to travel between planets without using additional rocket motors. Gravity assist is a method of propulsion in which the gravitational pull of one planet is used to propel a spacecraft toward its target.

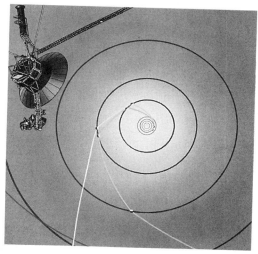

An illustration of the paths taken by *Voyager 1* and *Voyager 2.*

Sources: Angelo, Joseph A. *The Extraterrestrial Encyclopedia,* Rev. and updated ed., p. 219; Neal, Valerie, et. al. *Spaceflight: A Smithsonian Guide,* pp. 178-79.

• What is the message attached to each *Voyager* spacecraft?

Voyager 1 (launched September 5, 1977) and *Voyager 2* (launched August 20, 1977) are unpiloted space probes that explored the outer planets: Jupiter, Saturn, Uranus, and Neptune. The two space probes then traveled beyond the solar system. Each *Voyager* carries a gold-coated, copper phonograph record. The records contain information about Earth, as well as a message to any possible extraterrestrial civilization the spacecrafts may encounter.

Each record comes with a needle and instructions, in the language of symbols, for playing the record. The contents of the record were selected by a National Aeronautics and Space Administration (NASA) committee headed by the late astronomer Carl Sagan (1934–1996).

The records begin with visual images. There are pictures of Earth, the solar system, and the Milky Way galaxy; human anatomy and reproduction; examples of vegetation and animal life; human-made structures (from grass huts to the Taj Mahal and the Sydney Opera House); and means of transportation. Next comes greetings from Jimmy Carter, then president of the United States, and Kurt Waldheim, then Secretary General of the United Nations. Brief messages in 54 languages, ranging from ancient Sumerian to English, are included.

The next section is a series of sounds common to the Earth, such as thunder, rain, and barking dogs. The record concludes with approximately 90 minutes of music, taken from a broad spectrum of cultures.

It will be tens of thousands, or hundreds of thousands, of years before either *Voyager* comes close to another star. While the message may never be heard, the records are a sign of humanity's hope to encounter life elsewhere in the universe.

To obtain your own copy of *Voyager's* record on CD-ROM, as well as *Murmurs of Earth*, the book that tells about the record, call the Planetary Society at (818) 793-1675.

Sources: *Murmurs of Earth: The Voyager Interstellar Record*; Rudd, Richard. Voyager Project Home Page. [Online] Available http://vraptor.jpl.nasa.gov/voyager/voyager.html, July 2, 1996.

• What is the mission of the *Galileo* spacecraft?

The mission of the *Galileo* spacecraft is to make a detailed study of Jupiter and its rings and moons over a period of two years. *Galileo* was launched on October 18, 1989, and took almost six years to reach Jupiter. Using the gravity assist method (allowing the gravitational field of one planet to propel it toward another), it looped past Venus once and the Earth twice, before heading to Jupiter. *Galileo* traveled 2.5 billion miles to reach Jupiter, when Jupiter was only a half a billion miles away from Earth.

On December 7, 1995, *Galileo* released a barbeque-sized probe to analyze the different layers of Jupiter's atmosphere. *Galileo* is taking many measurements of the planet, its four largest moons, and its mammoth magnetic field. The mission is scheduled to continue through the end of 1997.

Sources: Mallon, Thomas. "Galileo, Phone Home." *The New York Times Magazine*, December 3, 1995 pp. 57+; *Scientific American*, vol. 273, December 1995, pp. 44-49.

ASTRONOMERS AND SKYWATCHING

• Who is considered the greatest **ancient Greek astronomer?**

Hipparchus (fl. 190–120 B.C.), who lived about 100 years after Aristotle, is considered to have been the greatest ancient Greek astronomer (a scientist specializing in the study of matter in outer space). Hipparchus was the first to develop a detailed explanation of how the planets and other objects move throughout the solar system. He was mistaken, however, as were most astronomers of the day, in placing the Earth (rather than the sun) at the center of the solar system.

Hipparchus measured, with remarkable accuracy, the directions of objects in the sky. He compiled the first catalog of stars, containing about 850 entries. He recorded each star's celestial coordinates, indicating its position in the sky. Hipparchus also categorized the stars according to their apparent brightness, or magnitudes.

One of Hipparchus's greatest achievements was to create a calendar with 365.2467 days in a year. This was based on his study of lunar and solar eclipses, as well as the solstices (the two days each year when the sun is at its highest and its lowest points in the sky, respectively, marking the beginning of winter and summer) and equinoxes (the days marking the start of spring and fall and the two days of the year in which day and night are of approximately equal length).

Sources: Abell, George O. *Realm of the Universe*, 5th ed., p. 16; *Dictionary of Scientific Biography*, vol. 16, suppl. 1, pp. 207-9; Engelbert, Phillis. *Astronomy and Space: From the Big Bang to the Big Crunch*, vol. 1, pp. 13-14.

• For whom is the **Hubble Space Telescope** named?

American astronomer (a scientist specializing in the study of matter in outer space) Edwin Powell Hubble (1889–1953) was the first to detect galaxies beyond our own. He studied faint, distant patches, known as nebulae (clouds), and found they were actually large groups of stars. Hubble found that these groups of stars were so distant, they had to be beyond the bounds of our own galaxy. Hubble revolutionized astronomy by illustrating that the universe (all matter and energy including Earth, the galaxies, and the contents of space as a whole) is much larger than anyone had previously imagined, and that it is growing larger all the time.

Hubble developed a famous equation, called Hubble's Law, which describes the expansion of the universe. It establishes a distance-to-speed relationship showing that the more distant a galaxy is from our solar system, the faster it's moving away from us. The speed of a galaxy's movement is measured by its redshift—the shift of its visible light spectrum toward the red, or longer, wavelengths.

The Hubble Space Telescope, named after astronomer Edwin Hubble, was deployed by the space shuttle *Discovery* on April 25, 1990. The telescope was designed to see deeper into space than any telescope on land possibly could. (Land-based telescopes are hindered because light is distorted by the Earth's atmosphere.) However, on June 27, 1990, the National Aeronautics and Space Administration (NASA) announced that the telescope had a defect in one of its mirrors which prevented it from focusing properly. Although other instruments, including one designed to make observations in ultraviolet light, were still operating, nearly 40 percent of the telescope's experiments had to be postponed until repairs were made.

On December 2, 1993, astronauts on the space shuttle *Endeavour* were able to repair the ailing telescope. Four of Hubble's six gyroscopes (navigational instruments consisting of a wheel that spins around a rod through the center) were replaced as well as two solar panels. Hubble's primary camera, which had a flawed mirror, was also replaced. The repairs were a huge success. The space telescope now regularly makes headlines with its startling discoveries.

Sources: Engelbert, Phillis. *Astronomy and Space: From the Big Bang to the Big Crunch*, vol. 2, pp. 253-59; Famighetti, Robert, ed. *World Almanac and Book of Facts 1995*, pp. 43-44; Parkinson, Clair L. *Breakthroughs: A Chronology of Great Achievements in Science and Mathematics*, pp. 494-95, 508; *Time* (July 9, 1990), p. 43.

• Who invented the **telescope**?

Hans Lippershey (ca. 1570–1619), a German-Dutch lens grinder and spectacle (glasses) maker, is generally credited with inventing the telescope. This is because in 1608 Lippsershey became the first scientist to apply for a patent for the telescope. (A patent is a grant made by a government that allows the creator of invention the sole right to make, use, and sell that invention for a set period of time.) Two other inventors, Zacharias Janssen and Jacob Metius, also developed telescopes around this time. Modern historians consider both Lippershey and Janssen to be likely candidates for the title of "inventor of the telescope," with Lippershey possessing the strongest claim.

In 1609, Italian astronomer Galileo (1564–1642) developed his own refractor telescope for astronomical studies. A refractor telescope is the simplest type of telescope; light enters through one end of a tube and passes through a glass lens, which bends the light rays and brings them into focus. The light then strikes an eyepiece, which acts as a magnifying glass. Although small by today's standards, the telescope enabled Galileo to observe the Milky Way and to identify craters on the moon's surface.

Sources: *The Great Scientists*, vol. 7, p. 162; Travers, Bridget, ed. *World of Invention*, pp. 618-19.

• Who is **Stephen Hawking**?

Stephen Hawking (1943–), a British physicist (a scientist who studies the interactions between matter and energy) and mathematician, is considered to be the greatest theoretical physicist of the late twentieth century. In spite of being severely handicapped by amyotrophic lateral sclerosis (ALS), a

Stephen Hawking.

muscular disorder also known as Lou Gehrig's disease, he has made major contributions to the field of astronomy. In particular, Hawking has vastly increased our understanding of black holes. He has also explored the origin and evolution of the universe (all matter and energy including the Earth, the galaxies, and the contents of space as a whole) through his research into the nature of space-time (the four-dimensional construct involving the three dimensions of space, plus time).

For instance, Hawking proposed that a black hole (the remains of a massive star that has collapsed into a single point of infinite mass and gravity) evaporates and gives off radiation, called "Hawking's radiation." He predicted that a black hole would completely disappear after all its mass has been converted into radiation, at which point it would unleash a tremendous explosion.

Hawking is currently working on his monumental Grand Unified Theory, an effort to explain the beginnings of space and time. This involves combining quantum mechanics (the study of the behavior of subatomic particles) with Einstein's theory of relativity (the theory that gravity is the result of curved space-time) into a theory of quantum gravity.

Hawking is the author of several books including the popular best-selling work *A Brief History of Time*, which has been made into a movie.

Sources: Iver, David F. *Dictionary of Astronomy, Space, and Atmospheric Phenomena*, p. 32; McMurray, Emily J., and Donna Olendorf, eds. *Notable Twentieth-Century Scientists*, vol. 2, pp. 877-79; Porter, Roy, ed. *The Biographical Dictionary of Scientists*, 2nd ed., p. 313; Simon, Sheridan. *Stephen Hawking: Unlocking the Universe*, pp. 9-10, 93-94.

• Is anyone looking for **extraterrestrial life?**

Despite the fact that alien life forms have never been discovered, the search for extraterrestrial intelligence (or SETI, as it is called) remains a popular

---

What is a "close encounter of the third kind"?

Unidentified flying object (UFO) expert J. Allen Hynek (1910–1986) developed the following scale to describe encounters with extraterrestrial beings or vessels:

Close Encounter of the First Kind—sighting of a UFO at close range with no other physical evidence.

Close Encounter of the Second Kind—sighting of a UFO at close range, but with some kind of proof, such as a photograph, or an artifact from a UFO.

Close Encounter of the Third Kind—sighting of an actual extraterrestrial being.

Close Encounter of the Fourth Kind—abduction by an extraterrestrial spacecraft.

Source: Rovin, Jeff. *Laws of Order*, p. 219.

---

pursuit. Astronomers (scientists specializing in the study of matter in outer space) believe that if life does exist on other planets, we now possess the technological capability of finding it and perhaps even communicating with it.

Most modern SETI missions use radio telescopes—instruments consisting of a large concave dish with an antenna at the center, tuned to a certain wavelength, that receive and process radio waves. The radio telescopes, tuned to nearby stars, listen for signals that may have been sent by alien civilizations.

The first large-scale SETI experiment, called Project Ozma, was begun by astronomer Frank Drake (1930–) in 1960. Drake conducted Project Ozma at the National Radio Astronomy Observatory in Green Bank, West Virginia, where a radio telescope was poised to receive signals from outer space. Drake detected one signal he initially thought was from a distant star, but it turned out to be coming from Earth.

A current SETI project is under way at the Harvard-Smithsonian radio telescope 30 miles (48 kilometers) outside of Boston, Massachusetts. The project is called BETA, the Billion-channel Extra-Terrestrial Assay. It uses an 84-foot-diameter (25-meter-diameter) radio antenna dish that sweeps the sky for signals. If the antenna picks up a strange signal, the computer alerts the project coordinators.

Other SETI research is being carried out by two private groups: the SETI Institute in Mountain View, California, headed by Frank Drake; and the Planetary Society, an organization of amateur astronomers, formerly led by astronomer Carl Sagan (1934–1996).

The search for extraterrestrial life was energized in late 1995 and early 1996, when three new planets were found in our galaxy. The planets orbit nearby stars, between 35 and 40 light-years from Earth. (A light-year is the distance light travels in one year, about 5.9 trillion miles.)

These discoveries show that our planet may not be unique, as was previously believed, and suggest that many more planets remain to be discovered. As a result, the National Aeronautics and Space Administration (NASA) has increased its own efforts to find new planets, particularly those that may be able to support living beings. NASA's proposed Origins Project, for instance, will use space-based telescopes to search for extraterrestrial life.

Sources: Engelbert, Phillis. *Astronomy and Space: From the Big Bang to the Big Crunch,* vol. 1, pp. 158-60; *Life,* vol. 15, no. 9, September 1992, pp. 60-67; *The Planetary Report,* vol. 5, no. 5, September-October 1985, pp. 10-12; *The Planetary Report,* vol. 16, no. 2, March-April 1996, pp. 4-7.

INDEX

A

Abacus 3: **577-78,** 577 (ill.)
Absolute zero 2: 400; 3: 449,
476-77, 478
Accelerated Mass Spectrom-
eter 1: 8
Accidents 2: 264
Acetic acid 3: 441
Acetone 1: 122
Acetylene 1: 122
Achilles 3: 579
Acid rain 2: 275, **282-84,**
283 (ill.)
Acne 1: 158
Acquired immunodeficiency
syndrome 1: 114, **116-17**
Acre 3: **574,** 614
Actinium 1: 138
Active solar energy systems
2: **258-59**
Adams, John Couch 2: 379
Adiabatic process 3: **479-80**
Adrenal gland 1: 46
Adrenals 1: 94
Adrenocorticotropic hor-
mone 1: 94
Aerosol 2: 281
Afghanistan 1: 81

Africa 1: 39, 44, 46, 59, 65,
121; 2: 231, 233, 241,
274, 277, 298
African American, first in
space 2: **405**
African American surgeon,
first 1: **149**
African elephant 1: 37, **45;**
2: **298-99**
Africanized honeybee 1: 61
Agent Orange 2: **293-95**
Ageratum 1: 80
Agriculture 1: 71, 78
AIDS 1: 114, **116-17**
AIDS-related complex
1: 116
Air conditioner 2: **246**
Aircraft 2: 312; 3: 506,
514, 535
Aircraft carrier 3: 535
Airolo, Switzerland 3: 548
Air bag 3: **521-22**
Airplane 2: 362-63; 3: **531-**
32, 541-42, 619
Airplane flight 3: **529**
Air pollution 2: 280, 282,
289-90, 361
Air pressure 2: 273, 333, 364;
3: 460, 477, 493
Air Venture Museum 3: 532

Akashi-Kaikyo Bridge 3: 544
Akron, Ohio 3: 450
The Alamo 3: 464
Alaska 1: 42; 2: 214, 229,
235, 237, 241, 274, 287,
335, 347
Alaskan malamutes 1: 42
Alaska Range 2: 214
Albatros fighter 3: 542
Alchemists 3: 465
Alchemy 2: 312; 3: 470
Alcock, John W. 3: 528
Alcohol 2: 325; 3: 478
Alcoholic beverages 1: 186
Aldehydes 2: 253
Aldosterone 1: 94, 96
Aldrin, Buzz 3: 458
Aleutian Islands 2: 235
Alfalfa 1: 168
Algae 1: 4, 70
Algal blooms 2: 275
Alkali metals 3: **482-84**
Alkaline earth metals 3: **484**
Alkaloids 1: 157
Allegheny River 3: 547
Allergies 1: 139
Allies 3: 542
Alligators 1: 55
Alloys 2: 312
Alphabet 3: 502

Nuclear material *3:* 452
Nuclear power *1:* 137; *2:* 245, 256, 262-64, 268, 314
Nuclear-powered automobile *3:* **523**
Nuclear-powered vessels *3:* **535**
Nuclear power plants *2:* **261,** 267
Nuclear reactors *2:* **263-66;** *3:* **487**
Nuclear waste storage *2:* **268-70, 268** (ill.)
Nuclear war *3:* 468
Nuclear weapons *2:* 265, 269
Nuclear winter *3:* **468**
Number, magical *3:* **583**
Number theory *3:* 565
Nuthatches *1:* 52
Nutmeg *1:* 187-88

O

Oak, *1:* 85, 175
Oats *2:* 254
Obermayer, Arthur S. *3:* 440
Obsidian *2:* 317; *3:* 439
Ocean currents *1:* 53; *2:* 335; *3:* 456
Ocean, depth of *2:* **230**
Ocean kelp *2:* 259
Oceans *2:* 221, 228, 230, **232,** 240
Octahedron *3:* 574
Office of Civilian Radioactive Waste Management *2:* 269
Ohio *1:* 155; *2:* 353; *3:* 549
Ohio River *2:* 241; *3:* 547
Ohm *3:* 613
Oil *2:* 246-47, **249,** 256, 280, **286-87,** 306
Oil fire *1:* **187**
Oil spill *2:* **287-88, 288** (ill.)
Oil well *2:* **251-52, 251** (ill.)
Oklahoma Agricultural and Mechanical College *3:* 525
Olbers, Heinrich *2:* 387
Old Faithful *2:* 306
Oldsmobile *3:* 518
Old World porcupines *1:* 39
Oleo *1:* **164-65**
Olkhon Crevice *2:* 232
Olympic Games *3:* 608
Onions *1:* 109, 177; *3:* 436

Onizuka, Ellison *2:* 407
On the Origin of Species *1:* **9-10**
Oodaq *2:* 219
Oort cloud *2:* 389
Oort, Jan *2:* 389
Operation Ranch Hand *2:* **293-95**
Ophthalmologist *1:* **149**
Opossums *1:* 41
Optical Society of America *3:* 435
Optician *1:* 149
Optometrist *1:* 149
Oral cavity cancers *1:* 133
Oranges *1:* **168-69,** 187
Orangutan *1:* 29
Orb web *1:* 59
Orchids *1:* 75, 178
Oregano *1:* 183
Oregon *1:* 90; *2:* 226
Organic compound *3:* **470-71**
Organometallic chemistry *1:* 72
Orient Express *3:* **537-38**
Origins Project *2:* 416
Orion *2:* 395
Orphan Drug Act of 1983 *1:* 159
Orphan drugs *1:* **159**
Osmium *2:* 312
Osteopathic medicine *1:* 146
Osteoporosis *1:* 158
Ostrichs *1:* 47, 49
Otis, Elisha *3:* 553
Oughtred, William *3:* 576
Ovaries *1:* 74, 94
Owens Illinois Glass Company *2:* 327
Owls *1:* 52
Oxygen *1:* **81,** 92-94, **136;** *2:* **217,** 227, 274, 281, **286, 311,** 371; *3:* **470, 472, 481, 486**
Oxytocin *1:* **94**
Ozone *1:* 135-36; *2:* 274-75, 280-84

P

Pacific Coast *2:* 348; *3:* 548
Pacific Ocean *1:* 55; *2:* 214, 221, 229-30, 232, 235-36, 273, 299

Pacific yew *1:* 158
Pacini, Franco *2:* 401
Pagemaker *3:* 586
Paint *2:* 331
Pakistan *1:* 46, 59
Paleontologists *2:* 227
Palitzsch, Johann *2:* 391
Palladium *2:* 312, 316, 330
Palmer, Daniel David *1:* 147
Palmer, Nathaniel *2:* 239
Palmer Peninsula *2:* 239
Palomar Observatory *2:* 402
Pancreas *1:* 94
Pangaea *2:* 220
Pantothenic acid (B5) *1:* 178
Papain *1:* 155
Paper *2:* 292, 323
Papillae, *1:* 106
Papillomavirus *1:* 127
Paraheliotropism *1:* 73
Paralysis *1:* 153
Parasite *1:* 93
Parathyroid hormone *1:* 95
Parathyroids *1:* 94
Paricutin *2:* 235
Paris, France *3:* 501, 521, 517, 528, 537
Parkes, Alexander *2:* 325
Parkesine *2:* 325
Parking meter *3:* **525**
Parsons, William S. *3:* 542
Partial eclipse *2:* 368
Pascal, Blaise *3:* 573, 573 (ill.), 584, 613
Pascaline *3:* 584
Pascal's triangle *3:* **572-73**
Passive solar energy systems *2:* **258-59**
Pasteurization *1:* 21, **163-64,** 191
Pasteur, Louis *1:* 20, 163, 163 (ill.); *3:* 471
Patellar tendon *1:* 152
Patent and Trademark Office *3:* 453
Patents *1:* 159, 187; *3:* **451-54**
Pathogens *1:* 115
PCBs *2:* **285**
PCP *1:* 160
Peanut butter *1:* **174**
Peanuts *1:* 78, 167
Peapods *1:* 166
Pearl Harbor *3:* 532
Pearson, Allen *2:* 353

440